Abbass F. Alkhafaji,

Strategic Management
Formulation, Implementation, and Control in a Dynamic Environment

Pre-publication REVIEWS, COMMENTARIES, EVALUATIONS . . .

"This book will be very helpful to those who teach strategic management. It will be an important tool, with its up-to-date text and new cases. It is prepared in a straightforward manner yet is comprehensive in nature. An extremely strong point is its coverage of global strategic matters."

Gene Murkison, PhD
Professor of Management,
Georgia Southern University,
College of Business Administration

"*Strategic Management* succeeds where so many other texts fail. It is scholarly yet succinct, free from the esoteric language and obfuscation often associated with textbooks. The author has done an excellent job of incorporating contemporary issues, specifically international strategy. The use of real-world examples will greatly assist students and instructors alike in applying the content to modern business practices."

Dr. David Whitlock
Dean, College of Business
and Computer Science,
Southwest Baptist University,
Bolivar, MO

NOTES FOR PROFESSIONAL LIBRARIANS AND LIBRARY USERS

This is an original book title published by The Haworth Press, Inc. Unless otherwise noted in specific chapters with attribution, materials in this book have not been previously published elsewhere in any format or language.

CONSERVATION AND PRESERVATION NOTES

All books published by The Haworth Press, Inc. and its imprints are printed on certified pH neutral, acid free book grade paper. This paper meets the minimum requirements of American National Standard for Information Sciences-Permanence of Paper for Printed Material, ANSI Z39.48-1984.

Strategic Management
Formulation, Implementation, and Control in a Dynamic Environment

THE HAWORTH PRESS
Promotional Management
Richard Alan Nelson
Editor

Strategic Management: Formulation, Implementation, and Control in a Dynamic Environment by Abbass F. Alkhafaji

Strategic Management
Formulation, Implementation, and Control in a Dynamic Environment

Abbass F. Alkhafaji, PhD

The Haworth Press®
New York • London • Oxford

The Haworth Press, Inc., 10 Alice Street, Binghamton, NY 13904-1580.

Cover design by Jennifer M. Gaska.

Library of Congress Cataloging-in-Publication Data

Strategic management : formulation, implementation, and control in a dynamic environment / Abbass F. Alkhafaji.

p. cm.

Includes bibliographical references and index.

ISBN 0-7890-1809-8 (hard: alk. paper)—ISBN 0-7890-1810-1 (soft : alk. paper)

1. Strategic planning. I. Alkhafaji, Abbass F.

HD30.28 .S7299 2003

658.4'012—dc21

2002068852

CONTENTS

Preface

This book is carefully designed to meet the needs of undergraduate students, as well as those of practicing managers. It provides an in-depth analysis of strategic management concepts substantiated with real-world examples to enrich the discussion. Business policy and strategic management, as a subject, has become a required course in undergraduate and graduate business curricula. It has also become a vital part of the corporate environment. "Almost all organizations of any reasonable size have some kind of strategic plan."[1]

The issues presented in this text directly face the managers of today and those of the future. They apply to all types of organizations, whether large or small, profit or not-for-profit, domestic or global. In addition, this text should provide helpful insight into today's strategic management decision making and should be a key to the development of successful organizational effectiveness. For the purpose of this book, strategic management is defined as the process of assessing the corporation and its environment to meet the firm's long-term objectives of adopting and adjusting to its environment through exploitation of opportunities and reduction of threats.

Instructors have used a variety of approaches in teaching this course, but the critical issue is to expose the student to a theoretical framework. This strong foundation will in turn enable the student to function effectively in the business world. This book develops in detail a framework for the formulation, implementation, and control of strategies for all types of domestic and global organizations.

For any company to succeed in today's global market, it must develop a competitive advantage. The market is going global, and increasing competition will affect every business, no matter how small or large, public or private the firm is. The increasing globalization of business has created a need for effective overseas managers. Protected markets no longer exist anywhere in the world. Successful global managers need to be capable, devise creative strategies, have effective communication skills, and possess self-awareness together with an understanding of foreign cultures, languages, and customs. The international marketplace is *highly competitive* and operations are managed in widely *varying* economic, social, political, and cultural environments. It must be noted that successful domestic managers do not necessarily become effective global managers unless they are well trained and open-minded. This book examines how companies expand their operations abroad and the need for appropriate strategies.

History and business literature is replete with evidence showing that vision, efficacious planning, and realistic goal setting can positively influence organizational performance. It is also evident that business organizations, both small and large, that employ strategic planning outperform their counterparts who operate without any formal planning.

In the present turbulent, globalized, and rapidly changing business environment, organizations can easily lose a sense of mission and direction. Strategic management is an instrument for controlling an organization's destiny. It has a lighthouse effect and forces members of an organization to think futuristically, highlights new opportunities and threats, and enables organizations to refocus on their mission. Strategic planning enables firms to remain proactive, be competitive, and develop calculated methods to resolve interrelated sets or problems and issues from an eagle-eye perspective.

Organizations of the twenty-first century will have to make fundamental changes in their operations and strategies. For many companies, poor-quality change has caused their downfall. "Forty-seven percent of the companies that appeared on the Fortune 500 a decade ago have disappeared from today's list."[2] CEOs must become the leaders of change. They must leave the traditional organizational system behind and become more progressive and flexible with the changing times. Objectives need to be redefined to meet the challenges of global competition. The role of employees and managers must change as well to better accomplish organizational goals in quality improvement and efficiency.

The past fifteen years have seen dynamic environmental changes. Foreign companies are proliferating and are stronger. The increased competition is fierce, product life cycles are shorter, product development cycles are faster, domestic and world economies are less stable, technological advances are faster, change occurs more often, and deregulation and economic liberalization abroad are common. Faced with declining profits and loss of market share, businesses today can no longer rest complacently on their laurels. Strategic planning is a process of thinking through myriad choices and developing appropriate alternatives to resolve issues and problems.

Planning also has a coalescing quality. It brings innovative leaders together and enables them to share and promote their vision. Good planning promotes teamwork, improves knowledge of the organization, fosters better communication across functions, and improves managerial skills. It establishes a pattern of success and growth and helps firms to influence and control their environment. The twenty-first century will bring dramatic advances and changes in technology and will usher business organizations into a globalized economy, with no governing body to smooth the transformation, which will require firms to adopt appropriate strategies to align themselves to the new shifts in the paradigm.

Characteristics of a Dramatically Changing Global Environment

The nature of strategic management today is seen in the environment-driven strategies of successful firms competing in a diverse market. The following are some of the characteristics of the dramatically changing global environment:

1. Change is an important constant factor, and therefore its effective management will require constant monitoring of the firm's internal and external environments. We can know neither the outcome of this change nor the direction, but we can be aware of the nature of our circumstances. Change will also necessitate employee participation, empowerment, and total quality management.
2. Strategic management is a necessary process for gaining competitive advantage, requiring the active participation of all functional areas.
3. The environmental, ethical, product quality, and integrity aspects of business practice are a critical concern requiring active support, commitment, and involvement of top management. In essence, all things must be considered, known and unknown, sins of commission and omission.
4. Environmental turbulence will dictate strategies to be constantly evaluated from a stakeholder's point of view.
5. Development of international strategies is a complex process because of the existence of trade blocks such as the EU, ASEAN, and NAFTA, and the likely emergence of new integration between China and the Soviet bloc countries, along with the African continent, the Middle East, and South America.
6. Restructuring the traditional organization into multifunctional, flexible teams is reforming the traditional hierarchical organization.
7. Strategies increasingly involve interorganizational teams and strategic alliances on a global scale, redirecting the company focus on customer and global competition.

We must understand that (1) faulty assumptions and false information can result in the formulation of poor or even disastrous plans, and (2) change is constant and continuous—that yesterday's good plan may not be relevant or of any value today. Consequently, firms need to continuously monitor, evaluate, and control their strategic plans if they are to result in positive goal achievement.

In short, the world of business and competition is in a vortex of dynamic change that will destroy those who do not carefully chart their course of action through the maelstrom. Those who remain proactive and adapt and adjust to the changing environment will succeed. We have to realize that we live in a changing world and business organizations, governmental units, and other entities, just like people, have to adjust and adapt to survive. Through strategic planning and strategic thinking we can anticipate the future, and through proactive efforts we can manage change to our advantage.

The Text

This book is an important educational tool for undergraduate business students. It is intended to assist students to integrate and apply their knowledge in different business functional areas. The book will assist students in learning the different analytical tools applied in the practice of strategic management. It is also intended to provide an answer to the many challenges business organizations face. Among these challenges are (1) the acutely competitive environment in the domestic as well as international markets, (2) the changing nature of the workforce and organization, and (3) the advances in technology and information systems that have transformed the market from an industrial to a knowledge-based society.

Included are the following distinctive features that separate this book from the traditional texts:

- *Managerial applications.* I have tried to treat the content as comprehensibly as possible while using a simple writing style that enables a student to form a clear picture of the topic area. The tone of the book is simple yet succinct. The real-world examples help students see how theory relates to practice and add relevance to the analysis presented.
- *International aspects.* While international and globalization aspects are included in different chapters, a separate chapter is devoted solely to discussing the strategic management aspects of the international environment.
- *Contemporary focus.* Current concepts such as total quality management, ethics and social responsibility, corporate governance, reengineering, globalization, international strategies, etc., are used and their relationship to strategic management is shown.
- *Content organization.* Each chapter presents an overall framework of the topic area, e.g., assessing the environment, international strategies, implementation, corporate culture, and the general manager. Subsequent sections analyze the impact of strategic management on this di-

mension, raise policy implications, and consider management tools and mechanisms.

The book is suitable for academics (with footnotes and references) and practitioners and students (no esoteric jargon or abstruse statistical analysis). The content is designed for undergraduate business students. It is a summary of experience gathered from my work expense, students, the books I have used, and the class notes I have prepared over numerous years.

Chapter 1 presents a broad overview of strategic management to prepare the reader for the remaining chapters. Chapter 2 begins by presenting the strategic management process and discussing its characteristics. It is imperative that students in business administration recognize the components of the strategic management process and be able to recognize and understand mission statements, strategic objectives, and organizational policies. This chapter also discusses the relationship between strategic management and total quality management.

Chapter 3 presents an in-depth study of the external and internal forces that affect the strategic plan and the importance of accurate and timely information to the organization. This chapter discusses the SWOT analysis in some detail.

Once the mission, goals, and objectives have been set for the organization and the environmental forces have been assessed, the corporate, business, and functional strategies must be developed and applied. This is the topic of Chapters 4 and 5. Global aspects of designing strategy have been integrated into many of the chapters. However, the specific focus of Chapter 6 is managerial strategies as applied to organizations that operate in a global environment.

Chapters 7 and 8 provide the student with a framework for implementing a formalized strategy. They discuss the structure, culture, and leadership requirements for successful implementation. Chapter 9 discusses the evaluation and control process, including the types of evaluation available.

Finally, strategic management in not-for-profit organizations is discussed in Chapter 10. This chapter shows the importance of developing strategy for not-for-profit organizations and how they are different from their for-profit counterparts.

Section II of the book is devoted to cases that illustrate various principles.

NOTES

1. Peters, J. (1993). Business policy in action. *Management Decision,* 31(6), 3.
2. Moravee, M. (1994). Leaders must love change, not loathe it. *HR Focus,* 71(2), 13-15.

ABOUT THE AUTHOR

Abbass F. Alkhafaji, PhD, is Professor of Management at Slippery Rock University in Pennsylvania. He also teaches at Sharjah University in the United Arab Emirates. Dr. Alkhafaji teaches a range of courses with special emphasis on strategic and international management. He is the author of several books and numerous articles on strategic management, corporate governance, and international management, and has received many awards for his research. He has conducted seminars in the United States and abroad. Dr. Alkhafaji is also Founder and Executive Vice President of the International Academy of Business Disciplines (IABD).

Acknowledgments

This book is a result of contributions from many students, graduate and undergraduate, and from other authors of books I have used in the business policy and strategic management areas. They have helped to sharpen my ideas over the years and helped me to acquire the knowledge and expertise to write this book. I am especially grateful to Slippery Rock University for providing good academic environments for teaching and research.

My greatest debt and gratitude go to my wife and family for their understanding and support in finishing this project. This project is dedicated to my family whom I love very much.

I am also grateful to the students of Slippery Rock University for reviewing various chapters and providing feedback and changes to strengthen the book. A special thank you to Dr. Ron Sardessai, of the University of Houston–Victoria, for his contribution to the book in general and to Chapter 6 in particular.

I am indebted to my talented assistants Carrie Kane and Georgette Hinkle for their diligent work in typing and organizing the book into its final format. I also thank the following colleagues, without whose help and support this book would not have been possible: Richard Alan Nelson, Abbas Ali, Manton Gibbs, Abdalla Hagan, Shahid Siddiqi, Mohammad Ibrahim, Parameswar Krishnakumar, Ram Mohan Kasuganti, Richard Ramsey, Louis K. Falk, Donald Heckerman, Ron Sardessai, Dharam Rana, Jamaluddin Husain, and Rogene Buchholz. I would like to extend my appreciation to Michael Polishen and Puja Schams for their technical assistance.

I also wish to express my thanks to Haworth Press editors Karen Fisher, Peg Marr, and Jennifer Durgan for their efforts in editing the entire book.

SECTION I: STRATEGIC MANAGEMENT FRAMEWORK

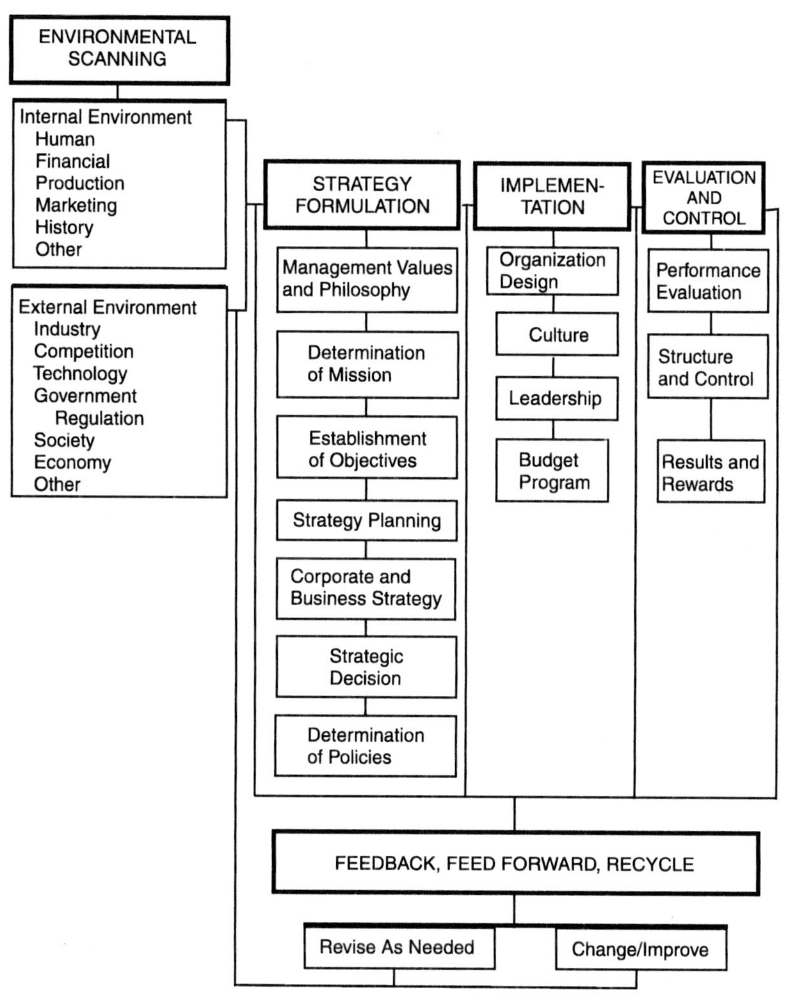

Chapter 1

Introduction to Strategic Management

The twenty-first-century realities of globalization, rapid changes in technology, increasing competition, a changing workforce, changing market and economic conditions, and developing resource shortages all increase the complexity of modern management. Whereas strategic planning was a competitive advantage in the past decade, it is a necessity of global thinking in this century. Planning strategically is certainly a new requirement in the global business world. In order to survive the new business challenge, global thinking and practice must permeate all corporate activities. Successful companies are, of course, the first to consider the global marketplace as their arena for competition. In addition, recent studies have concluded that organizations engaged in strategic management have outperformed those who do not.[1] According to John Peter, strategic management has become a vital part of most, if not all, organizations. "Almost all organizations of any reasonable size have some kind of strategic planning."[2]

WHY IS IT IMPORTANT TO STUDY STRATEGIC MANAGEMENT?

Traditional business disciplines—accounting, economics, finance—have been recognized for centuries. Management per se first appeared in the patriarchal familial structures of earliest civilization, with records of management following soon after. Hammurabi's (2123 B.C.) Codification of Law mentioned accounting practices; Sun Tzu (600 B.C.) recognized such management techniques as division of labor, specialization, and the benefits of sound planning; Confucius (552 B.C.) advocated competition through merit systems while bemoaning the inherent problems of bureaucracy. In India, Kautilya (332 B.C.) wrote extensively about public administration techniques and the necessity of job descriptions.[3] However, strategic management and business policy are relatively "foreign" concepts. Why? First, the subject matter is relatively new compared to traditional business topics. Second, strategic management and business policy integrates the traditional subjects with the main purpose of providing a practical, real-world view of business management.

The study of strategic management and business policy is a capstone course designed to integrate all prior learning into one subject suited for application in the modern business environment. Further, strategic management is designed to develop an awareness of the processes by which organizations can achieve synergies of the whole through the effective cooperation and interaction of the many departments within an organization. Today's managers must have and/or develop the ability to see the interdependent and interrelated nature of organizations. In addition, managers must develop the necessary skills to closely interact with people from differing backgrounds. Therefore, the study of strategic management is designed to prepare current as well as future managers to meet the challenges of today's competitive and ever-changing environments.

HISTORY OF STRATEGIC MANAGEMENT AND BUSINESS POLICY

The study of business policy is relatively new, and the discipline finds its roots in the early American business colleges. Harvard started a course similar to Business Policy in 1911 and, by the 1920s, required it for second-year students. Harvard hoped to demonstrate how the internal and intradivisional functions of business were closely interrelated in practice and how top management had to recognize and manage these interrelationships to work effectively and efficiently.

In 1959, a Ford Foundation and Carnegie Corporation-funded study indicated that business school curricula resulted in various disciplines with course content that students understood only in isolation. The study found that when students were presented with problems requiring integrated subject matter, they had trouble applying the individual course content to the business as a whole entity.[4] In reaction to this study, the American Assembly of Collegiate Schools of Business (AACSB) launched the business policy course as an organized capstone course intended to provide an important and lasting role in schools of business. Subsequently, the field of business policy passed through an evolutionary process and today business policy course content is again evolving into the study of strategic management.[5] This new field contributed to other business disciplines such as management, marketing, accounting, and finance, among others.

According to Gluck, Kaufman, and Walleck, strategic planning and strategic management evolve through four consecutive phases.[6] Increasing change and complexity in the corporation's external environment most likely cause the development of these phases. The first phase involves developing the annual corporate budget. This is called *financial planning.* At this stage the company collects information internally, such as this year's sales and next year's expectations. Also collected is information about personnel, production capacity, raw materials, and other related matters.

The second phase is similar to the first except the plan covers a longer period, three to five years. This type of planning is called *forecast-based planning.* This stage involves collecting information from outside the organization but on limited scale.

The third phase of planning, called *externally oriented planning* or *strategic planning,* is developed mainly by top-level management with the help of consultants. At this stage the company collects information about the external environment and the changes in its competitive market. The main criterion of this stage is the top-down approach to planning. This type of planning does not focus on implementation, which is left for lower-level management and employees to discuss. The third phase also features long-period forecasting, five years or longer.

The final phase is the *strategic management approach,* in which all management and key employees participate to develop a sequence of strategic plans to achieve the various objectives of the corporation. At this stage a comprehensive analysis of the corporate external environment takes place.

PURPOSE OF BUSINESS POLICY COURSE

To understand why Business Policy is taught, one needs to examine what is learned in the course. Business Policy provides practice in decision making (DM) because it primarily covers the job of the general manager and analyzes potential problems from the perspective of the business as a whole. It provides decision makers with the needed information to pursue clarity, accuracy, greater consistency, and speed in the DM process.

The course offers the views of general management. Therefore, instead of getting a functional or operational point of view, the student receives an overall point of view, from the top of the corporation. The course enables the student to develop an eagle-eye perspective that a chief executive officer (CEO) requires in order to be successful. During the course, the student will analyze a wide range of business policy cases, which will help the student acquire a much broader general knowledge about business practices domestically and internationally. Because of this wider view, the student's creativity and imagination will be additionally stimulated when faced with real problems in working situations.

The central theme of the business policy course is corporate strategy. Strategy is not a theory but is the corporation's general approach to achieve its mission and objectives. The strategic management process is important, not only for top-level management, because it filters down to the middle and operating levels as well as the shop floor employees and their supervisors. An understanding of domestic and international competition is important to everyone involved in the organization. Understanding the strategic process can provide employees with direction as well as the needed incentives to work hard and be more competitive.

The course stresses the development of the top manager's ability to relate the processes of management to the common problems that top managers face. This is probably the reason that most of the exercises completed by the student consist of case analyses. Analyzing cases enables the student to utilize processes and theories learned in earlier courses to strategically solve problems from an organizational standpoint.

Business Policy has been designed to create an awareness of and an interest in the strategic problems of a business and its relationship with society. It is hoped that students will learn to evaluate both qualitative and quantitative evidence when conflicting points of view are encountered. This course will teach a student to become proficient at decision making, while learning all the basic concepts in the field of business policy and strategic management.

Strategic Management Models

Scholars feel that the strategic management process is best understood and applied using models. Therefore, several strategic management models have been introduced. Each model has several components that are interrelated, dynamic, and continuous. A change in any of these components may result in a change in other components. For example, the company's objectives and strategies may change if it obtains a new technology or other capabilities that improve its competitive advantage. Therefore, the four major elements of strategic management (environmental analysis, formulation, implementation, and evaluation and control) should be considered interrelated and continuous. These models do not guarantee success. However, they do represent a clear and practical approach to formulating, implementing, and evaluating control strategies. Although different models exist, they do have common elements. Almost all of the models focus on the environmental analysis of the organization. Most of them start by identifying an organization's mission, goals, objectives (hierarchy of purpose), and the various levels of strategies (hierarchy of strategies). Understanding the organizational environment and its hierarchy of purpose will help the company to adopt or avoid certain strategies in order to take advantage of the opportunities in its environment. By understanding the previous strategies of the organization and assessing its current position in the market, management can better forecast the future.

Most scholars present a clean picture of how these various elements relate to each other and how they should work. It is important to understand that the strategic management process is more complex than a simple drawing of a relationship. To ensure success in the formulation and implementation of any strategy, everyone in the organization must be involved. Operating-level management and employee involvement and feedback are essential to any strategy. Since competitive position is dynamic and ever changing, the means to support the competitive position of today's organization must be comprehensive and relevant because the organization must deal with the global aspects of the business environment. Relevancy involves the analysis of current and potential competitors inside and outside the industry. Strategy needs to be developed by talented individuals who are familiar with corporate internal and external realities, who should consider the global marketplace as the proper domain of analysis. You cannot have an effective strategy unless each of the other managers and employees of the organization participates in his or her capacity.

In this book, the strategic management framework consists of four connected, dynamic, and continuous elements: *environmental analysis, strategy formulation, strategy implementation,* and *evaluation and control.* Although each of these strategic management elements can be considered individually, they are all interrelated and must build upon one another to form the overall, integrated process. This model (see Figure 1.1) is shown in more detail at the beginning of Section I and will not be repeated in the other chapters.

The Elements of Strategic Management

Three terms are prominent in almost all business organizations today: *business policy, strategic planning,* and *strategic management.* All of them deal with management efforts to confront situations that arise in the organization's daily routine while trying to achieve the organization's goals and objectives. Thus all of the terms are related, but each has its own unique definition.

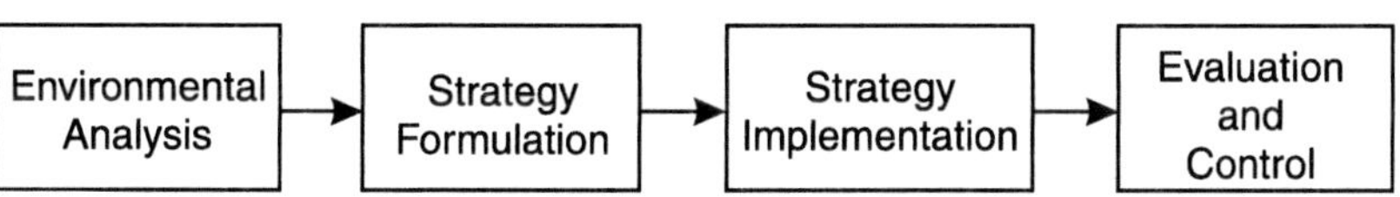

FIGURE 1.1. Strategic Management Framework

BUSINESS POLICY

Business policy guides certain continuous actions in the organization to assist managers in ascertaining corporate objectives and to support and enhance corporate strategies. In other words, business policy is the set of rules designed by the organization to confront a recurring situation that threatens the organization's mission. It is a supporting instrument to aid in accomplishing the company's objectives and formulating, implementing, and controlling strategy. Business policies are usually the last resort for the organization in confronting problems that have occurred frequently. An example of a business policy is the refusal of convenience stores to accept any currency larger than a $20 bill after 10 p.m. Another example of business policy is a company commitment to distribute a certain percentage of net earnings (i.e., 50 percent) as a dividend to shareholders. Other examples include these:

- A company will not consider any cost reduction options if it means compromising quality.
- A company decides to grow only through retained earnings.
- A company will not consider adding new products with less than 10 percent return on investment.
- A company sells exclusively on cash terms.
- A rental company charges a deposit for rented material.
- A rental car company charges extra money for delivering the rented car in another location.
- A company hires personnel with experience only.
- A company prepares guidelines on how to collect debts from its customers.
- A company will not question customers' returns of items purchased earlier.
- A company responds to 50 percent of customer inquiries within three working days.

Strategy refers to the method or route a company chooses to achieve its objectives after careful assessment of its resources and environment. Strategy therefore refers to the determination of long-term corporate objectives and the methods along with the functional policies proposed by the company to realize these objectives. Strategy is a comprehensive, long-term plan indicating how the corporation will achieve its missions and objectives. Alfred Chandler defined strategy as the "determination of the basic long-term goals and objectives of an enterprise, and the adoption of courses of action and the allocation of resources necessary for carrying out those goals."[7] Planning is the end result of strategy design.

Policy versus Strategy

From a conceptual standpoint, the terms *strategy* and *policy* have different and distinct meanings. However, on the more practical level of day-to-day usage, their distinctiveness often becomes blurred. Frequently, these words are erroneously used as if they were interchangeable.

In general, policies are drafted to be used as broad guidelines by the organization's decision makers. These general guidelines indicate how an organization should deal with recurring problems in its routine operation. By providing a prescribed path for handling repetitive matters, they save time and effort. Thus, policies streamline and help focus the decisions made and the consequent actions taken by an organization. In theory, these guidelines are used to help organizational leaders make all other decisions; they represent a framework for decision making.

In contrast, strategies represent an organization's specific plans of action. Strategic planning permits the organization to chart a course of action into the future that coordinates and balances all the contributions made by the entire organization, yet strategic planning must be flexible enough to absorb and respond, drive the organization forward, and adapt to the current business environment.[8] Strategies denote a general program of action to achieve long-term objectives of the companies, the deployment of resources to attain these objectives, and major policies to be followed in using these resources. We can say that all strategic decisions and subsequent actions of the organization should revolve around and occur in accordance with the guidelines provided by policy.

Events That Define or Alter a Company's Strategy

The strategic plan is the result of strategic design and it includes a statement outlining the company's mission, future direction, performance targets, and strategy selection. *The strategy will change when the following events take place:*

1. When the company attempts to strengthen its long-term competitive position and secure competitive advantage
2. Through any actions intended to improve profitability, customer services, and products

3. Because of any actions of expansion, change in leadership, and change in ownership
4. Through any action that responds to changes in industry conditions (i.e., change in demand, globalization of competition, government regulations, or new entry or exit in the industry)
5. When company resources and capabilities change
6. When a company moves to counter imitation by rivals and new demand for quality in product and services at a reasonable price
7. Through actions to capitalize on new opportunities, such as new technology, product innovation, the purchase of a new company, new opportunities that open up, new markets, or a change in market condition (free market)
8. When the company goes through restructuring, mergers, and buyouts
9. When defensive action to counter the moves of rivals and to defend against external threats is taken
10. Any time the organization does not accept its current strategy

Measuring the Effectiveness of Policy

The effectiveness of a policy can be measured by determining how closely the company comes to achieving its goals and objectives. Is the company surviving as an entity? Is the company making an acceptable rate of profit? Objectives can be measured and, therefore, one can determine if their outcome is positive or negative. Companies impact a large part of our economy. They utilize much of society's resources, such as land, labor, capital, and technology. We must learn to be efficient in the allocation of resources to benefit society. We must learn how to plan wisely.

Formal planning is increasingly necessary in today's society with accelerated technology, rapid social change, and turbulent organizational environments. Guidelines are set in terms of broad parameters of strategic planning. More effective strategic planning probably represents one of the greatest profit improvement opportunities for business organizations today. One valuable lesson worth mentioning at this early stage is that a strategic plan is only of use when it can be implemented. Strategy is based on policy, and both play an important role in assuring the success of the organization. They deal with functional elements of how a company intends to reach its objectives.

A good example of strategic failure is the strategy designed by Disney executives to establish Euro Disney in April 1992 north of Paris. Euro Disney is the fourth Disney amusement park in the world. The first two parks were created in the United States and the third one was established in Japan.

Those three parks have proven to be very successful. When the company expanded to the European market it experienced many difficulties during the first two years of operation. An insufficient number of visitors and huge investments, which mounted to more than $3.68 billion, resulted in huge losses for the company. The strategy established in 1995 to rescue the company was partially successful.

Another example is the failure of the U.S. automobile makers to plan strategically, which allowed the Japanese and others to gain U.S. market share in the 1970s and 1980s.

STRATEGIC PLANNING

Strategic planning is a management tool to look at the future and see tomorrow's opportunities or challenges to gain competitive position. Managers who think in terms of today are behind the times tomorrow.[9] Competitive strategic planning not only predicts future events but also influences them and energizes resources and activities. The evolutionary process integrates decisions and actions into a vision of where the organization wants to be in the future, rather than allowing daily demands to determine the organization's future direction and position in the marketplace. While the *mission* represents the concept of the business, the *vision* refers to the future direction of the company. Sometimes they are combined in one statement, although they may have separate statements.

Strategic planning, the result of strategy formulation, requires strategic thinking, which is a continuous process that deals with corporate events in a comprehensive manner. *Strategic thinking* refers to the question, "Where do you want to go?" How to get there is the planning. Strategic thinking leads managers to successful strategy planning now that corporations must compete in an expanded marketplace. Understanding the driving force in such markets enhances the firm's global competitive position. Strategic thinking, therefore, is the matching of opportunities with corporate resources in order to envision the future direction that leads to improved corporate performance and enhanced competitive advantage.

Strategies are essential ingredients for success in a global market. Companies learn from each other through benchmarking (comparing your company to others in the market and learning from the best practices). A number of studies indicate that companies that formulate strategic plans outperform those who do not. Strategic planning helps organizations to be more focused and to successfully pursue desired results.[10] Successful companies are, of course, the first to consider the global marketplace as their arena for competition.[11] Companies without strategic planning are no longer guarded. Strategic planning is the company's road map to see where it is now, how it got here, where it wants to be in the future, and how they *plan* to get there. Strategic planning has four main purposes:

1. To find, attract, and keep customers
2. To ensure that the company is meeting the needs and wants of its customers, which is a cornerstone in providing the quality product or service that customers really want
3. To sustain a competitive position
4. To utilize the company's strengths and take full advantage of its competitor's weaknesses

In planning, management is in need of reliable and relevant information about the company's *internal environment* (skills, equipment, financial capabilities, etc.) and its *external environment* (position within its industry, and the overall opportunities and threats). Environmental information is important in forecasting the future, which is often unpredictable.

To build competitive advantage in business today, organizations are turning to strategic management technologies. Early systems focused primarily on support functions such as accounting and record keeping. These activities contributed to the firm's competitiveness only indirectly, with insignificant reductions in costs. Today, systems are integrated throughout all levels of the organization and have become essential tools for the business to survive.[12] This includes all technologies such as information systems and advanced manufacturing technology that keeps a company on the cutting edge.

The Mission Statement

A key component, critical to any strategic plan, is the organization's *mission statement.* A firm must have a stated mission from which it sets goals and objectives (see Figure 1.2). The mission statement must include the following: Who is the company? What does it want to accomplish? What type of commitments does the company provide its customers and employees?[13] A mission statement is a clear definition of the organization's business. It involves stating the business's overall strategy, and may include what strengths the company has, what areas it wants to be in, who it is, and what it is trying to do. A mission can be described as an organization's raison d'être, or reason for being. It reflects the organization's purpose and should describe its major areas of interest or intended actions. A mission should also include methods used to satisfy market needs.

SUBJECT: The Nutrition/Dietetics Department

Mission Statement

The basic purpose of this department is to use its resources to promote good nutrition. This, of course, must be done in cooperation and coordination with other hospital departments. All activities must take place under the auspices and within the greater framework of the hospital organization as a whole. Attention must be given to total patient care, as well as to financial matters, as is appropriate for a profit-oriented health care center.

Promoting good nutrition is a multifaceted task. It extends from providing nutritious, appealing, in-hospital food (for both patients and staff) to educating patients about the proper diet to follow at home. It includes nutritional screening of incoming patients to determine if nutritional intervention is necessary and the further assessment of those found to be at risk. It includes making nutritional recommendations and consulting with nurses, physicians, and other professionals. It also includes continuous training and education of the dietetics staff.

Resources of the department include the expertise of a competent, caring staff of registered dietitians, and a well-trained complement of technicians, food service employees, and other workers. Supplies, equipment, and financial resources provided by a multimillion-dollar budget, as well as support and goodwill contributed by the parent hospital organization, also assist the department in successfully fulfilling its mission.

Goals

1. Timely delivery of patient meals that are both nutritious and appealing
2. Successful operation of a convenient cafeteria that serves nutritious and appealing meals to employees
3. Operation of an effective program of nutritional screening and assessment
4. Operation of an educational program to benefit patients, the dietetics staff, other hospital staff, and the community
5. Operation of the department in a financially responsible manner
6. Operation of the department in a manner that complements overall hospital goals
7. Operation of a comprehensive quality control program

Objectives

1. Breakfast, lunch, and dinner tray service will commence precisely at 7:30, 11:00, and 4:30 respectively at least 95 percent of the time.
2. A staff dietitian will evaluate patient menus for nutrition and value with computer-assisted programs. Menus will be published in advance.
3. Responses on patient questionnaires regarding food acceptability will increase from 65 to 75 percent positive.
4. Improvements in cafeteria food quality and convenience will promote a 25 percent increase in cafeteria revenues.
5. A dietetics chart note will be placed in the medical record of 97 percent of the patients who are admitted on restricted diets.
6. At least fifteen complete nutritional assessments will be performed by the department each week.
7. A new, department-sanctioned, nutritional assessment worksheet will be developed and in use by July 31.
8. A continuing education meeting will be held for registered dietitians once each month. Ninety percent attendance will be attained.
9. Food service supervisors will conduct in-service programs at least two times per month.
10. Availability of community nutrition services will be advertised in the local media once each week.

FIGURE 1.2. Example of Strategic Planning in a Nutrition/Dietetics Department of a Large Hospital

FIGURE 1.2 *(continued)*

11. A balanced budget for the department will be submitted on June 1 of each year.
12. A report from each area supervisor indicating compliance with the budget will be submitted each month.
13. Two hundred patient questionnaires regarding food quality will be collected and evaluated each quarter.
14. A system of peer evaluation will be developed by September 1 and in use by December 1.
15. A representative from the Dietetics Department will attend 90 percent of the hospital meetings and functions to which the department is invited.

Stone advocates that for a mission statement to be effective it must be simple to comprehend, relevant, and reliable, and that it should set the company apart from its competitors, as well as the fact that it should be written in a positive tone to encourage commitment and energize all employees toward fulfilling the mission. The mission statement should also be enduring and adapted to the target audience. The target audience has a "bearing on the length, tone, and visibility of the statement." It is important to know who you are writing for before you decide what to write.[14]

Some of the important elements of the mission are the corporation's goals and objectives, philosophy, and its basic values, ambitions, and beliefs. The goal provides, in general terms, the basis for implementing its policies, objectives, strategies, and planning. The mission must be carefully worded to provide proper direction. It should be designed with the participation of all members of the organization. Top-level management sets the vision and acts as a mentor, leaving the details to the various levels of management and/or committees. People involved and participating from the beginning are more responsive and supportive of strategic planning and the change it brings.[15]

In formulating strategic plans, management must encourage productive communication. Many well-intentioned ideas are counterproductive without the direction of a strategic plan. Since its inception in 1975, Microsoft's mission has been to create software for the personal computer that empowers and enriches people in the workplace, at school, and at home. Similarly, Saturn Corporation has done well even though it is a relatively new car company. It has established itself as a different kind of company with a different kind of car. The company's mission statement follows:

> Saturn was created with one simple idea: to put people first. In the beginning, the focus was on creating a different kind of company, one dedicated to finding better ways for people to work together to design, build, and sell cars. . . . Saturn believes in taking better care of their employees and paying more attention to their customers' needs. Today the company is dedicated to designing vehicles that complement customers' daily lives.[16]

Saturn's main purpose is to focus on the small-car niche market, which wants to buy a small, inexpensive, and reliable car.

The mission statements of both companies strongly emphasize commitment to providing the customer with a quality product through enthusiastic, productive teamwork. This should enable these firms to remain strong and continue to grow. Both companies have reached a high degree of success for many reasons, but chiefly due to excellent employees, continuous improvement, and dedication to achieving worthwhile goals. This dedication benefits customers, the company, and employees' personal lives.

The mission of a financial institution could be to meet the financial service needs of its customers (individuals and businesses). The institution pursues a leadership position in the markets where it chooses to compete by providing high-quality, differentiated products and exceptional customer service. The institution seeks to penetrate existing markets, deliver products and services to new geographical markets, and strategically manage the business mix to achieve superior results. Notice that the goals of this institution are directed to its customers, future expansion, and industry dominance. It plans to meet customer needs by providing superior customer service and by offering different types of products and services. The institution plans to dominate the industry by expanding market share in the current market and expanding into new geographical areas. It also plans to maintain stability while doing this by the use of strategic management.

Every organization must have a purpose and stated mission. Peter Drucker asserts that even though the question "What is our business?" is simple, it is one that causes the most "frustration and failure" in an organization. Drucker said that the answer to "What is our business?" begins by investigating customers' needs and wants.[17] Derek Abell expanded this idea by using three dimensions: "(1) customer groups, or *who* is being satisfied, (2) customer needs or *what* is being satisfied, and (3) technologies, or *how* customer needs are satisfied."[18] A clear and concise mission statement is invaluable. It will give the company a firm foundation on which to stand.

Objectives and Goals

The company's mission must be turned into objectives and goals, the second step in strategic planning. *Goals* are broad statements that present what needs to be pursued in certain areas. Most businesses express their main goal as maximizing stockholder wealth. The focus on maximizing short-term *return on investment (ROI)* will overlook corporate competitiveness. American managers are accused of focusing on short-term results rather than a company's long-term survival as a vital entity. They tend to establish strategies that expand the size of the company rather than profitability and stockholder satisfaction. An organization's goals depend on the nature of its business and will stem from its mission. The organization's market share, technology, productivity, and profitability are all components of a desired goal. Saturn's goal is to infiltrate and dominate the market. They want to sell cars at a very affordable price from extremely well-staffed and maintained showrooms, with the auto industry's best after-sales service. They also plan to keep things simple and easy for their customers. Microsoft's main goal is to produce a product that customers want.

A company always has a large number of objectives, which are stated in a hierarchical fashion, from the most to the least important. They indicate the desired result of planned activity. Not-for-profit organizational objectives might not be specific or measurable. The objectives of for-profit organizations are the specific intended results. They are measurable and have a time frame. There are three levels of objectives within an organization:

1. *Strategic or long-term objectives* are usually set for the entire organization and broadly stated.
2. *Intermediate objectives* are usually more specific and increasingly complex and detailed. They are set for various strategic units or functions.
3. *Operational or short-term objectives* are more specific than the previous two and should be done on an individual or group level.

Objectives and strategies are formed from strategists' consideration of mission, strategic policy, and appropriate information. When a firm operates outside its parent country, the objectives and other strategies might be different. While the strategic management process is the same for domestic and international management, the environment is often different. For example, companies must adhere to different rules when operating abroad. Therefore, strategies must be altered. Many multinational companies depend on the superiority of some resources abroad such as capital, labor, or technology. These organizations capitalize on advantage in order to overcome weaknesses at home.

Corporations conduct business abroad to achieve economies of scale, increase market share, and reduce overall cost. Operating abroad may impose limitations on organizations in setting objectives and designing strategies because the host country's needs and priorities may be different from those of the parent country. For example, the host government, because of extra cost, may limit efficiency levels. The utilization of certain resources may be set at specified levels. Growth may be legislatively set, etc.

Corporate Philosophy

Corporate philosophy is an important element of the corporate mission statement. Corporate philosophy represents the basic beliefs, values, and aspirations of the chief executive officer and top-level management. It shows how the company proposes to conduct business in the future as well as its priorities. A *philosophical creed* is often developed to reflect the company's corporate culture. The creed usually describes a company's responsibility to its stakeholders (i.e., stockholders, employees, customers, management, and communities at large). For example, a company's responsibility to its stockholders can be to provide them with a fair return on their investment, to introduce a new product, to purchase new equipment, etc. A company's responsibility to its employees can be to provide them with a sense of security on the job, give them safe working conditions, honor their dignity, appreciate their merit, and provide fair compensation. Delivering immediate and quality service, continuing to reduce costs, and maintaining reasonable prices are good examples of corporate responsibilities toward customers.

The *learning-curve theory* stipulates that efficiency (and thus cost savings) results when people continuously repeat a task. This applies to management decision making, as well as to assembly-line labor. There is evidence, however, that the learning curve has limits—the significance of the learning curve effect is greater in complex tasks and tends to decrease over time.[19]

The Learning Organization

Organizations need to continuously learn from their past experiences and need to be willing to adapt a new position if they are to survive and prosper. The *learning organization* is relatively a new trend in business that emphasizes systematic problem solving. This means that everyone in the organization is engaged in identifying and solving problems, enabling the organization to continuously improve and increase its capability. The interacting systems that make up the learning organization resemble a network in which each group communicates to and influences every other group. While top-level management provides the vision for the development of strategies, employees assist in scanning the environment for critical information that is vital to the process. Information sharing requires adjustments on the part of managers for the inclusion of employees, suppliers, and customers. Employee empowerment will encourage participation in the process of designing strategies as well as in implementation. Transformational change involves redesign and renewal of the total organization in which horizontal structure replaces the familiar hierarchical pyramid. This concept is similar to total quality management, which is discussed in Chapter 2.

STRATEGIC MANAGEMENT

Strategic management is the process of assessing the corporation and its environment in order to meet the long-term objectives of the organization. It refers to the series of decisions taken by management to determine the long-term objectives of the organization and the means to achieve these objectives. Once a mission has been established, strategies are developed to pursue it. An organization must develop a form of strategic management to control these strategies.

Through strategic management, an organization can handle its mission while at the same time assessing the relationship of the organization to its environment. The *environment,* in this case, means any internal or external force that may cause an organization to stray from the path of its stated mission. Thus, strategic management becomes a component of an organization's mission. Without it, an organization would have great difficulty implementing and controlling strategies. In addition, one important point to keep in mind is the difference between intended strategy and the strategy actually realized. Peter Wright and colleagues addressed the *intended strategy* as the one that was originally planned and could be emergent in its original, modified, or an entirely different form. On the other hand, *realized strategy* is what is actually implemented because of changed external or internal events.[20]

An example of intended versus realized strategy is Honda's entrance into the American motorcycle market. When Honda entered the market in 1959, its intended strategy was to market its motorcycles with 250 cc and 305 cc engines even though it was selling the 50 cc model in Japan with great success. However, the intended strategy failed because, despite what Honda management believed, the U.S. market preferred the smaller model. It was not until Sears Roebuck expressed an interest in selling the smaller model that Honda changed its mind about the model to sell. So, the intended strategy was modified and the realized strategy met with positive results.[21]

The traditional approach indicates that each of the elements of strategic management constitutes a planned and organized step in the process. The strategic management process begins with defining vision, missions, and goals followed by strategy formulation, strategy implementation, and evaluation and control.

Proponents of *emergent strategies* believe that the initiation of such strategy does not require going through the steps mentioned above in a sequential fashion. They are usually suggested by operating-level management and/or employees. However, such a strategy does not diminish the role of the strategic (general) management. Management has to evaluate the emergent strategy in the context of the already established strategy (intended strategy) and determine whether it fits the organization's needs, criteria, and capabilities. This will necessitate a thorough evaluation of the organization's internal and external environment. Usually, the formulation of intended strategies is a top-down procedure, whereas the formulation of emergent strategies is a bottom-up approach. Therefore, the effectiveness of such a strategy depends on the type of communication and leadership available in the company. In most cases, strategies are a mix of both intended and emergent strategies. Figure 1.3 shows the difference between intended and emergent strategies.[22]

An important aspect of the strategic planning process is the *strengths, weaknesses, opportunities, and threats (SWOT)* analysis, which is discussed in more detail in Chapter 3.

Possibly the most dominant forces behind the strategic management process are the personal values and philosophies of top management. These values influence every stage of the process and limit or direct the organization's progress accordingly. There are many good examples of a top manager's philosophy affecting the strategic direction of an organization. Lee Iacocca's influence upon Chrysler Corporation is well known. Chrysler, during the 1980s and early 1990s, was a reflection of Iacocca's personal management philosophy and vision. Jack Welch had a similar impact on General Electric (GE) during the same period.

In many businesses where organizational objectives are merely an extension of their founders' objectives, the influence of management values and philosophies is even more apparent. Bill Gates, founder and president of Microsoft, is a good example. In the 1990s, Gates was the primary driving

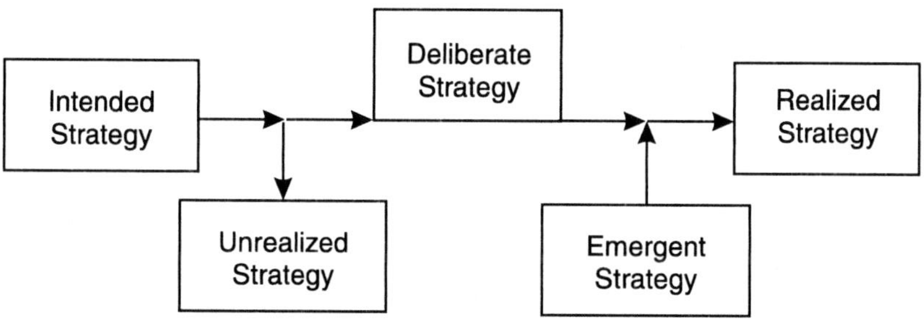

FIGURE 1.3. The Difference Between Intended and Emergent Strategy

force behind Microsoft—the man with the vision of what his company would become.

Strategy Formulation

Strategy formulation and strategy implementation are two sequential stages of the strategic management process. *Strategy formulation* consists of determining the organization's mission, goals, and objectives, and selecting or crafting an appropriate strategy. *Strategy implementation* is followed by evaluation and control. Although each of these strategic management stages can be considered individually, they are all interrelated and must build upon one another to form the overall, integrated process.

Strategy formulation involves much research and decision making, yet it is primarily a process to answer the question, "How are we going to accomplish our goals and get where we want to go?" Before this question can be asked, however, the goals and objectives must already have been determined. Essentially, crafting the strategy can be thought of as a continuous effort to develop a set of directions, draft a blueprint, or draw a road map.

Strategy formulation is influenced by many factors, including (1) evaluating the internal and external organization (especially the projected future environment); (2) establishing the predetermined mission and goals of the organization; (3) setting the organization's strategic policies or guidelines; and (4) assessing the needs, values, and skills possessed by those who develop the strategy. The same factors influence development of the strategic objectives.

According to William Bogner and Howard Thomas, there are two competing models of strategy formulation. The *objective model* is based on economic concepts (i.e., supply and demand, competition factors, etc.). The model begins with a company objective, which will eventually be affected by competition. The competition will have an impact on the strategy formulation process. The industry structure (combined competitors) will directly impact the formulation process, which in turn will affect resource allocation decisions (how the money is spent). This process will continue until an external factor (i.e., technological change) disrupts it, at which time a new objective model will be formulated.[23]

The second model is the *cognitive model.* It exposes a flaw in the objective model (i.e., the inability to capture the significance of the changes causing the objective formulation process to begin again). The cognitive model follows the same principle as the first model. However, it also consists of a collective view of objective strategies, which are consolidated into one formulation process. This process is to define one's own place in the industry and cognitively organize one's understanding of competitive strategy.[24]

A model introduced by Robert Grant is *resource-based strategy formulation*. This strategy formulation process can be applied to any resource of the company. Resources are defined as human, financial, physical, technological, reputation, and organizational. The process consists of a series of steps that present a flow of decision making that contributes to an overall strategy of the firm as follows:

1. The firm's resources should be classified and its strengths should be appraised in relation to the weaknesses of its competitors. Also, opportunities for better utilization of resources should be defined.
2. The firm's capabilities should be identified, as well as the inputs to each capability.
3. The rent-generating (profit-making) potential of each resource should be identified in terms of
   a. its competitive advantage, and
   b. its probability of returns.
4. At this point, a strategy should be selected that best uses the firm's resources relative to its external opportunities.
5. Once a strategy is formulated, the resource gaps among the first four steps need to be filled. After this is done, each step is then updated and the process begins again for new resources.

This process is termed the resource-based view of the firm. The key to resource-based strategy is to understand the relationships between the resources and determining how competition and the market environment will affect them.[25]

It should be noted that management's perception is very significant in this process. A strong body of research suggests a bias (or distortion) may occur between objective reality and the manager's perception of reality in the strategy formulation process.[26] Howard Stevenson noticed a wide variance in senior management's perception of the organization's competencies, which frequently fall victim to a false perception of what the company is in comparison to the industry.[27]

After determining how the goals will be accomplished, actual tasks must be performed to convert the goals into reality. In short, the predetermined strategy must be implemented.

Strategic Planning and Uncertainty

An integrated approach to strategic planning must be established encompassing issues of profitability, productivity, quality, advanced production processes, innovation, market growth, corporate downsizing, public image, social responsibility, and other business goals. An organization's strategy must be thought of as a tool to realize its competitive goals.[28]

Many companies approach today's uncertainty in two ways: (1) totally ignoring strategic planning, they concentrate on short-term profitability; or (2) they rely on the government to either predict future business environments or protect them from competition. For example, Lee Iacocca appealed for government protection of the domestic automobile industry from Japanese competition during the 1980s. However, in most instances, the more appropriate corporate response to uncertainty is to obtain better and more organized information from both internal and external sources, since superior information usually reduces uncertainties, thus enabling the company to maintain a proactive response posture toward important environmental changes.

Internal sources of information include the organization's research and development, marketing, finance, accounting, operations, public relations, and information systems operations. External sources include published materials, such as magazines, trade journals, newspapers, libraries, and online databases. Also, suppliers, distributors, salespersons, customers, and competitors are good sources of information. Obtaining better information will reduce uncertainty, produce calculated risks in continuing areas of uncertainty, and enable the company to respond quickly to important changes in the environment. *Certainty* is a situation in which a manager has complete knowledge and control of the outcome of a decision. *Uncertainty* is the degree of change and complexity in a company's environment of which management has no complete knowledge or control. Whenever the environment changes, it will lead to some changes in the strategies adopted. Corporate strategies must be flexible.

Management has to prepare for these kinds of conditions by collecting enough information and using appropriate forecasting techniques. Two types of forecasting techniques can be used, quantitative techniques and qualitative techniques. *Quantitative techniques* are useful when forecasts are not available, and *qualitative techniques* are based on the assumption that the future will be like the past. *Risk* is a situation in which the managers or decision makers do not have all the information or knowledge needed for a secure decision. Therefore, they have to estimate the likelihood of certain outcomes in evaluating decisions.

In conclusion, strategy formulation is affected by many different factors. Some external factors are environmental threats, social obligations, or opportunities or resources available to the firm. Perhaps the most important internal factor affecting formulation is the manager's personal values and aspirations (see Chapter 2). Ultimately the test of good strategy formulation and implementation is whether there is a "fit" between the chosen strategy and the manager to produce the desired performance levels and achieve corporate objectives.

Strategic Planning in the United States

Important changes in the environment occurred in the United States in the 1960s. Economic growth began to slow down, and domestic and international competition began to increase in some major American industries. In the 1970s, energy and environmental problems became a concern to society. It was during this period that the height of excitement over strategic planning occurred, as groups such as GE, Boston Consultant Group (BCG), and others were developing strategic planning models. From this, a new breed of professionals, called strategic planners, emerged. These new professionals were quickly hired as many firms began to establish corporate strategies.

However, results did not meet expectations. In fact, a "reassessment of thirty three strategies described in *BusinessWeek* in 1970 and 1980 found that nineteen had failed, ran into trouble, or were abandoned, when only fourteen could be deemed successful."[29] One-third of the Fortune 500 companies in 1970 had vanished by 1983. In 1982, Peter and Waterman identified forty-three excellent companies that had demonstrated superiority on six critical financial yardsticks for a period of twenty years. Five years later, only fourteen were still excellent on the basis of those measures. In ten years some had disappeared entirely and many of the remaining were in trouble.[30]

This initial failure of strategic management was attributed to hostility between strategic planners and operating managers. Operating managers did not implement the strategic plans they were given, which caused many firms to miss some tremendous opportunities. Today, companies are more aware of the need for strategic planning but have shifted the origination point from the strategic planners to the operation level. Organizations perceive this shift as necessary to capitalize on ever-changing economic conditions. Michael E. Porter, a Harvard Business School professor, said that a corporate strategy should be "more than a compilation of individual business unit plans. It should be a device to integrate business units that enable the parent company to capitalize on synergies so that the whole of the corporation is more than the sum of its parts."[31]

Implementation of Strategy Formulation

To be effective, a strategic plan must be action oriented. Implementation of the plan in a particular business must be a priority, geared to the specific aspects of producing finished goods. Strategic plans must be specific and articulate, yet they are instruments meant to help steer an organization to prosperity. Plans must be flexible enough to allow an organization to seize new opportunities and react to changing market conditions. The planning process is one of evolution; adjustments are made to achieve the mission.

The starting point in formulating strategy is to develop a clear concept of (1) what the business is, (2) what it should be, and (3) how the company will get where it wants to be. Next is to implement the crafted strategy. Implementation refers to the arrangement of tasks and responsibility to the individuals or groups in the organization. Implementation through organization structure is the second major step in the strategic management process. This is discussed further in future chapters.

Corporate Stakeholders

Stakeholders are groups who have direct interests in the organization and without whose direct involvement the company would have difficulty surviving. Stakeholders are stockholders, employees, management, major creditors, major consumers, major suppliers, etc. Those stakeholders expect the company to satisfy their demands. Stockholders, for example, provide the company with needed capital and expect an appropriate return on their investment in exchange. Employees provide the company with the needed labor and skills and expect fair wages and job satisfaction in return. Major creditors provide the company with financial support when it needs it and expect more value and timely payment. Major customers buy a company's products and services and expect value for their purchases.[32] Therefore, the company must take stakeholder interests into account when formulating its strategies. If it does not, those stakeholders may withdraw their support of the organization. For example, stockholders might sell their shares, employees might leave their jobs, creditors might discontinue their support, customers might buy from competitors, suppliers will seek more dependable buyers, and so on.

If the stakeholders' interests are taken into consideration, the company will send a clear message that its strategies will be formulated with the stakeholders' claims in mind. A successful manager is able to understand the various stakeholder demands and balance their conflicting interests in formulating and implementing strategy. For instance, employee or union demands for higher wages may conflict with consumer expectations for reasonable prices. In practice, few organizations have the resources to fulfill and manage all stakeholders' interests. It is therefore important to decide which claims to satisfy first. This can be done after a thorough analysis of the various groups in the organization. A *stakeholder analysis* involves identifying the major internal and external stakeholders, their interests and concerns, and how these groups can be satisfied.

Corporate Social Responsibility

Corporate social responsibility is a term that has emerged over the past forty years to describe an increasing interaction between corporations and their stakeholders. It refers to corporate actions to improve the welfare of society along with advancing the company's own interests. People in corporations are being held responsible for policies or strategies that are now seen as socially unacceptable. It is becoming necessary for corporations to develop new ways of dealing with and meeting increasing social needs. The strategic decisions of companies certainly involve social and political as well as economic consequences. Companies are therefore invited to be socially responsible and to build certain social criteria or goals into their strategy formulation processes.

It is in the long-term interest of a company to behave in a socially responsible manner. This means that corporations must do more than simply obey the law, which may be lagging behind society's values and expectations. The social responsibility of business encompasses the economic, legal, ethical, and discretionary expectations of society at a given point in time. Social responsibility is a healthy investment strategy. Many investors (such as not-for-profit organizations, cities, states, churches, universities, and mutual funds) view companies that are not socially responsible as riskier investments. Thus, if a company desires to preserve the support of its investors, it must behave in a socially responsible manner. Because being socially responsible may result in sacrificing short-term profits, companies need to examine the economic and social impacts of particular strategies. Consider the impact of some incidents on the reputation and image of many companies, such as Exxon's oil leak in Alaska, the faulty tires of Firestone, Ford recalling millions of their trucks, the Union Carbide gas leak in India, and many other similar cases.

MORAL AND ETHICAL DUTIES

Business has an ethical responsibility to its stakeholders. Therefore, strategies must be ethical and socially responsible. They should involve right and responsible actions. For example, as the strategy takes the owners/shareholders into consideration by providing them with reasonable returns on their investment, it should consider the employees' concerns as well. The strategy should emphasize the dignity and respect of all company employees and reassure their economic well-being, health, and job security. Happy employees will result in happy customers, which results in good financial performance. In addition, major customers expect high-quality products and services, which are safe and durable, at reasonable prices. Companies should provide a commitment to satisfy their customer needs and expectations all the time. Similarly, in dealing with major suppliers, quality and not price alone determine the source of supply. It is unethical to force your suppliers not to deal with your competitors. Strategy formulation should reflect good citizenship, waste removal, and problem solving. Exercise care, because discriminatory actions in a diverse society are not humane and tend to prove costly for everybody involved.

Being ethical and socially responsible involves not only satisfying legal requirements, but also going beyond the law to meet your responsibilities to society as a whole. A proactive approach is required and expected by society.

CORPORATE GOVERNANCE AND STRATEGY

Stockholders provide capital to businesses. They are, therefore, the owners of the organization who face the challenge of keeping managers' desires for excessive growth under control. Theoretically, they have the power to remove ineffective and incompetent managers. In order to do this, several *governance mechanisms* are used. The first of these mechanisms is *stockholders' annual meetings,* which are designed to allow shareholders to voice approval or disapproval of management's performance. Often opposition to management does not materialize because stockholders find it very expensive to finance their own challenges. In addition, many of them hold few shares, not nearly enough to hold any real influence over corporate policy. Stockholders are many and widely distributed all over the world.

However, this situation started to change. Since the 1970s, institutional investors such as pension funds, insurance companies, and college endowment funds have expanded to hold more than one-half of many corporate stocks.[33] For example, 63 percent of Ford Motor Company stock, 81 percent of Digital Equipment Corporation, 79 percent of Kmart, and 72 percent of Citicorp were held by institutions. These investors would like to see the value of their stock increase. Therefore, they have begun to play a more powerful role in governing the corporations in which they own shares. After Exxon's 1989 oil spill in Alaska, public pension funds, led by the New York City Employees Retirement system, persuaded the company to include an environmentalist on its board.[34]

In the 1980s and 1990s, institutional investors became more involved in corporate activities than ever before. When they are not satisfied with corporate performance they usually let management and the company know. General Motors Chairman Roger Smith met with a group of institutional investors in 1987 because the group was angry that GM made a $700 million "hush mail" payment to H. Ross Perot when he left his position on the GM board. They also reprimanded Smith for decreasing profits and market share, weak stock price, poor productivity, and the big bonuses received by senior executives. The result was that GM announced a series of major policy changes including stock buybacks and capital spending cuts.[35]

The next mechanism is the *board of directors*. Because these persons are elected through stockholder votes, they are subject to legal accountability for the company's actions. Both the inside and outside directors provide valuable information and resources to the institution. However, critics claim that insiders (officers of the company and those tied economically to the CEOs) often abuse their position and sometimes present information that puts management in a favorable light. In reality, outside members of the board are selected carefully by the CEO and not the stockholders. Critics therefore claim that CEOs dominate the company and the board of directors. For example, a Delaware court ruled in 1985 that Trans Union Corporation was too quick to accept a takeover bid. As a result, board members were forced to pay the difference between the price received and the price that might have been received in the sale.[36]

Today, corporate boards are becoming more active in the corporate governance role. After GM market share declined to 33 percent in 1992, from 44 percent in 1981, shareholders started complaining. The eleven outside members of the board of directors met privately and decided to replace Robert Stempel, chairman of the board's executive committee, with John Smale, retired chairman of Procter & Gamble, and promote John F. Smith Jr., head of GM's international operations, to CEO.[37] As the threat of legal action grows, boards have begun to assert independence from company management and from the CEOs. Although many boards are beginning to take their responsibilities more seriously, there are still a number of weak boards. An effective board should take on the following responsibilities: (1) setting the corporate strategies and missions, (2) hiring and firing the CEO and top management, (3) supervising the top managers, (4) reviewing and approving the use of resources, and (5) caring for stakeholder interests.[38]

In conclusion, strategic management is taught to provide a sampling of various situations encountered by managers. The value of the course lies in exposing students to the practical world of business. The student should learn strategy in problem solving that is beneficial to different groups in the

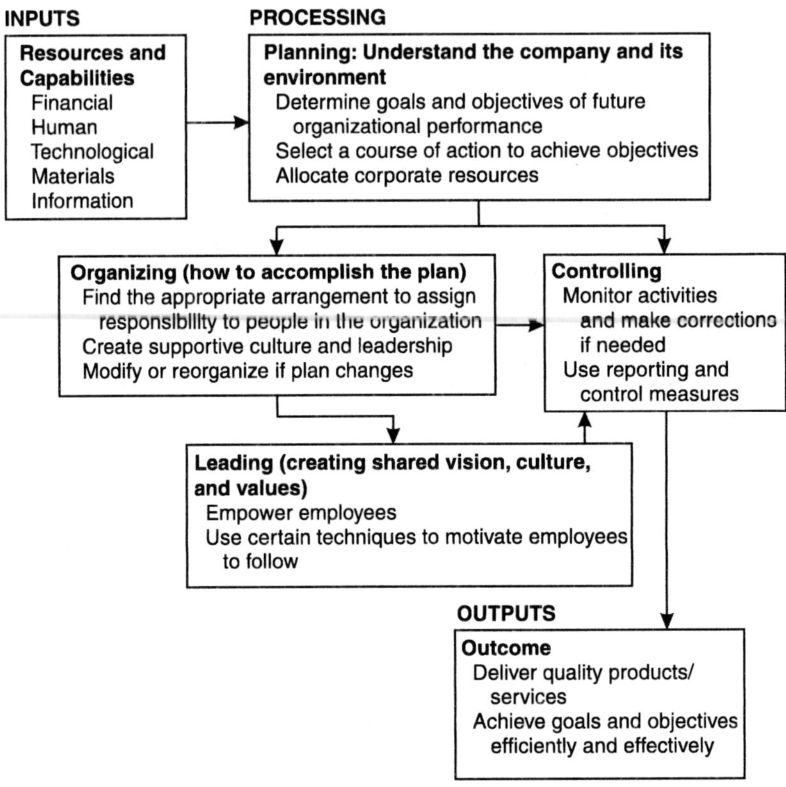

FIGURE 1.4. Management Activities in Modern Organizations

business community. Figure 1.4 summarizes management activities in a modern organization.

REVIEW QUESTIONS

1. Explain why business students should study strategic management.
2. Explain the difference between the terms *strategy* and *policy.*
3. Define business policy, strategic planning, and strategic management. How are they similar? Dissimilar?
4. Describe what is meant by an organization's "mission." How is it developed? Why is it useful to have a clearly stated mission?
5. Define goals and objectives. How do they differ from one another?
6. Define and differentiate between an intended, an emergent, and a realized strategy. Give examples of each.

NOTES

1. Miller, C. C. and Cardinal, L. B. (1994). Strategic planning and firm performance: A synthesis of more than two decades of research. *Academy of Management Journal,* 34(6), 1649-1665.

2. Peter, J. (1993). Business policy in action. *Management Decision Journal,* 31(6), 3.

3. Wren, D. (1972). *The Evolution of Management Thought.* New York: Ronald Press Co.

4. Gordon, R. A. and Howell, J. E. (1959). *Higher Education for Business.* New York: Columbia University Press.

5. Schendel, D. E. and Hofer, C. W. (1982). *Strategic Management: A New View of Business Policy and Planning.* Boston: Little, Brown. Also Leontiades, M. (1982). The confusing words of business policy. *Academy of Management Review,* 7(1), 46.

6. Gluck, F. W., Kaufman, S. P., and Walleck, A. S. (1982). The four phases of strategic management. *Journal of Business Strategy,* 2(3), 9-20.

7. Chandler, A. (1962). *Strategy and Structure.* Cambridge, MA: MIT Press.

8. Edgley, G. (1990). Strategic planning. *Association Management,* 42(3), 77-80.

9. Scharf, A. (1991). Secrets of strategic planning: Responding to the opportunities of tomorrow. *Industrial Management,* 33(1), 9-10.

10. Daly, N. R. (1991). Planning for action. *Association Management,* 43(4), 59-62, 107.

11. Balsmeier, P. W. and Borne, B. J. (1997). 1990's corporate planning styles. *Business Research Yearbook,* 4, 304.

12. Chan, F. T. S., Chan, M. H., Mak, K. L., and Tang, N. K. H. (1999). An integrated approach to investment appraisal for advanced manufacturing technology. *Human Factors and Ergonomics in Manufacturing,* 9(1), 69-86.

13. Scharf, Secrets of strategic planning.

14. Stone, R. (1996). Mission statement revisited. *S.A.M. Advanced Management Journal,* 61(1), 31-38.

15. Edgley, Strategic planning.

16. Saturn Web site: <http://www.saturnbp.com/company/our_story/>. Accessed August 21, 2002.

17. Drucker, P. F. (1980). Managing for tomorrow—Managing in turbulent times. *Industry Week,* 205(1), 54.

18. Abell, D. (1980). *Defining the Business: The Starting Point of Strategic Planning.* Englewood Cliffs, NJ: Prentice-Hall.

19. Abernathy, W. J. and Wayne, K. (1974). Limits of the learning curve. *Harvard Business Review,* 52(5), 109-119; Alchian, A. A. (1963). Reliability of progress curves in airframe production. *Econometrica,* 31(3), 679-696; Hall, G. and Howell, S. (1985). The experience curve from the economist's perspective. *Strategic Management Journal,* 6(3), 197-212.

20. Wright, P., Pringle, C., and Kroll, M. (1998). *Strategic Management: Text and Cases.* Boston: Allyn and Bacon; Hill, C. W. L. and Jones, G. R. (1997). *Strategic Management: An Integrated Approach,* Second Edition. Boston: Houghton Mifflin Co., pp. 32-36.

21. Ibid.

22. Mintzberg, H. and McHugh, A. (1985). Strategy formation in an adhocracy. *Administrative Science Quarterly,* 30(2), 160-197.

23. Bogner, W. and Howard, T. (1993). The role of competitive groups in strategy formulation: A dynamic integration of two competing models. *Journal of Management Studies,* 30(1), 51.

24. Ibid., p. 58.

25. Grant, R. M. (1991). Resource based theory of competitive advantage: Implications for strategy formulation. *California Management Review,* 33(3), 114.

26. Duhaime, I. M. and Schwenk, C. R. (1985). Conjectures on cognitive simplification in acquisition and divestment decision making. *The Academy of Management Review,* 10(2), 287-295.

27. Byars, L. (1991). *Strategic Management Formulation and Implementation: Concepts and Cases,* Third Edition (p. 79). New York: HarperCollins Publishing.

28. Balsmeier and Borne, 1990's corporate planning styles.

29. Ibid., p. 306.

30. Alkhafaji, A. F. (2001). *Corporate Transformation and Restructuring: A Strategic Approach.* Westport, CT: Quorum Books, p. 6.

31. Balsmeier and Borne, 1990's corporate planning styles, pp. 306-307.

32. Alkhafaji, A. F. (1989). *A Stakeholder Approach to Corporate Governance: Managing a Dynamic Environment.* New York: Quorum Books, p. 65.

33. Fromson, B. D. (1990). The big owners roar. *Fortune,* 122(3), 67.

34. Dobrzynski, J. H., Schroeder, M., Miles, G. L., and Weber, J. (1989). Taking charge. *BusinessWeek,* Issue 3113, p. 66.

35. Hill and Jones (1997). *Strategic Management,* Chapter 2.

36. Alkhafaji, *A Stakeholder Approach to Corporate Governance,* p. 65.

37. Tayler, A. III (1992). What's ahead for GM's new team. *Fortune,* 126(12), 58-61.

38. Demb, A. and Neubauer, F.-F. (1992). The corporate board: Confronting the paradoxes. *Long-Range Planning,* 25(3), 9.

Chapter 2

Strategy Formulation

INTRODUCTION

This chapter covers the strategic management process as defined by the strategic management framework. This management model encompasses the nature of strategic decisions derived from the general concept of strategy and its structure. In addition, this chapter answers the questions: What is strategic management? What is the strategic management process? Who are the strategists? The chapter further analyzes and explains the necessity for management to anticipate and adapt to the ever-changing environment.[1] It describes the composition and benefits of the strategic management process. It also discusses a number of recent trends that command attention, as they influence the process of strategic management. Some of these trends are global competition, total quality management, and reengineering.

Definition and Meaning

Strategic management is the process of assessing the corporation and its environment in order to meet the firm's long-term objectives of adapting and adjusting to its environment through manipulation of opportunities and reduction of threats. Furthermore, this process requires a careful evaluation of the firm's environment before making managerial decisions and taking actions. This process results in the formulation and implementation of strategies designed to achieve the objectives of the organization. Other definitions of strategic management include the following:

- Higgins and Vincze: "the process of managing the pursuit of the organization's mission while managing the relationship of the organization to its environment, especially with respect to its environmental stakeholders: the major constituents in its internal and external environment affected by its action."[2]
- Harvey: "process of formulating, implementing, and evaluating business strategies to achieve future objectives."[3]

- Pearce: "the set of decisions and actions resulting in formulation and implementation of strategies designed to achieve the objectives of an organization."[4]
- Chandler: "the determination of the basic long-term goals and objectives of an enterprise, and the adoption of courses of action and the allocation of resources necessary for carrying out these goals."[5]
- Quinn: "the pattern or plan that integrates an organization's major goals, policies, and action sequences into a cohesive whole."[6]
- Glueck: "a unified, comprehensive, and integrated plan designed to ensure that the basic objectives of the enterprise are achieved."[7]

Characteristics

Strategic management possesses the following characteristics:

1. *Futurity:* The process of strategic management deals with future events and their consequences, thus requiring top managers to possess a long-term concept of decision making. Strategic management attempts to scan the broad future of the corporation using a written corporate scenario. In essence, strategic planning involves anticipating future events.
2. *Long-range impact:* Strategic management encompasses long periods of time, often exceeding five years. It attempts to predict events in the long run and analyze the potential impact of such events on the corporation.
3. *Iterative process:* Strategic management must be a continuous and repetitive process to be effective. A new strategic plan is developed while the current plan is in action. New plans are usually adopted and improved based upon the feedback obtained during the implementation phase.
4. *Systematic and rational:* Systematic is characterized by the use of orderly planning or by the use of a methodical approach, whereas rational implies possession of unemotional and logical reasoning ability. Thus, strategic management is a systematic and rational process because it consists of systematically processing decision inputs, which lead to rational and expected outputs.
5. *Integrated function:* Integration encompasses the concept of bringing all the parts together to create a whole, i.e., to establish "a set of policies and methods used by management to facilitate communications and to coordinate the activities of individuals or groups within the company."[8] Thus, the strategic management process serves as a foun-

dation for the other activities and functions of the corporation, such as organization, staffing, and control.

6. *Means to an end:* Strategic management is not an end unto itself. It is a means, or a tool, to be used to achieve corporate objectives.
7. *High stakes:* Due to the long-term nature and the broad organizational scope of strategic management, strategic decisions inherently involve the long-term commitment of a substantial proportion of organizational resources.

The Process

Strategic management is the domain of top-level management, and the process involves four basic components:

1. *Environmental scanning* consists of analyzing internal and external factors that may affect the organization and its ability to pursue a given course of action. Scrutinizing the environment includes the appraisal of the composition of competition within the firm's industry and also involves assessing the impact of globalization on the industry and the company's performance.
2. *Strategy formulation* (strategic planning) involves making strategic decisions concerning the organization's mission, philosophy, objectives, policies, and methods of achieving organizational objectives. Formulating a strategy is an important step to enhancing organizational position and building competitive advantages not only in the national but also in the global arena.
3. *Strategy implementation* is concerned with making a variety of managerial decisions such as the type of organizational structure, the type and source of information systems, leadership "fit," and the type of control mechanism that should be employed.
4. *Evaluation and control* is concerned with the evaluation systems that are to be used to ensure the operation of strategic planning to effectively achieve the organization's objectives. Evaluation consists of comparing the predicted results to the actual results. Strategic management is a process of appraising the corporation as a whole, taking the environment into consideration. It usually focuses on opportunities and problems related to the achievement of corporate objectives in the long run.

This chapter provides brief descriptions of these components. In-depth study of each component is covered in following chapters.

At the corporate level, the strategic management process involves activities that range from the initial statement of the corporate mission to the evaluation of the firm's actions to meet the terms of that mission. To determine the corporate mission, top management scans both the internal and external environments, followed by an evaluation of the pertinent strategic factors. This is how the process of strategic management is continuous and repetitive.

Throughout the strategic management process, the organization must focus intently on all its activities, searching for answers to four basic questions:

1. *Who are we?* The question is an attempt to identify the company's competitive position. How do we differentiate ourselves from competitors, focusing on our strengths and weaknesses? What is our natural market? Looking at threats and opportunities, how do we fit in this market? Simply, it is the mission of the company.
2. *Where are we now?* Are we maximizing opportunities and reducing threats to the success of the organization? Where is the company compared to the rest of the industry? Are we leading or lagging behind the industry, or just holding our own? Is our strategy adequate to counter our shortcomings? Where is the company standing right now? Is it an acceptable position? What is our current strategy?
3. *Where do we want to be?* If the current strategy is not appropriate, especially in the long run, what strategy should we adopt? This is simply stating objectives.
4. *How do we get there?* How can we turn threats into opportunities? This question isolates the means to achieve objectives efficiently and effectively, *the choice of new strategy, and how to implement it.*

The strategist must analyze corporate objectives in light of the environment. Management must determine the company's strengths, weaknesses, opportunities, and threats (SWOT). Then the strategist will match the corporate strengths to the environmental opportunities available and reduce the corporate weaknesses facing environmental threats. This process is known as *SWOT analysis.* Management uses SWOT analysis to make decisions about developing the overall strategy of the corporation.

WHO ARE THE STRATEGISTS IN ANY ORGANIZATION?

Those individuals who are familiar with the corporate environment must design the strategy. It is important that all members of the organization play a part in designing the strategy. This will energize resources and activities, increase communication, and ensure success in the planning process. In designing the strategy, management needs to act as a mentor, or coach, to guide the rest of the organization in designing and implementing organizational strategy. People who are involved and participating from the beginning are more responsive and supportive of strategic planning and the change it brings.[9]

In any organization, the strategists include all the people who influence an organization's overall strategies. These include the board of directors, the CEO, various managers, outside planners and consultants, and sometimes those in middle management positions. The duty of strategist is to see the organization as a whole, to understand the interdynamics of the organization, and to make decisions in light of the environment in which the organization operates.

In theory, the board of directors is the representative and the protector of stockholder interests in the firm. The board can be held legally accountable for corporate strategies. Its directors are responsible for approving the financial decisions on issues important to stockholders, i.e., dividends, issuing stocks, and major strategic investments. The board has the authority to hire, fire, and compensate company executives. It is positioned at the top to participate and monitor corporate strategies.

In the past, most of the board members were selected indirectly by the CEO of the firm. The board, therefore, could be dominated by management and might serve as a rubber stamp for management decisions. There is evidence that corporate boards are actually becoming aware of their power and are starting to influence strategic decisions in the organization.[10] Separating the roles of the CEO and the chairman of the board can help prevent a concentration of power in one individual and create more accountability.

The primary strategist in small or medium-size companies and in most large ones is the CEO. Usually, the corporate strategies of all multiple strategic business unit (SBU) companies are determined by corporate CEOs along with other strategists. General managers or the CEO of each SBU will determine its business strategy.

In most companies, groups of top management emerge informally to play a role in designing the strategy. These informal groups, called coalitions, work as strategists. In order to accomplish organizational objectives, it is sometimes necessary to compromise among SBUs in an organization. Theorists also believe that the use of coalitions proactively, through empowerment and sense of ownership, not only assists in adjusting strategy but helps form the vision and mission of the organization.

Mintzberg expands on the coalitions that were mentioned. He has grouped his coalitions into two primary segments, external and internal. The external coalition consists of four basic groups: owners, associations or suppliers, employee associations or unions, and public groups such as consumer, government, and special interest groups. Mintzberg's internal coalition consists of six groups, the CEO, the operators or production managers, line managers, analysts, support staff, and finally those who determine the ideology of the organization.[11]

Top managers have a constant role in formulating strategy and analyzing its success or failure once a strategy is chosen. Another strategist is the professional planner, who has been charged by the board or the CEO with the functions of strategic planning, implementation, and adjustment. This role is almost a direct contrast to the empowerment theory, actually taking strategy responsibilities away from certain line managers and in some cases actually creating conflict.

Other people are involved in designing the strategy such as investors, mid-level managers, and various coalitions in the organization. However, their participation depends on the overarching philosophy of the organization, as established by the CEO and the board. Management philosophy determines the extent to which people within the organization are involved in the development of the vision (the future direction of the company) and strategies for the organization. Strategists include all those who are involved in development, implementation, evaluation, and adjustment of strategy.

ENVIRONMENTAL SCANNING

Internal environments refer to the quantity and quality of an organization's physical and human resources, including finances, managerial talents, and expertise in marketing, production, research and development, etc. The external environment consists of the operating environment (forces and conditions within the specific industry) and the remote environment (forces and conditions beyond a specific industry). Although it may be difficult at times to distinguish between the internal and external environments, usually the issue of control is one of the deciding factors. Variables that are, to a certain degree, under management's control are internal; those outside of management's control are external. Assessing the internal environment includes evaluating the internal strengths and weaknesses of the organization, whereas assessment of the external environment involves examining the conditions and forces affecting the organization's strategic options that are typically beyond the firm's control. SWOT analysis typically generates strategic alternatives, which become the basis to forecast the future as it relates to the organization and to formulate the strategies and objectives that best match the organization with its environment.

Open and Closed Systems

In the past, management has considered the business environment to mean merely internal areas (production, finance, marketing, and personnel) where the elements are controllable by management. This is a closed-system view of the organization, predicated upon the doctrine that these internal elements decide the success of the company. This model presents a relationship between inputs, organization, and outputs, all of which management can control to a certain degree (see Figure 2.1).

Today, managers understand that organizations are not that simple and that they face a dynamic, constantly changing environment over which management has little control. Managers realize that an organization cannot exist in isolation. Because there are external variables beyond management control, management must identify and adapt to these environmental changes and prepare for future change. This is the open-system model, which examines the relationship between the internal and external environment (see Figure 2.2).

Managers need to comprehend the various elements of the environment to understand which ones have a direct influence on operations and which ones have little or no influence. Some of these variables may have more or less influence than others depending on the type of business. Generally, the more local the business, the less influence the external environment has. For example, a cookie business in a small town such as Slippery Rock, Pennsylvania, is less likely to be affected by international competition. Conversely, the larger the business, the more likely it is that the external environment will have a greater influence on it. For example, aluminum companies in Pennsylvania are subject to strong competition (domestic and international) as well as government regulations in addition to their internal environments. This is discussed in more detail in Chapter 3.

Information systems provide strategists with information concerning the status and the results of a company's operations in order to assist them in their decision making. It is important for strategists to establish strategic de-

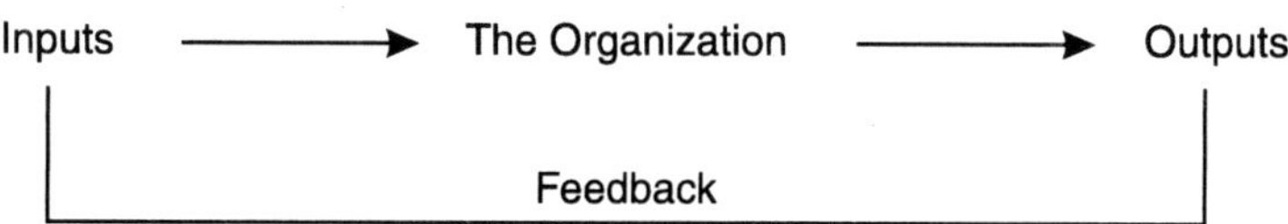

FIGURE 2.1. Input-Output Model: The Company As a Closed System (*Note:* An example of a closed system is setting a temperature in a room after closing all access to the outside such as doors or windows.)

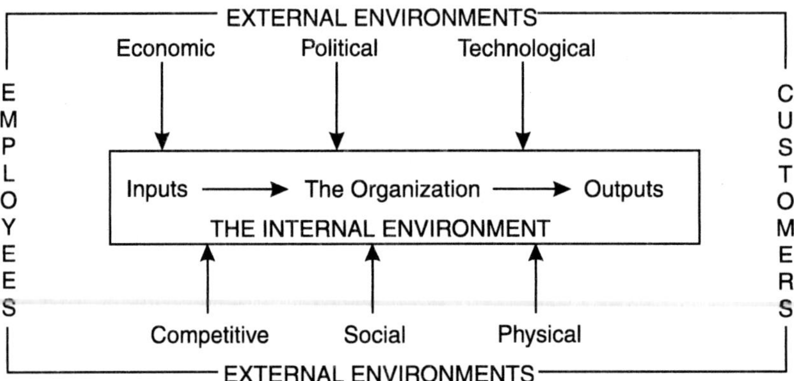

FIGURE 2.2. Input-Processing-Output Model: The Company As an Open System

cisions based on relevant information that will assist in the forecast of the company's future strengths, weaknesses, opportunities, and threats.

Importance of Information and Forecasting Techniques

The ability of the strategic manager to plan for and adjust to change will influence the degree of the organization's success in the market. To cope with change, the strategist must be able to forecast the future. Forecasting techniques are specifically designed to predict the future based on the data gathered by the strategist. Once data are accumulated, they must be converted into information that enables strategists to determine objectives and formulate strategies from which to make choices. Strategists need to be well aware of changes taking place in their organization and the industry, as well as the macroenvironment. Strategists therefore should have the skill to understand the information provided and to question the assumptions before making a decision. Many companies have started an information system to provide current information to various levels of management through computers. Usually the strategists' decisions affect the allocation of resources in various divisions and departments. It is therefore required that strategists develop the skills of compromise to keep the management of these divisions satisfied.

Methods used to provide information about current situations are called *descriptive techniques*. Analysis of current data by descriptive techniques enables the decision maker to apply today's knowledge to future situations. Forecasting is an aid to reduce uncertainty and assist in decision making.

Unfortunately for the decision maker, the environment is becoming increasingly volatile and thus the predictions become more difficult.

Forecasts are assumptions about the future, based upon past trends, and as such they are subject to a margin of error. The accuracy of assumptions made by strategists and the degree to which the strategic plan is based on these assumptions can determine the success or failure of a company. The inputs used in conjunction with the selected forecasting techniques will influence the accuracy of the resulting assumptions for a company. Assumptions about future growth rates, economic status, the gross domestic product, interest rate, and the company's market should be assessed periodically, especially in the formulation stages to ensure their validity.

Regression is a statistical means of relating changes in one variable with the changes in one or more variables upon which its value depends.[12] By utilizing this technique, forecasters can predict the trends in the short term. This knowledge can be used to predict trends for the long term based on the anticipated changes in the external environment.

Another means of predicting future trends is *simulation modeling*. Simulations allow the strategist to answer "what if?" questions based on the internal and external environmental data gathered. These simulations are computerized models that allow the forecaster to quickly see what changes to anticipate given a change in one of the variables. The complexity of the simulation model requires that the decision maker analyze carefully the relationships of the internal and external environments influencing the company. Although microcomputers enable forecasters to analyze more information in a relatively short period of time, they do not ensure that the resulting decisions will be better. They do, however, provide the means by which to make better decisions.

A number of techniques are available to strategists. Regression and simulation modeling are only two of the analytical forecasting techniques utilized by strategic planners. Several factors are involved in formulating forecasting models to be used in strategic planning.

In developing a strategic plan, decision makers need to choose the techniques that are most applicable to their situation. In addition, they should try to employ more than one technique to improve the quality of the decisions. No matter what techniques are used, the value of the resulting output is no better than the data put into the model.

Regardless of the time and money invested in the forecasting process, the volatile nature of the corporate environment will affect the validity of the decisions. No matter how extensive the process, the human factor still exists. The strategist uses forecasting techniques to make assumptions. Remember: The uncertainty of the future can never be eliminated from decision making. As a result, strategists must analyze the environment with the realization that the strategic plan must remain flexible to adjust to change.

STRATEGY FORMULATION

Strategy formulation is the process of developing long-term plans to deal effectively with environmental opportunities and threats.

The Mission Statement

As discussed in Chapter 1, the mission describes the organization's identity, product, market, and the particular methodology or technology of emphasis. The mission usually reflects the values and priorities of the strategic decision makers and outlines the vision and future direction of the company. Of all the steps in the process, this first step is perhaps the most difficult and most critical. Defined by top management, the mission statement incorporates specifics about the organization that make it unique.

The mission statement also describes what the organization hopes to achieve, such as (1) the size of the organization, (2) the scope of endeavor, and (3) the number and diversity of the organization's businesses, markets, and customers. This delineation of purpose, or reason for being, is extremely important because it forces the entire organization to focus its goals, objectives, and strategies in a unified direction.

A mission statement that is too broad or too restrictive can result in organizational inefficiency or lead to lost opportunities. Thus, formulation of the mission statement is extremely important since it will be the guiding force, or umbrella, under which all other organizational decisions will be made. The mission statement acts as an "invisible hand" that guides widely dispersed employees to work independently while at the same time ensuring that the collective efforts contribute to realizing the organization's potential. Since any organization exists to accomplish something in the larger environment, the organization's mission statement describes specifically and concisely what the organization intends to supply to the larger environment.

Five key elements shape the organization's mission statement. First, the organization culture and the history of the organization influences the mission statement through its past goals, policies, and accomplishments. Second, those who direct the company have personal goals and vision, which also play a part in the formulation of the mission. Third, the external environment defines the main opportunities and threats that must be taken into consideration, and the internal environment determines the organization's strengths and weaknesses. Fourth, the organization's resources play a vital role because they make certain missions possible and others impossible. Fifth, in the formulation of a mission statement, an organization should base its choice of purpose on its distinctive competencies, meaning a company's unique capability to compete.

Development of the mission statement should begin with an explicit recognition of (1) the organization's present range and composition and (2) the desired range and composition for the future. Understanding of the current position should answer the question "What is our business now?" Delineation of the future position should clarify the question "Where do we want to be in the future?"

Overall, a well-stated mission should explain clearly, concisely, and cogently what the organization is all about, for both its competitors and its stakeholders. In Chapter 1 I listed some key elements that make a mission statement more effective. The mission statement needs to be simple to comprehend, relevant, and current, and it should be written in a positive tone to encourage employee commitment to fulfilling the mission's requirements.

As the global market continues to change, the companies who do not have full commitments to designing and implementing a strategic mission statement will suffer the most. The companies that will succeed in the twenty-first century are the ones with a clear vision and well-written missions, goals, and objectives.[13]

Strategic goals, also developed by top management, further define the mission statement. Goals are driven by mission statements that reflect the general direction of the organization in many areas, i.e., market standing, product and service innovation, productivity levels, physical and financial resources, profitability, manager and employee performance and attitude, and public and social responsibility. To ensure that the strategic management process remains dynamic and current, upper management must evaluate and update the mission statement and goals if the environment so dictates.

Strategic Objectives

The second phase, the establishment of strategic objectives, further defines the organization's mission and goals. More specific than goals, good objectives must be measurable within a stated time frame. Objectives are based upon the mission, goals, strategic intent, and internal and external analysis. Strategic intent refers to the company's ability to maintain a long-term advantage over its competitors in the global market. Objectives are the ends or the desired results. Long-term objectives cover a multiyear period, typically exceeding five years, whereas short-term objectives denote a time span of less than one year. Such short-term objectives, often called *annual objectives,* are the smaller targets necessary to achieve the long-term objectives. An organization's success in reaching short-term objectives will determine the overall achievement of the longer-term objectives. The executive officers, top-line managers, or strategy specialists most often prepare objectives.

Therefore, a good objective should be a clear written communication understood throughout the organization. Above all, the objective should be achievable and measurable. For example: A company that attempts to achieve an 8 percent rate of return in the third year of existence has a *corporate* objective. Similarly, doubling company sales (units or $ amount) in four years is another corporate objective. Increasing divisional sales or revenues by 30 percent this year and 50 percent by the end of next year is a *business* or *divisional* objective. Reducing absenteeism from 15 to 5 percent in two years is a *functional* objective. Improving public understanding of a company's position on a public policy issue from 33 to 65 percent in six months is a *communication* objective.

Objectives provide direction and motivation and may incorporate internal and external processes of the organization. To be effective, objectives should be arranged according to priority and, like the mission and goal statement, reviewed frequently for appropriateness. Objectives may be pursued singularly or simultaneously.

Strategic Planning

In the third phase of strategy formulation, the organization creates its plan of action based upon the detailed analysis of the internal and external environments. Such strategy is designed to reach the organizational objectives, which by design must also support the adopted mission and goals. Strategy usually includes short-range, intermediate, and long-range goals. Strategy is "an approach to using resources within the constraints of a competitive environment in order to achieve a set of goals."[14] Relying on assessment of the external environment and the company profile, strategy identifies a range of possible opportunities from which the firm can plan long-term objectives. As a subset of strategy, policies are designed to guide managers' thinking, decision making, and actions toward the implementation of the organization's strategy.

Strategy can be subdivided into three major categories: corporate, business, and functional. Sometimes an additional layer of strategy such as the enterprise strategy or operating strategy is included. Therefore, I will discuss all of these strategies.

Different Types of Strategies

Enterprise strategy encompasses the dealings of a corporation and its social responsibility such as pollution control, safety measures taken by the company, or its contribution to solve particular problems such as energy shortages or education needs. This strategy is the scope of stakeholder satisfaction achieved by a corporation at any one time. Enterprise strategy should address the question, "What do we stand for?" This strategy tends to have a positive effect on the overall performance of the organization. The stakeholder relationship is moderated by the firm's *grand strategy*.[15] The type and range of stakeholder groups varies from firm to firm and situation to situation, but there are four fundamental stakeholder groups that every organization must consider: (1) owners, (2) employees, (3) major customers, and (4) major creditors. For example, Mentor Graphics Corporation was founded on the principle or long-term vision "build things people will buy." This was a very successful company in the design automation industry in the 1980s. As competition increased and the Daisy Corporation overtook Mentor Graphics as the industry leader, the corporate strategy of Mentor became "beat Daisy." Companies must be careful that their grand, abstract vision is not too inspirational, or the company may wind up making more poetry than product.[16]

Corporate strategy describes what business the firm is in, or should be in, and how the corporation intends for its business to be conducted. Corporate strategy includes the overall aspects of integrating its business into a unified position in relation to the environment and competition. There are two main strategic concerns at the corporate level. The first concern is with the executive management and deals with the scope, mix, and emphasis among the various activities. At this level, decisions are concerned with the appropriate strategic approach for each different business unit and the improvement of performance for the overall organization. The second major strategic concern is prioritizing corporate resource allocation across various corporate activities. For example, multiple-SBU organizations must determine in what areas the organization wishes to compete and then arrange the various SBUs to produce a balanced portfolio. Here the corporate strategist's essential task is to determine the business mix, establish investment priorities, and allocate corporate resources among the various SBUs. Thus, in determining corporate strategy, the organization endeavors to coordinate the business portfolio and to provide direction to the individual SBUs. Various generic strategies are labeled *growth, stabilization, investment, reduction, turnaround,* and *takeover* (to be discussed in later chapters). Typically, the

CEO, the board of directors, owners, corporate staffs, and/or strategic planners are involved in the development of corporate strategy (see Table 2.1).

Business strategy is management's plan both at the corporate and SBU levels for directing and running a particular business unit of the corporation. The primary focus of business strategy is to assess the strategic advantages of the individual unit. It is also concerned with the issues of (1) how the SBU expects to compete in a specific business, (2) what each SBU must contribute to achieve success for the organization, and (3) how to obtain resources from the corporation and allocate them to achieve the SBU's objectives. A major component of business strategy at the SBU level is a marketing orientation. It specifies how the individual business unit will compete in the marketplace. At the business level, strategies tend to be action based in an attempt to gain advantage over the competition. As a result, business strategies are built upon market factors (buyer needs, market share, product differentiation, and economic resources) and are of the utmost importance. The owners, directors of SBUs, divisional managers, or divisional staff are involved in the development of business strategy.

Functional strategy, which supports business strategy, does so by managing each principal activity within the business. The functional level is more specific than business strategy and assists the organization in performing the critical functions necessary to run efficiently. Functional strategy involves planning for maximum resource utilization. Examples of functional areas af-

TABLE 2.1. Various Strategies

Type of Strategy	Organization Hierarchy	Theme of Strategy
Enterprise strategy	Board of directors	Stakeholder domain, i.e., social responsibility, environment, education, etc.
Corporate strategy	CEO of the company	Overall strategy
Business strategy	Various SBUs	How each SBU competes in its industry
Functional strategy	Various functions	Each function, such as production, marketing, public relations, finance, etc., develops its own strategy. It is more specific to support the business strategy.
Operation strategy	Different departments or divisions	More specific and short term in nature. It supports the functional strategy. It deals with day-to-day operations.

fected by this strategy include human resources, marketing, production, finance, public relations, physical resources, and research and development. There should be a functional area strategy for every major functional area. Functional area strategy also indicates how each major sub-activity of the business will contribute to achieving the overall business strategy. Managers at the functional level develop this strategy.

Operational strategy is the most detailed of the strategies and breaks down the related plans and practices into departments and supervisory levels. These positions manage the day-to-day requirements of functional-area support strategies—the nuts and bolts of various facets of the organization's functional areas. An example of an operating-level strategy is an inventory control system, i.e., just-in-time (JIT).

Strategists must also consider an overall strategy, which is the combination of strategic actions that define the direction of the organization. Examples are changes in consumer preferences, product innovations, technologies, and market entries and exits, along with the overall rate of change within the industry. Numerous other substrategies exist within these main strategic categories.

International strategy. Companies have been entering the global market for more than two decades. Nike and other shoe manufacturers make shoes in Asia. McDonald's gets more than half of its revenue from outside the United States by selling burgers in large foreign cities such as Moscow and Beijing. Coca-Cola also sells 50 percent of the world's soft drinks. More people all over the world want world-class goods. There have never been as many borders open to free trade as there are today. The North American Free Trade Agreement of 1993 removed trade barriers between the United States, Mexico, and Canada. The General Agreement on Tariffs and Trade (GATT) of 1993 and the World Trade Organization (WTO) have eased trade throughout much of the industrialized world. Europe is now moving toward borderless trade with the implementation of a single currency. Even Japan is now more open to foreign goods than ever before. Peace dividends—the reallocation of resources from military purposes to consumer ones—are major forces behind the escalating globalization of the world today.[17]

Communications technology and falling trade barriers are changing the rules of international strategic management. Companies that operate domestically and abroad have developed new criteria for determining where and how they compete in the twenty-first century. The location of the country where they operate is crucial to their strategic importance. A country's strategic importance is a function of overall market size and its ability to provide easy access to high-value inputs such as labor, energy, capital, etc. Strategy for an international company is a hierarchy that includes corporate-level and business-level strategies. The emphasis of corporate strategy is on selecting the industry in which the company will operate and how the various businesses within the company will coordinate activities. The emphasis of business strategy is on market share and how to compete domestically and internationally. The primary drive of international strategy is determined by business unit strategy.[18]

When a company originates in one country and decides to transfer valuable skills and products to another, it is called an international company. Usually, the company transfers a product that was developed at home to other overseas markets, at the same time maintaining firm control over marketing and product strategies. Sometimes the international company establishes manufacturing and marketing functions in another country in which it operates. These companies are called multinational companies (MNCs). Initially, companies begin with export-import activities (becoming international companies). This can be done either directly, using a sales subsidiary, mail order, and telemarketing, or indirectly, selling through distributors or agents. Companies can also expand their operations through licensing and franchising. Then they expand further through partnerships or joint ventures with foreign companies. This can be done through a distribution alliance, manufacturing alliance, and/or joint venture.

Some companies expand overseas by establishing production pace in response to local demand. This can be accomplished by establishing subsidiaries abroad. Such companies first develop products for their home market and then offer them overseas. Because of the duplication of production facilities, these companies might incur higher production and marketing costs. Examples are the automobile companies. If the company decides to further penetrate a particular foreign market because of the opportunities and the availability of resources, it might initiate direct investments and establish subsidiaries. This can be done through assembly, complete manufacturing, or acquisitions. This type of company is called a *multinational enterprise*. The subsidiaries of a multinational firm operate independently from one another. Examples are Xerox, IBM, Procter & Gamble, Apple, and Motorola.

A global company is a borderless business with many subsidiaries abroad, which complement each other and have some kind of control with their own operation. They are more sensitive to their localities. This type of company tends to standardize its product worldwide so that the firm can maximize international efficiency by locating activities in low-cost countries and producing standardized products from world-scale facilities.[19] When control and research are transferred to the local subsidiary, the company has moved closer to becoming a global company. For example, Intel, Texas Instruments, Motorola, Levi Strauss, all of the watch companies, all brand-name clothes companies, and semiconductor producers have established subsidiaries abroad.

A Strategic Alliance

A strategic alliance involves any cooperative linkage between corporations to achieve common objectives. Various types of alliances include distribution, manufacturing, R&D, and joint venture, which is the most common form. A joint venture is basically a partnership in which two or more firms carry out a specific project or cooperate in a selected area of business. Joint ventures can be temporary, disbanding after the project is finished, or long term. Such an alliance is usually formed to exploit the strengths of one partner and to mitigate the weaknesses of the other.

The need to enhance technology, research and development, and management skills may also bring two or more firms together. This was illustrated by the cooperation of IBM, Apple, and Motorola in the creation of the PowerPC. By cooperating in technological research, the companies created a single platform that enables computers with different platforms to communicate with one another.

An alliance is especially useful in developing global competitiveness. Governments rise and fall rather quickly in many developing countries because of unstable economic or political environments. Under these circumstances, companies prefer safer types of investment methods such as joint ventures.

An example of this would be the successful alliance between KLM and Northwest airlines that allows both airlines to fly freely through each other's national markets. Both have benefited greatly, with KLM profits increasing by $49 million. This alliance also enables both carriers to share know-how in reducing costs and using flight connections efficiently. If the alliance continues to work, it could force the hands of envious competitors around the world.[20]

An example of global strategy at work is the Ford Motor Company. It introduced the Contour as "A world car for the 21st century." After watching the performance of the Contour in Europe, promotions bringing it into Ford's U.S. market stated that the Contour was the result of a $6 billion investment and eight years of development. Ford and Mitsubishi also established a joint venture agreement. In this agreement, Ford produced the Probe while Mitsubishi produced the Eclipse. The two cars had the same design, but were considered to be different because of their names. The global market presents the ability to have larger production runs while keeping costs down, as Ford has done with its global business strategy.[21]

Total Quality Management

Total quality management (TQM) refers to the systematic improvement of quality and cultural transformation in management techniques through the involvement of everyone in the organization and in all aspects of the business operation. This concept refers to the philosophy that promoting quality values in all organizations should be the driving force behind managing, planning, designing, and improvement initiatives. TQM is a long-term concept and not a quick fix for corporate problems. Evidence of the importance of TQM can be seen in the enthusiastic response to the Malcolm Baldrige National Quality Award, which was initiated August 20, 1987, to recognize high quality in American industry. Some of the companies that won the Baldrige award include Globe Metallurgical Inc. (1988), Federal Express Corporation (1990), GTE Directories Corporation (1994), and ADAC Laboratories (1996).

Robert C. Stempel, the former chairman of General Motors Corporation, was quoted as saying, "The worldwide quality revolution has permanently changed the way we all do business. Where once quality was limited to technical issues, it is now a dynamic, perpetual improvement process involving people in all aspects of the business."[22] In 1989, the American Society for Quality Control conducted a survey which showed that 54 percent of the executives rated service quality as extremely critical and 51 percent gave U.S. products less than an 8 on a 10-point scale. Correspondingly, some Fortune 500 executives said U.S. products merited no better than a C+.[23]

"Total quality" in the business world has become an important and competitive issue. The concern for quality has been around for centuries. However, the emphasis on worldwide quality revolution is permanently changing the way we do business. When Edward Deming and Joseph Juran talked about quality control in the 1950s, few American companies were listening. American businesses at that time were booming. They were the front-runners in innovation and industry. They did not foresee the future consequences of not adopting such a system.

Role of TQM in strategic management. An organization must apply a strategic management plan to be able to implement TQM. Companies might need to change their strategy in order to improve the current system, or redesign the system from scratch.[24] Typically, the TQM process starts with defining a problem, setting objectives, gathering data, setting certain standards, examining the environment, allocating resources, and taking a course of action. Strategic planning is the process of developing and maintaining a strategic fit between the organization and its changing environment. Bushnell and Halus argue that the steps involved in designing and implementing a strategic plan can be seen to closely parallel many of the key concepts involved in TQM.[25]

Barrett argues that one aspect of the strategic planning process should be to implement a TQM program.[26] Chalk states that strategic planning is essential for TQM.[27] Henderson argues that the basics of TQM can govern executive-level strategic planning and goal setting. He states that TQM can be reduced to the following strategic management objectives:

1. Continuous improvement in quality goods and services
2. Company responsibility to its customers
3. Flexibility in adjusting to customer needs and expectations
4. Cost reduction through improved quality and non-value-added waste elimination[28]

The TQM approach has companies moving toward *proactive* improvement to match customer needs and provide superior customer value. Momentum has built as the U.S. Department of Commerce's Malcolm Baldrige National Quality Award and local initiatives were launched. Managers began to respond and quality improvements proliferated. Organizations that successfully incorporated TQM practices share some common positive effects:

1. When employees are more involved in the process of improvement, productivity and consumer satisfaction will increase. This also gives the employees a sense of importance and leads to higher motivation, reduced employee turnover, increased productivity, and increased profits.
2. Employees gain a personal understanding of TQM, which in turn leads to more effective worker involvement.
3. TQM offers employees greater participation in decision making and thus makes the implementation of company's objectives much faster.[29]
4. TQM allows for in-time consideration of potential problems.
5. TQM reduces management bureaucracy. Teams are self-managing and do their own hiring and firing.[30] TQM promotes reduction in the production cycle. Empowered workers feel responsible for the quality of their processes; they strive for defect reduction and delay reduction.

TQM and strategic management are management-led processes. The senior leaders in a company must create clear and visible quality values, as well as high expectations. Reinforcement of the values and expectations requires substantial personal commitment and involvement. Leaders in

TQM, as in strategic management, are guided by clear, visible statements of values, usually in the form of mission statements.[31]

Policies that support the goals and objectives of an organization provide the necessary direction for the TQM process. These guidelines ensure that every employee understands and is responsible and accountable for TQM in daily business activities. For example, McDonald's has incorporated environmental policies into its TQM process to emphasize part of its corporate mission. The policy, as stated by Bennet, Freierman, and George, says, "McDonald's believes it has a special responsibility to protect our environment and future generations. . . . We will lead in word and in deed." The policy further states that the company is guided by four principles: "effectively managing solid waste, conserving and protecting natural resources, encouraging environmental values and practices, and ensuring accountability procedures."[32]

TQM and the strategic management process are not two separate structures. Quality is made part of the business through integration in the strategic planning process, according to George and Weimerskirch.[33] One of the goals of TQM is continuous improvement toward the ideal of zero defects. This concept plays a major role in the strategic plans that guide a company. Further, strategic management defines policies and ensures the acceptance and implementation of TQM throughout the company.

The TQM approach, like strategic management, involves extending the improvement process into the future. Achieving the highest levels of quality and competitiveness requires a well-defined and well-executed approach to continuous improvement, a process that must contain regular cycles of planning, execution, and evaluation. These same cycles are vital to the strategic management process.

Therefore, the benefits of TQM mirror the overall goals of strategic management. They consist of improved (1) customer satisfaction, (2) organizational effectiveness, and (3) competitiveness.

Reengineering and Strategic Management

In today's competitive environment, corporations are being required to find new and improved methods of doing business. Although this may not be that difficult, it adds to the necessity of reducing cost while being innovative and this task becomes extremely difficult. Reengineering is the term used to describe the concept and method of radically redesigning business processes.

Reengineering plays a critical role in the strategic management process to help organizations significantly change. The goal is to develop and create superior business processes to produce unique goods and services customers value highly.

Some companies have turned to work reengineering to pave the way for TQM. Although

> no single generally accepted definition has yet emerged for the concept . . . work reengineering [can be defined as] the practice of modifying company policies, procedures, methods, practices, processes, structure, organization, systems and technology to achieve dramatic improvements in performance relative to appropriately defined critical success factors and performance measures.[34]

Work reengineering differs from other process improvement methodologies in that it is typically approached from a project perspective, with process improvement goals and objectives and a limited time frame firmly in mind. This project orientation keeps work reengineering focused on getting real results.

Work reengineering also seeks to attain dramatic step-change increases in performance rather than the incremental change advocated by continuous improvement. This concept helps an organization to revitalize its process. It seeks the optimal solution to operational problems without regard to what exists today. It allows a company to address policies and procedures, organization and structure, people and culture, system and technology, all of which are subject to review and change in the search for improvement. Work reengineering recognizes the risks but seeks the rewards associated with rapid and substantial change.

The success of reengineering depends not only on management's ability to lead the corporation in change, but management's ability to diagnose what that change should be. Before reengineering takes place, management must determine the primary purpose and the focus of the business, the culture, and organizational culture. Before reengineering, Union Carbide made a strategic decision to focus on commodity chemicals and exit from many of its specialty chemical markets. Union Carbide was then able to focus the reengineering to meet its strategic goals. Both Kodak and IBM assumed that their visions were correct and that they could reengineer their way to prosperity. They were wrong and their employees and shareholders have suffered.

Once the vision and strategy are finalized, then companies can begin planning the reengineering. This type of change does not come about from moving a few people around or changing a couple of boxes on the organizational structure. This type of success comes from completely redesigning the organization from scratch. That means beginning with the corporate vision and strategy.

Management needs to start with a blank piece of paper and design the organization that will best accomplish those strategies. Many companies claim they are reengineering when in reality they are squandering corporate resources on projects that have too narrow a scope to have any impact on the bottom line. In order to affect the results of the business unit or corporation, you must restructure the things that are fundamental to the functioning of the unit. Anything less will have little impact on the bottom line.

During this process, it is critical that management not only creates the right vision and the right structure but also is involved in communicating why change is necessary. Management must realize that this type of change is very upsetting to the employees. Failing to provide information only increases anxiety and makes the changes more difficult to implement.[35] Here internal communication through effective public relations is crucial. Reengineering can be successful when the participants of the company share the vision and the mission of the company and strive diligently to make it succeed.

Strategic management is a process by which an organization keeps itself aligned with changing conditions. Reengineering is linked to strategic management because reengineering is doomed to failure if corporate strategy is not part of the process. Successful reengineering must be aligned with mission and vision, which are part of strategic management, to help an organization change those business processes that are fundamental to the success of the organization.

Reengineering and TQM. Unlike TQM, which can take three, four, or even ten years, reengineering is well suited to situations that warrant dramatic improvement in a relatively short time. TQM offers productivity improvements, increases in quality, improvements in flexibility and reductions in response time, improved quality of life, increased employee satisfaction, and enhanced control over the business. Reengineering can result in reduced processing lead time, productivity increases, improved quality of decision making, increased employee satisfaction, and improved visibility of process problems.

While reengineering differs from TQM, it is not in conflict with TQM. The two can and have been used to complement each other very effectively. Reengineering can be employed to generate improvements to a process before initiating a long-term TQM effort. Reengineering can pave the way for TQM. It produces tools for process improvement when a radical change is needed. Reengineering can be used to jump-start an existing TQM process that has been less than successful. It is important to mention that those in charge of reengineering do not create conflict with the basic tenets or principles of TQM. In fact, several of the tools and techniques employed by reengineering are the same as those used by TQM. Employee involvement teams and statistical process control are two prime examples.

In a high-performance workplace, graduates entering the workforce will be expected to have competencies in managing resources and information, monitoring their own performance, improving systems, and selecting and applying technology. They will need interpersonal skills and communication, as well as reasoning and problem-solving skills.

Management needs to understand international requirements to do business overseas. In 1987, the International Standards Organization published the ISO 9000 series of Quality Assurance and Quality Management Standards, which has brought agreement on an international scale, enhancing quality as a factor in safety and consumer expectations in international trade. In the competitive world of national and international trade, quality and standards are becoming increasingly important to customers. Companies supplying products or services need to be able to demonstrate that they are at least as good as their competitors in these areas, or preferably better. At the same time, they must maintain their profitability and improve the efficiency of their operations.

Organizational Policy

The fourth part of strategy formulation defines organizational *policy*. Policy provides the basic assumptions and guidelines for use by all levels of the organization in an effort to achieve the designated strategic objectives. Management writes policies to assist organization members in formulating, implementing, and controlling phases. The owners, board of directors, or the top management team usually creates strategic policies. Strategic policies focus on many areas, including these:

1. The qualifications of products to be offered, including national and international requirements, e.g., ISO 9000 quality assurance procedures.
2. The organization's culture and management philosophy.
3. The geographic location of the basic actions.
4. The role of the organization in society. Organizations must provide information about their product and services in a language that is understood by the user, and on the educational level of the user.
5. The industries to be entered.
6. The organizational goals and objectives.
7. Performance criteria.

STRATEGY IMPLEMENTATION

Implementation involves transforming the chosen strategies into action and refers to the methods and techniques the organization adopts to execute management's selected strategy. Implementation is a process of selecting (1) the most appropriate structure for the chosen strategy, (2) support systems for resource allocation, and (3) suitable motivation. Inherently, implementation is critical to goal attainment since even the best strategy is worthless if implemented incorrectly.

In 1993, Mercedes-Benz implemented a strategic marketing plan to increase the percentage of cars produced outside of Germany. As part of the strategy, Mercedes-Benz expanded into new geographical markets and new market niches, such as sport-utility vehicles, minivans, and a subcompact city car. Mercedes-Benz anticipated an increase in U.S. sales of 13 percent with the implementation of the new strategy. The merger of Mercedes-Benz with Chrysler in 1998 was a continuation of that strategy.

No matter how great the strategic plan appears to be, it is useless unless all levels of the organization are committed to its implementation. To properly implement a strategy, five key areas must be addressed:

1. The organizational structure must be able to support the strategic action. In addition to an appropriate structure, the strategy should include the degree of autonomy allowed for each individual to carry out his or her portion of the required activities.
2. Implementation systems must be in place to ensure that the firm's activities, from the decision-making process to output, are in accord with the agreed-upon strategy.
3. The organization's management style must focus on leadership, planning, organizing, controlling, communicating, and problem-solving activities.
4. The organization's culture must be in tune with, and supportive of, the strategic process.
5. There must be a match between the strategy and the implementation.

Thus, successful implementation of strategy requires a planned effort with commitment from all members of the organization, not just from management. However, management must ensure that the proper tools, support mechanisms, and lines of authority exist within the organizational structure to implement the strategy.

EVALUATION AND CONTROL

Evaluation and control entails monitoring the organization's performance to ensure that the chosen strategy achieves the desired objectives. The corporation evaluates and appraises its mission, goals, objectives, strategies, and policies in light of its dynamic and ever-changing environment. Thus, the strategic management process goes full circle as a continuous and repetitive cycle of vision, planning, implementing, and evaluating.

Evaluation is an essential function for validation of the success or failure of management's strategy. If results are below expectations, the organization has the opportunity to reassess its direction and, if necessary, alter the strategic plan.

DECISION MAKING

The decision-making process may be viewed simply as making a choice. More comprehensively, decision making is a systematic process that begins with identifying a need or problem and ends with implementation of the chosen alternative. Decision making should not be confused with problem solving. Problem solving is a less complex process directed toward the solution of an immediate problem, most often involving a trial-and-error approach. Strategic decision making always involves the evaluation of several possible solutions and ultimate selection from the existing alternatives.

Decision making permeates all functions of management, especially where top management is confronted daily with choosing the course of action that will best achieve the goals to which the company is dedicated. Further down the managerial ladder, a decreasing number and quality of alternatives are available, but making correct decisions at any level is, nevertheless, essential to the well-being of the organization.

Decision making is the most important activity of management. Organizational decision making is quite complex and occurs within constraints that include psychological, environmental, and decision-related factors. Environmental constraints include organizational factors such as objectives and policies, the organization's environment and structure, reference groups, group dynamics, and roles. Decision-related factors include the relative importance of the decision, the time and information available to make the decision, and the involvement of multiple decision makers. As a result, the decision-making process is very complex.

Ethical decision making involves the general nature of morals and of the specific moral choice to be made by the individual in relation to others. Ethical dilemmas involve interrelationships in which there are conflicts and tension. Ethical standards may be different for different cultural groups; e.g., one group may believe that lying is acceptable behavior while others may feel that it is very unethical.

Thus, in conclusion, strategic management can be implemented successfully. However, it takes time, hard work, and commitment at all levels of the organization. In addition, failure to appropriately assess the environment and to make appropriate changes can lead to failure in the marketplace and may ultimately threaten the survival of the organization.

REVIEW QUESTIONS

1. What is strategic management? What does it consist of?
2. What are some of the characteristics of strategic management?
3. List and discuss the four basic components of the strategic management process.
4. What is meant by open and closed systems?
5. Explain the SWOT analysis.
6. What is the importance of information and forecasting techniques?
7. Name and describe the five key elements of the mission statement.
8. What are the components of strategic objectives?
9. List and explain the five categories of strategy formulation.
10. What is organizational policy?
11. What are the key areas of strategy implementation?

NOTES

1. Scharf, A. (1991). Secrets of strategic planning: Responding to the opportunities of tomorrow. *Industrial Management,* 33, January-February, 9-10.

2. Higgins, J. M. and Vincze, J. W. (1993). *Strategic Management: Text and Cases,* Fifth Edition. Chicago: Dryden Press, p. 5.

3. Harvey, D. F. (1988). *Strategic Management and Business Policy.* Columbus, OH: Merrill Publishing Co., p. 6.

4. Pearce, J. A. III and Robinson, R. B. Jr. (1988). *Strategic Management: Strategy Formulation and Implementation,* Third Edition. Homewood, IL: Richard D. Irwin, Inc., p. 8.

5. Chandler, A. (1962). *Strategy and Structure: Chapters in the History of the American Enterprise.* Cambridge, MA: MIT Press, p. 6.

6. Quinn, J. B. (1980). *Strategy for Change: Logical Incrementalism.* Homewood, IL: Richard D. Irwin, Inc., p. 9.

7. Glueck, W. F. (1980). *Business Policy and Strategic Management.* New York: McGraw-Hill, p. 8.

8. Hayden, C. L. (1986). *The Handbook of Strategic Expertise.* New York: The Free Press, pp. 5-7.

9. Edgley, B. (1992). Strategic planning. *Association Management,* 11, March, 77-80.

10. Alkhafaji, A. (1992). The effectiveness of the board of directors: Management views. *Pennsylvania Journal of Business and Economics,* 2(1), 11-20.

11. Mintzberg, H. (1978). Patterns in strategy formulation. *Management Science,* 24, 934-948.

12. Granof, M. H. (1983). *Accounting for Managers and Investors.* New Jersey: Prentice-Hall, Inc., p. 507.

13. Stone, R. (1996). Mission statement revisited. *S.A.M. Advanced Management Journal,* 61(Winter), 31-38.

14. Hayden, *The Handbook of Strategic Expertise,* pp. 14-15.

15. Judge, W. Jr. and Krishean, H. (1991). Enterprise strategy, grand strategy, and financial performance. *Southern Management Association Proceedings,* 14-16.

16. Langeler, G. H. (1992). The vision trap. *Harvard Business Review,* 70(2), 46-48.

17. Maney, K. (1997). Technology is "demolishing" time distance: Global is local in a new world order of business. *USA Today,* April 24, 2B-3B.

18. Beamish, M. and Rosenzweig, P. M. (1997). *International Management.* Burr Ridge, IL: Robert D. Irwin, Inc., p. 32.

19. Alkhafaji, A. (1995). *Competitive Global Management.* Delray Beach, FL: St. Lucie Press, p. 242.

20. Stewart, T. (1995). Flying high: Why KLM's global strategy is working. *BusinessWeek,* February 27, 90-91.

21. Hagen, A. and Kedia, S. (1998). Technology Transfer and Development Strategies for Microelectronic Industry. *Business Research Yearbook.* Lanham, MD: University Press of America, p. 407.

22. Maney, Technology is "demolishing" time distance, pp. 2B-3B.

23. Ross, J. E. (1995). *Total Quality Management: Text, Cases and Readings,* Second Edition. Delray Beach, FL: St. Lucie Press, p. 3.

24. Bounds, G., Yorks, L., Adams, M., and Ranney, G. (1994). *Beyond Total Quality Management: Toward the Emerging Paradigm.* New York: McGraw-Hill, p. 46.

25. Bushnell, D. S. and Halus, M. B. (1992). TQM in the public sector: Strategies for quality service. *National Productivity Review,* 11(3), Summer, 355.

26. Barrett, M. J. (1993). Continuous quality improvement as an organizational strategy. *Healthcare Financial Management,* 47(9), 20.

27. Chalk, M. B. (1993). Establishing a quality climate. *Journal of Property Management,* 58(5), 14.

28. Henderson, G. (1992). Girobank: Quality is the key. *Banking World,* 10(12), 26.

29. Elrich, E. (1993). The quality management checkpoint. *International Business,* 6(5), 50-62.

30. Niven, D. (1993). When times get tough what happens to TQM? *Harvard Business Review,* 71(3), 20-24.

31. George, S. and Wemerskirch, A. (1994). *Total Quality Management: Strategies and Techniques Proven at Today's Most Successful Companies.* New York: John Wiley and Sons, Inc., pp. 1-65.

32. Bennet, S., Freierman, R., and George, S. (1993). *Corporate Realities and Environmental Truths: Strategies for Leading Your Business in the Environmental Era*. New York: John Wiley and Sons, Inc., pp. 35-38.
33. George and Weimerskirch, *Total Quality Management,* pp. 1-65.
34. Greengard, S. (1993). Reengineering: Out of the rubble. *Personnel Journal,* 72(12), p. 48B.
35. Ibid.

Chapter 3

Assessing the Environment

INTRODUCTION

The globalization of markets and interdependence of economies have continued to increase over the years. This has resulted in increased competition, revolutionized technologies, rapid changes in organizational structure, diversity of the workforce, new demands, and changes in market and economic conditions. These developments also add to the complexity of the organizational environment. The environment of an organization, or of any system, includes all of the circumstances or influences that surround and/or affect it. The environment is segregated into two components, the internal and the external, and refers to all variables that affect the strategy of an organization.[1]

As stated in Chapter 2, environmental analysis is based on systems theory, which includes the concepts of open and closed systems. A system or organization exhibits a patterned "energic input-output in which the energic returns from output reactivate the systems."[2] This input-output-recycle behavior is patterned and is primarily concerned with the interdependence of the organization's relationships and structures. Closed systems, theoretically self-contained and requiring nothing from the outside, fail to recognize the interdependency of the relationship between the internal and external environments. Open systems, however, not only recognize that the outside environment is essential to survival, but constantly strive for goal achievement through control of or adaptation to the external environment. The external environment consists of all the stakeholders concerned with the organization, i.e., customers, creditors, communities, trade associations, competitors, suppliers, and stockholders, as well as the macroenvironmental factors, e.g., technology, socioeconomic, political, etc. (see Figure 3.1).

Strategic management includes continuous assessment of the corporation and its environment by top management. Strategic management is a process of making appropriate changes within the organization so that the organization can adapt to its environment and optimally exploit its opportunities in the market.

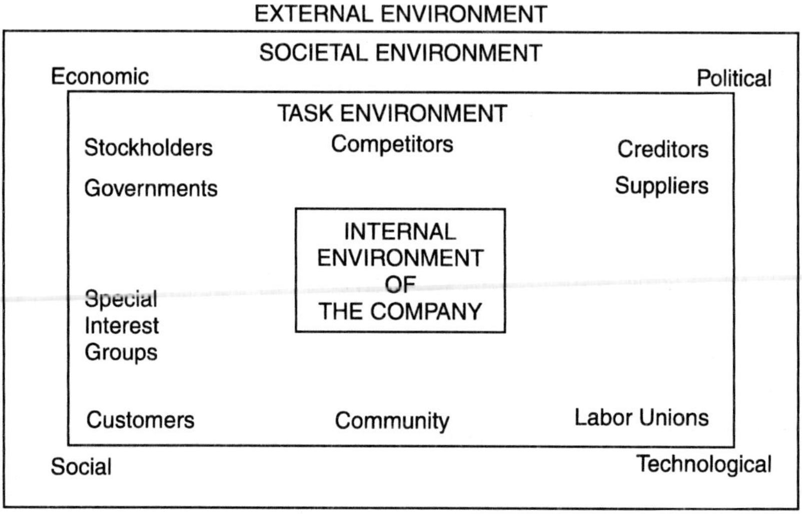

EXTERNAL ENVIRONMENT

SOCIETAL ENVIRONMENT

Economic

Political

TASK ENVIRONMENT

Stockholders

Competitors

Creditors

Governments

Suppliers

INTERNAL ENVIRONMENT OF THE COMPANY

Special Interest Groups

Customers

Community

Labor Unions

Social

Technological

FIGURE 3.1. The Business Environment

Strategists analyze the elements within the internal and external environments in search of relevant strategic information. The resultant findings are classified as organizational strengths, weaknesses, opportunities, and threats (SWOTs). The SWOT analysis becomes the premise upon which strategic objectives are determined and strategies formulated.

Every organization's environment contains a set of influential forces that affect what it can and cannot do. Thus the environment, as a whole, influences the organizational decision-making process, since every environmental factor or situation affects the organization and its management. Management makes decisions under dynamic conditions where variables are hard to isolate precisely and are thus frequently misunderstood. Not only do external forces affect the organization within its particular industry; these external forces may also affect the industry itself. In order to successfully manage the external forces, effective environmental scanning must be undertaken. Environmental scanning is a systematic method to monitor and forecast those forces that are external and consequently not under the direct control of the organization or its industry.

The external environment defines an organization's opportunities and threats. Generally speaking, every decision involves different sets of factors; hence every decision is made under different circumstances. Thus, management makes decisions based upon the organization's unique situation. Bridges concludes that this environmental complexity is a major factor in whether decision making is effective.[3] Due to this complexity, the decision maker must undertake environmental research. Management must use informative guidelines, standards, or criteria that aid in determining the actual conditions in the environment before formulating strategies and making relevant decisions.

DYNAMIC ENVIRONMENTS

A *dynamic environment* is an environment that is constantly changing and where variables create situations that force an organization to constantly change. Dynamic environments tend to impact larger companies more than smaller companies simply because the larger companies must usually deal with more factors that threaten their competitive advantage. In comparison, smaller companies do not have to deal with as many external or internal factors, and the rate of change is perhaps slower or less complex. For instance, smaller firms may have fewer social, international, or internal issues than the larger companies.

To illustrate the dynamic of this environment, consider the personal computer (PC) revolution of the past thirty years. Intel Corporation is the biggest and most successful computer chip manufacturer today. In 1971, Intel was able to pack 2,300 transistors onto a thumbnail-size sliver of silicon to make the first microprocessor. Between 1971 and 1991, the number of transistors able to fit in this small area was doubled every two years. This represents an increase of about 40 percent each year. In the past decade, the number of transistors has continued to rise but at the slower rate of about 21 percent each year. More than 80 percent of the company's revenue and practically all of its profits come from the sale of microprocessors. Intel sales and profit started declining in 1998. The biggest challenges the company faces today are wide use of the Internet and intense competition. Current digital communications and electronic commerce represent a new and fast-developing reality. Internet users have realized that they can use the World Wide Web to shop and to find information, and can send e-mail without upgrading to the latest and most powerful PCs. Intel's competitors such as Cyrix (a unit of National Semiconductor) and Advanced Micro Devices (AMD) began selling their PCs at about $1,000—machines packed with enough power and memory to compete with Intel $2,500 systems.[4]

In order for a company to compete in a dynamic environment, change should not only be encouraged, but actually incorporated into the working process of the business. Strategic planners forecast change to aid the organization in being an early adapter instead of being a laggard. In summary, in today's competitive and ever-changing world, organizations that wish to remain competitive must actively adapt by promoting a culture that enhances change development and acceptance. Hickman and Silva make a compelling case for strategy and culture to go hand-in-hand as the foundation of excellence. They suggest a series of exercises to train employees to be innovative, not necessarily in their work, but in their thinking process. The long-term result will be reflected in their approach to solving task-specific problems.[5]

THE INTERNAL ENVIRONMENT

The environment within the firm, the organization's *internal situation,* must be assessed before potential future strategies can be developed. Understanding the organization's internal environment is important in strategy formulation because an organization must be aware of its available resources to use them effectively.

Key internal variables that affect strategy formulation (determining organizational mission, goals, and objectives and crafting the strategy) are the corporation's structure, culture, and resources. The structure of a corporation is often defined in terms of its (1) communication processes, (2) work flow, and (3) authority and responsibility relationships. Although there are infinite varieties of organizational structure, certain types are predominant in modern, complex organizations: the simple, the functional, the divisional, the matrix, and the conglomerate. An organization may also be composed of a number of suborganizations, or SBUs, of various sizes. It is important for the various subdivisions to communicate and work in the most efficient, organized way. A corporation's culture is the collection of beliefs, expectations, and values shared by the corporation's members, which is transmitted from one generation to the next. These beliefs, expectations, and values constitute norms, or rules of conduct, that define acceptable behavior for all members of the organization. Corporate resources are typically considered in terms of financial, physical, and human resources as well as organizational systems and technological capabilities.

Before making strategic decisions, top management must scan the organization's internal environment for strengths and weaknesses. In addition, the strategist should attempt to determine why they are strengths or weakness, how each strength can be transformed into an opportunity, how each weakness can be turned into a strength, and how each strength can complement each of the others to help the overall mission of the organization.

Each of the individual internal factors must be analyzed to ensure that strategy formulation will fit the organization as a whole. For analysis purposes, internal environments are usually divided into categories by function, i.e., marketing, production, etc.

Marketing

Since marketing is concerned with making the product or organization known, the marketing function must be carefully evaluated for its strengths and weaknesses. Whether using local, regional, or national publicity, attempts are made to increase the organization's sales or goodwill. Once the marketing alternatives are evaluated and the best ones chosen, the marketing department must determine which strategy it will employ to achieve the mission and objectives for growth in the market. One approach for meeting growth objectives is the intensive growth method. Intensive growth could be achieved in several ways. One way is through market penetration, which seeks to increase the sales of the organization's present products through a more aggressive marketing effort. Another way is through market development, which takes existing products into new markets. When employing this strategy, the marketing department's main objective is to make the new target market aware of the product and its availability. Through product development, the last form of intensive growth, the existing product is improved through research and development. The marketing department must make the public aware of any changes to stimulate the purchase of the new product. An effective evaluation of the marketing function aids in the determination of the best approach to use. The product life cycle contains the following stages (see Figure 3.2):

1. In the introduction stage, the company attempts to gain initial market acceptance. The research and development department tests and monitors customer reaction to the new product. This requires the company to educate the public, that is, to create awareness and interest in the target market. It also requires careful pricing and distribution in the right places. At this stage, sales volume is still low while cost is high, and therefore profits are low.
2. After the new product has been introduced with success, sales in the growth phase are expected to increase rapidly from both repeat purchases and additional customers. The profit margin is higher at this stage. Competitors and potential competitors consider entering this market (depending on barriers to entry, i.e., patent protection, customer loyalties, etc.).
3. During the maturity stage, sales volume continues to increase slowly. Sales and profits peak and begin to fall as the competition increases.

4. During the decline phase, sales begin to decline and profits drop swiftly. Substitute products have been introduced and accepted by customers. Many companies consider leaving the market (depending on exit barriers).

Production/Manufacturing

When a company is operating in a dynamic environment, the strengths and weaknesses of the production or manufacturing function can ultimately determine not only the success of the company, but the existence of the company as well. The production/manufacturing function can be considered a strength when it produces cost-competitive goods that are sufficiently high in quality. If not, then it must be considered a weakness.

As a company escalates the product life-cycle curve and approaches the maturity stage, it should be gaining valuable experience that will lead to better cost efficiency and higher product quality. Of course, this improved efficiency and quality cannot be expected to escalate indefinitely, as shown in Figure 3.2. At some point, the company will reach the maximum attainable level, and at that point the company can only achieve higher efficiency and product quality with the advent or incorporation of better technology.

Finance

Finance is another key component to be overseen by top executives. If financial affairs are mismanaged, the organization is in jeopardy. Finances must be managed with knowledge about the internal factors so that budgets and disbursements are appropriate. Financial alternatives must be evaluated

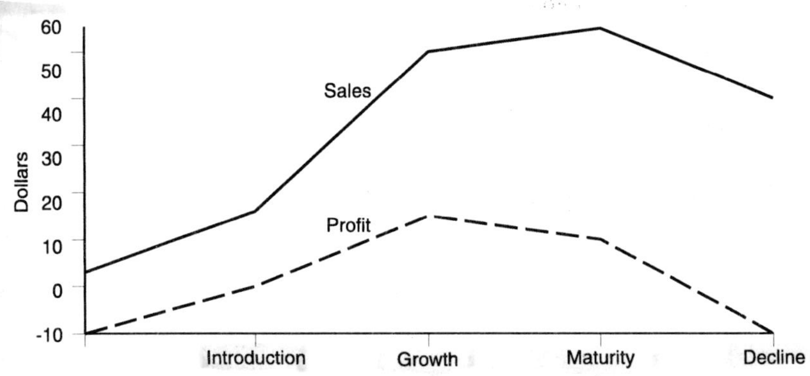

FIGURE 3.2. The Product Life Cycle

carefully to determine the optimal amount of disbursement to each division so the organization, as a whole, benefits and the organizational objectives are achieved.

The finance department must also consider long-term financial requirements. Too many firms are concerned with short-term financial performance and therefore ignore long-term financing. Long-term corporate financial planning can include building an investment portfolio of various stocks and bonds to diversify the organization's financial risks. Such an investment portfolio is often built by purchasing different types of bonds with staggered maturity dates and then selling them as the situation warrants. On the other hand, most companies establish preemptive stocks (holders of common stock will be given the first option to purchase new shares) so that when new issues come out, they can resume their percentage share and remain in control.

Some companies do not distribute dividends during economic downturns, while others maintain a balance so they can pay dividends regardless of the general economic condition. The latter strategy is preferred since investors prefer regular dividends. Financial analysis is an important part of analyzing the internal strengths and weaknesses of the organization. In the past, corporate performance was measured mainly by financial results. However, recently, with the increasing number of service sector corporations, financial and operational measures become important. This is called the balanced scorecard. Some of these measures are profitability, customer satisfaction, growth, market share, and job satisfaction.[6] The appendix briefly discusses the importance of financial analysis. It shows the ratio analyses that must be understood by managers.

Research and Development

Research and development is yet another critical internal factor that must be evaluated. Strategy formulation in this area is vital. Many questions must be evaluated and answered, such as: "What type of products do we want to produce?"; "How can we improve existing products?"; and "Do we have the skills and equipment to produce the desired new products?" All these questions and more must be addressed, and alternatives must be developed and evaluated.

The internal organization must always be creating and recreating ideas. Public demands, markets, and technology change drastically over brief periods of time, so products can quickly become obsolete. To remain viable, new products must be developed to replace them. "A number of survey respondents directed their R&D efforts primarily to customer needs and place little or no emphasis on engineering improvements."[7] This points out that organizations should adopt new technological improvements when these improvements offer a large reduction in cost through a gain in efficiency or when the improvements better meet customer needs. Technological improvements should also be adopted on an experimental basis, when possible, without endangering the present program. Organizations invest a sizeable amount of time, effort, and money into the formulation of strategies to improve and create new products or services. Organizations cannot survive and grow without a successful product or service strategy.

Human Resource Management

Management and personnel are two significant factors that affect the operation and internal environment of a corporation. Unions are just one part of the uncontrollable external environment that can put enormous strain on the internal environment. Caterpillar Inc. is a good illustration of a union's effect on a company's viability. Caterpillar's profitable years ended with the general economic recession of the early 1980s, which forced the layoff of 20,000 members of the United Auto Workers union. Concerned with the layoffs, wage ceilings, and stringent job transfer rules, the UAW called a strike, which resulted in large losses for Caterpillar. This situation was partially a result of management's failure to communicate the necessity of the cost-cutting measure to the union. The basic lesson in this example is that an organization must be aware of and seek to effectively manage its internal and external environments.

Managerial functions and roles affect the internal environment. Managerial functions are more generalized duties as compared to roles, which are specific categories of managerial behavior. Managerial functions include planning, decision making, organizing, staffing, communicating, motivating, leading, and controlling. The roles of top management and the board of directors are covered in Chapter 2. Internal organizational environments change rapidly. For example, employees' levels of education and expectations are rising. Therefore, management must change to meet the demands of their subordinates. Management could attend classes or seminars to stay up to date on current strategies and formulations. If an organization is not growing, not changing its strategies, and not implementing strategies, it may hinder its position as a vital entity and its existence may be threatened. A solid, proactive, and aggressive management system can prevent this from happening.

Managerial values and capabilities must also be evaluated. Although managers do not consciously articulate their values as they make decisions, their values greatly influence their decisions at a subconscious level. Managerial capabilities must be evaluated periodically by the board of directors' committees or upper-level management to ensure that management has the ability to plan, manage, and execute the strategies. Management performance will ultimately determine the fate of the organization. Unless management can induce subordinates to effectively execute their particular jobs, the organization cannot successfully achieve its objectives.

Employee Perspectives and Compensation

Employee capabilities and performance are tied to compensation plans. Fair and adequate compensation is essential to encourage maximum productivity from employees. Compensation is considered one motivator for encouraging maximum performance, even for the less aggressive employee. In the past, the preferred compensation plan was straight salary, but many are currently supplementing this with performance bonuses or other incentive schemes. Modern compensations may include such fringes as stock options, increased insurance plans, or longer vacation times. Appropriate compensation plans are believed to motivate employees to perform to organizational expectations and allow the organization to attract and keep good employees. The resultant benefits to the organization are lower turnover, lower absenteeism, and lower employee training costs.[8] In effect, the organization, as a whole, benefits.

Bonuses to reward employee performance may increase competition among the workers instead of promoting teamwork. Bonuses are also a short-term incentive. Mary Walton, in her book describing the management method of W. Edwards Deming, cites Deming as condemning performance evaluation. He feels that bonuses and merit rating encourage short-term performance at the expense of long-term planning.

> They discourage risk-taking, build fear, undermine teamwork, and pit people against each other for the same rewards. On a team, it is difficult to tell who did what. The result is a company composed of prima donnas and of sparring fiefdoms. People work for themselves, not the company.[9]

To reduce the risk of incurring the wrath of shareholders if CEOs are overcompensated, the SEC has enacted rules to allow shareholders to vote on the issue of company officers' compensation. Other valuable employee benefits to shore up the inner strength of the organization include: pay for college, university, and trade school tuition and books for willing employees, personal development and enrichment seminars, etc.

Communication

Communication within the organization is a significant internal factor. Since effective organizations are constantly changing, communication is essential to ensure that the interdependent and interrelated parts function as a whole. For example, the research and development department must communicate information concerning its products under development to marketing and, in turn, receive feedback as to the market potential for the products. In addition, communication between the organization and its external environment is essential for the organization to understand its customers and for the customers to become aware of products or services the organization has to offer. Many companies use public relations campaigns to convey their enterprise strategies to their stakeholders, which can improve the image as well as the reputation of the company.

In conclusion, to be effective, strategic management must be internalized by all organizational components and requires an assessment of the entire organization's internal environment to determine present strengths and weaknesses. Although each organizational component must develop its own strategic plan, the corporate level must ensure that the separate plans are sufficiently integrated to accomplish the overall strategy. Evaluation of the internal environment helps in the strategy formulation process by setting boundaries to work within and goals to work toward.

THE EXTERNAL ENVIRONMENT

We live in a dynamic environment that changes all the time. Businesses must understand the changes in the environment and how these changes affect their performance. Consider two major factors that impacted business in 2001 and 2002:

- The terrorist attacks on the World Trade Center and the Pentagon that occurred on September 11, 2001, affected the airline industry and its performance. These attacks forced the airline industry to rethink its security measures, with government guidance. It also encouraged the industry to find a reasonable way to satisfy customers while heightening security measures.
- The unethical and illegal manipulations of financial statements of many major American companies that have come to light since late 2001 have shocked the country. Top executives of these companies cashed in billions of dollars in stock even when their companies were not performing well in the marketplace.

As a result of these incidents, the federal government has enacted new financial regulations and required corporate CEOs to verify financial statements.

The *external environment* is composed of outside forces over which management has little or no control but which affect the organization's development and success. The external environment is constantly changing, and this means that companies must also change along with it.[11] Since the external environment contains information needed by management for strategic formulation, strategists must constantly scan the external environment to identify the threats and opportunities that might impact the corporation.

Because companies vary in their basic organization, competitive analysis begins with an overview of the industry's primary economic traits. Some economic traits to consider are *market size, market growth rate, number of rivals and their relative sizes* (i.e., is the industry fragmented by many small companies or by a few large companies?), *number of buyers and their relative sizes,* and *whether the product of rival firms is highly distinguished, weakly distinguished, or essentially identical to yours.*[12]

The Industrial Environment

Each company is part of an industry. An industry contains a group of companies offering similar products or services or close substitutes that satisfy the same basic consumer need. A model designed by Michael Porter highlights five forces that shape competition within an industry. These forces are discussed later in this chapter. The five forces are as follows:

1. The risk of new entry by potential competitor companies that are currently not competing in the industry but which have the capability to do so
2. The degree of rivalry among established companies
3. The bargaining power of buyers
4. The bargaining power of suppliers
5. The competitive force of substitute products[13]

Porter argued that when a company understands how each of these five variables work, it will be in a good position to identify strategic opportunities and threats. Product life cycle (PLC) analysis is an important tool that assists in understanding the company position within its industry and in designing a strategic plan. The following section attempts to provide a better understanding of the methods in which the PLC can be used in strategic planning.

Strategic Planning and the Life Cycle Concept

The life cycle concept is based on the assumption that a product's (or industry's) sales volume follows a four-phase cycle: embryonic (introduction), growth, maturity, and aging. Although there are some exceptions to this evolutionary sequence, they are not common enough to warrant any change in the life cycle; nor is the life-cycle concept restricted to a sales volume basis. Other financial data are also employed in the study of this phenomenon. Because the life-cycle concept (Figure 3.2) is comprehensive and flexible, it is applied to the strategic-planning function of many businesses.

Stage 1. The first phase is the *embryonic,* or *introduction, phase.* This phase is crucial to product survival and product profit margins. When introducing a product to the market, it is often necessary to do it slowly and secretively until it is well developed and can be introduced in mass quantities. By proceeding slowly, the company does not lose a phenomenal investment in advertising, promotion, production costs, and market testing if the product is not accepted in the market. Secretiveness in the introduction phase prevents competitors from taking advantage of the company's research and development. If pertinent information is not protected, competitors may quickly capitalize on the innovative idea, and if they can get a similar product to market faster, the competition may gain the larger market share with little or no R&D investment. If the developing firm determines that it cannot produce or promote the product efficiently, then an alternative is to sell its idea to a firm that can.

For example, in 1980 Texas Instruments tested their new personal computer 99/4 in Lubbock, Texas. They were not able to deliver the product on time as promised, which caused them to lose market share. Usually, testing in a small market will provide a company with the necessary feedback, while making it difficult for the competitors to find out about the new product development. Such strategies will ensure the first mover advantages in capturing a big market share. Also, it will give the company's research and development the necessary time to design the product according to consumer preference.

During the embryonic stage, sales volumes just begin to increase. Because the introduction of a product is initially very costly with little revenue generated, both profits and cash flow are negative. The strategy is to recoup the start-up costs and initial losses during the later, more profitable stages of the life cycle.

Stage 2. In the *growth stage* of the product life cycle, the product is on the market and is producing a margin of profit. If the product is successful, the entrance of other firms into the market is inevitable. If the product innovators choose to reinvest in additional research and development to maintain the competitive lead or to gain even greater market share, they may realize little rise in profits. This growth stage is characterized by a continuous increase in sales volume, usually at a rate greater than that realized in the embryonic stage. Also, profits and cash flow reach their lowest point before beginning to increase. Toward the middle and end of this phase, profits and cash flow enter into the positive range, with the firm realizing a positive return on its investment in the embryonic stage. Growing competition for market share inevitably accompanies the higher profit margins. When the competition entering the market reaches its peak, the next stage of the product life cycle is entered.

Stage 3. The *maturity stage* requires the organization to make major decisions concerning the product since it is during this stage that all three measures (sales volume, cash flow, and profit) peak and then begin to decline. Profits peak first, followed by cash flow and sales volume. Since the maturity stage is characterized by the existence of many competitors in the market, product sales level off and then start to slowly decline. Competitors engage in price-cutting wars to gain market share and to force inefficient producers out of the market. In this phase, competition is fierce, with only the strongest firms able to maintain their position. Weaker firms begin to search for a new niche in the market or some other way to strengthen their current situation. Further, when profits begin to decrease, management must decide the fate of the product. At this point, there are several alternative strategies to be considered. First, the company can attempt to differentiate the product from its competitors by promoting certain aspects such as the product's related service or its technological superiority. Complementary products may be developed, such as a beauty parlor for Barbie dolls. Second, companies may look for different geographic or demographic markets. Last, the company may develop new uses for the product, e.g., baking soda as an air freshener or a toothpaste. If these alternatives are not present, or are not feasible, the firm may drop the product as it enters the next stage, decline.

Stage 4. The final stage, the *aging* or *declining stage,* begins with a continuous decline in the entire industry's sales. With large decreases in sales and in an effort to maintain market share at others' expense, price-cutting wars eventually begin. This may result in sale prices at or below production costs, which eventually eliminates all but the strongest producers. During this phase, the three measures of sales volume, cash flow, and profits decline very sharply. Sales profits fall into the negative range, and sales volume and cash flow end up in the negative range as well. At this point, the firm must consider the two remaining options—liquidate or continue attempts to expand the market. In a few instances, firms can reverse the maturity process and return the product to the growth stage of the life cycle. For example, a company selling detergent can introduce an improvement on that detergent or perhaps change the packaging. Currently VCRs are being phased out, along with videotapes, as newer technology replaces them.

The lengths of these stages are not predetermined and vary with every product. Some products, such as Pepsi and Coca-Cola, have been in the maturity stage for years and are still making large profits. Other products may have a maturity period of two or three weeks, as in the case of movie action figures. The product life cycle length varies with product characteristics; e.g., fad items will have very short cycles, while durable goods such as washing machines will have a much longer life cycle.

An obvious application of the product life cycle is to find which stage a product is in and then select the appropriate strategy. Formulation of strategy will allow executives to know the exact strategy that should be followed in every situation if executives understand the environmental and organizational variables that have significant input on the context of strategy. For example, in the contingency approach, the most important single variable in the determination of strategy is the life-cycle stage of the product. Management should consider the following in each of the product life cycle stages: *the needs of the target market, buyer concentration, type of product, rate of technological change, market segmentation, market share,* and *elasticity of demand,* among other factors. In the general theory of strategy formulation, Michael Porter suggests competitive strategies for surpassing other competition.[14]

The Risk of New Entry by Potential Competitors

The established company in a particular industry should assess the possibility of a new entry by potential competitors in its market. If the possibility is high, then it cannot raise its prices and should prepare itself for less revenue and maybe severe competition. Therefore, a high risk of new entry represents a strategic threat. Other things being equal, a low risk of new entry allows established companies to raise their prices, so it represents an opportunity. Entering new markets is subject to the level of the *barriers to entry,* which is determined by the extent to which established companies have the following:

1. Brand loyalty
2. Economies of scale or cost advantage over potential entrants
3. Other factors, such as the level of capital investment, ease of existing in the future, and the stage of products in the life cycle

Threat of new entry. Management has to assess the possibility of new competitors joining the market. This means increasing industry capacity and preparing for intense battles for market share. The possibility of new entries depends on the existing barriers to entry into the industry and the possibility of retaliation from established companies in that market.

Barriers to entry. This refers to the industry attempt to block or deter new companies from entering the market. The higher the barriers to entry, the greater the potential profitability for the present member firms. When the barriers to entry are low and demand is high, the industry should expect many new entrants. The entrance of many companies into the same industry will increase supply and put pressure on prices and profits. There are six major considerations:

1. Whether the established companies have reached *economies of scale*. This refers to the increase in production volume to the point that the cost per unit decreases. Significant reduction in per unit cost will deter potential entrants. For a potential company to enter, it must risk either entering at a large scale or incurring a significant cost disadvantage by starting small.
2. Whether the established companies have *product differentiation*. A differentiated product or service, whether actual or perceived, will create brand loyalty among consumers. High customer loyalty will deter new entrants unless the new entrant is ready to incur high initial advertising and promotional costs to overcome this barrier.
3. Sometimes a higher *customer switching cost* prevents new entries. New entrants would have a difficult time convincing buyers to switch to their product or service.
4. Sometimes high *capital requirements* for entering a new market work as a barrier to entry. Technology cost might also work to prevent new market entrants.
5. If access to the distribution channels used by established firms is limited, this might work as a barrier to entry unless alternative channels are found.
6. Government policy may deter new entry to a particular market through licensing or other requirements. Common examples include health care organizations and the sale of liquor.

Rivalry Among Established Companies

Strong rivalry represents a threat to established companies, whereas weak rivalry constitutes an opportunity to raise prices and earn greater returns. The degree of competition depends on the number and size of companies within a particular industry and the level of demand conditions. The structures of industries have different implications for rivalry. These structures vary from fragmented (made up of many small and medium-sized companies) to consolidated (dominated by a small number of large companies). Rivalry is strong in fragmented industries because of the low entry barriers and products that are hard to differentiate. This level of rivalry between existing companies, along with the new entrants into a fragmented industry, will create excess supply, with the result that companies start cutting prices and reducing production. It may also result in a price war that will depress industry profits, force some companies to exit, and discourage any more new entrants. Reduction in production and prices will continue until overall industry capacity is brought in line with demand. Some companies choose to exit from such markets or are forced out through bankruptcies, at which point the prices may stabilize again.

The situation is different with the consolidated industries. They are more interdependent, as the competitive actions of one company will directly affect the profitability of others in the industry. When one company decides to cut its prices, for example, the other companies have little choice but to follow. Such a strategy results in a price war between the established companies (such as the airline industry has experienced). Particularly when demand is not growing at expected levels, companies fight to maintain revenues and market share. *Demand conditions* govern the intensity of rivalry among the established companies. The intensity of rivalry is more moderate if the demand is growing. This provides room for expansion to all companies. However, these companies usually send signals to one another to stabilize prices.

When products or services reach the decline stage in the PLC or because of severe competition, some companies choose to exit from the market. *Exit barriers* are a serious competitive threat, especially when demand is declining. However, exiting from current markets depends on the following:

1. The level of investments the company has in specialized fixed assets
2. Whether the output of a particular unit is needed as input in another
3. Whether the company has emotional attachments to the industry

Bargaining Power of Buyers

Buyers can be viewed as a competitive threat when they force down prices or demand higher quality and better service. The ability of buyers to make demands on a company depends on their power relative to that of the company.

Bargaining Power of Suppliers

Suppliers can be viewed as a threat when they are able to force up the price the company must pay for inputs or to reduce the quality of goods supplied. The ability of suppliers to make demands on a company depends on their power relative to that of the company.

Substitute Products

Substitute products limit the price that companies in an industry can charge without losing their customers to the makers of the substitutes. This threat comes more from another industry. The closer the substitutes, the greater the threat they pose.

Macroenvironmental Forces

Environmental scanning is usually split into four different major areas: economic, technological, political, and social. Although external environmental information is typically harder to gather, such information is essential to determine the optimal strategy. Therefore, management tends to continuously seek "perfect information."

The external environment impacts strategy formulation with four major forces: legal-political, economic, sociocultural, and technological forces. These forces can be either interrelated or interdependent. Of these four forces, the economic environment is the most significant for business organizations. The economic forces are the rate of inflation, the interest rate, the value of the currency, the unemployment level, the gross national product, and the business cycle. The economic cycle is usually divided into various stages, including depression, recession, recovery, and prosperity or peak. During any of these stages, the key variables affecting strategic decision making are the levels of unemployment, corporate interest paid, and consumer income. Since the inflation rate and the gross national product growth rate are significant indicators of the current economic stage, they are the two variables most influencing the strategic planning process.

Economic Forces

It is commonly agreed that the federal government exerts a powerful influence on the U.S. (and thus world) economy through the fiscal or monetary policies of the Federal Reserve Board. Also, the amount of spending by the federal government directly affects the level and composition of business activity within the economy. Where and how the federal government spends its money also influences the business environment. The national economic factors affect even multinational corporations that operate within the United States.[15] Companies are usually affected by the general condition of the national economy, either directly or indirectly. The value of the dollar might affect multinational corporation performance. Therefore, the firm's strategies are somewhat dependent upon economic conditions.

Technological Forces

Technology is a second aspect of the external environment that affects the organization in its strategic management process. In the past two decades, technology has changed drastically. Although technology is commonly interpreted as applying to automation, it has a broader meaning and is defined as the systematic application of scientific knowledge to practical purposes, including new ideas, inventions, techniques, and/or materials. The broader concept of technology could include a new method of planting trees. Since most industries' competitive advantages are predicated upon some type of advanced technology that changes rapidly, many industries are highly dynamic, e.g., electronics. Technological advances have in the recent past created entire new industries, such as biomedical genetics. Given the increasing rate of change of technology today, it is an important environmental variable for organizations. Competence and innovation in technology will provide an organization either a strategic advantage or a strategic disadvantage. For example, a firm that does not keep pace with technological development is destined to decline. On the other hand, a company that is a product innovator may become successful in the market by gaining a distinct advantage over the competition.

There are specific disadvantages for management in the area of technological advancement. Taylor and Hawkins believe that automation has a direct, and not necessarily positive, effect on corporate decision makers as "machines tend to duplicate mental as well as manual process."[16] As two examples, they cite (1) middle-aged, experienced, but change-resistant, managers who cannot, or will not, adapt to computer technology, and (2) the redundancy in management caused by "mergers arising from the search for technological economies [of scale]."[17] Furthermore, if a firm does not achieve a technological advantage, this technology gap becomes a major factor in altering the demand for a firm's (or industry's) products or services.

Political and Regulatory Forces

Political and regulatory forces are the third major area of the external environment. The political orientation of Congress or the executive branch ranges from conservative to liberal and generally splits down party lines (Republican and Democrat). The current political orientation of each branch of government should be considered in the strategic planning process. For instance, the Republican party is generally considered relatively probusiness, and when this party controls a branch of government, that branch will tend to be more favorably oriented toward business organizations.[18] In June 1998, Republicans in the Congress were able to kill the antitobacco bill that was highly debated and accepted by many as a solution to prevent teenagers from smoking. The tobacco industry lobbied against the bill and succeeded after spending millions of dollars.

Within the regulatory environment, all levels of government enact laws and regulations affecting business organizations. Primarily, regulations involve employment practices, tax revenue generation, or the legal structure within which the organization operates. However, as the government tends to move toward more concern with the physical environment and social issues, businesses will increasingly find themselves concerned with new laws and regulations in these areas.[19]

Although many governmental laws and regulations are restrictive, some have a direct, positive influence upon an organization. During the 1980s, greater emphasis was placed on the deregulation of businesses. Budget cuts in many agencies have reduced personnel, which has resulted in much government deregulation. Peter Drucker, in his book *Management in Turbulent Times,* says that ethical investors and public interest groups are moving strategic decision making from being just a private management matter to a more public interactive one. He asserts that in the international arena, multinational corporations must be aware of political risk and instability in foreign countries as well as political changes in the United States.[20]

Sociocultural Forces

Social and cultural forces are the last major external environmental areas affecting strategic management. Social forces are related to the values, attitudes, and demographic characteristics of an organization's employees and customers. Dynamic social forces can influence the demand for an organization's products or services, and such forces should modify the organization's strategic decision making.

Bryson states that social values are shifting in our society. For instance, he mentions how the baby-boom generation affected enrollment in universities.[21] Furthermore, women currently comprise about 52 percent of the workforce, and the trend for women to seek employment is forecasted to continue upward.[22] Moreover, today most people desire not only well-paying, but also personally stimulating jobs. Byars explains that most Americans want a higher quality of life. "To most American families, the balancing of work and leisure is important."[23] Assessing the changing values, attitudes, and demographic characteristics of an organization's customers is essential to establishing the firm's objectives and strategies.

Social responsibility covers a wide range of influences, from government regulation to pressure from organizations that, if not resolved, could lead to more regulations. Due to the threat of added, and sometimes contradictory, regulations, organizations must develop proactive strategies to deal with what others perceive to be the organization's social responsibility. In many instances, some external influences could be neutralized with proactive strategic management. The catalytic converter on cars is a good example of a social trend that affected the political structure, which in turn forced change upon a given industry. External sociocultural environments are reflected in changes in the social or cultural trends of a given population, e.g., lifestyles, consumer activism, career expectations, population growth rates or regional population shifts, age distribution changes, life expectancies, birth rates, etc. Social responsibility is an internal attitude or choice reflected in management attitudes toward the external environment, i.e., whether management has to conform to social norms via regulations, or whether management voluntarily selects to be socially responsible because it is inherently right and inherently good business.

Labor unions' work ethic underwent many changes in the 1960s and 1970s. Labor's stated objective was equal reward rather than equal opportunity. Although labor has become somewhat less combative and more cognizant of the business organization's needs, management and labor still need mutual trust to create the requisite team effort to effectively compete with those countries where labor-management relationships are less combative.

Motivating today's blue-collar workers calls for managers to be trustworthy. A good example of what will not work is upper management being compensated with large raises for a successful rollback of wages or fringe benefits. For example, in the United States, CEOs receive eighty-five times more than the average employee. In comparison, this rate is much lower in Japan (just seventeen times). In Germany, it is only twenty times.[24] This imbalance does not result in positive motivation for the majority of the organization.

Demographics are a significant social factor. For example, changes in preferences have a penetrating effect on some businesses, as does the average age of the population. The increased buying power of minorities has also had a profound effect on business. Such a change is a result of shifting social and legal forces. Due to these changes, pollsters have become a significant external influence.

Political, economic, sociocultural, and technological forces have a clear impact on strategic formulation (see Figure 3.3). Managers must cope with change in these external environments to effectively deal with threats and opportunities presented to the organization.

Other Significant Factors

There are still other, more specific, factors in the external environment that affect strategic management. Natural resource availability and international events are two such factors.

Natural resources include a range of naturally existing materials, minerals, or populations that an industrialized society requires to exist at a comfortable level. Although each society defines what "comfort level" is acceptable to them, the United States is faced with the real possibility of reducing its standard of living as emerging third world countries enter the global arena. With natural resources inherently finite in quantity and distribution, increasing global competition dictates that businesses and government strategists plan effectively for natural resource conservation. Since conservation is imperative, all societal levels must be concerned with the best possible utilization of natural resources under their control. In addition,

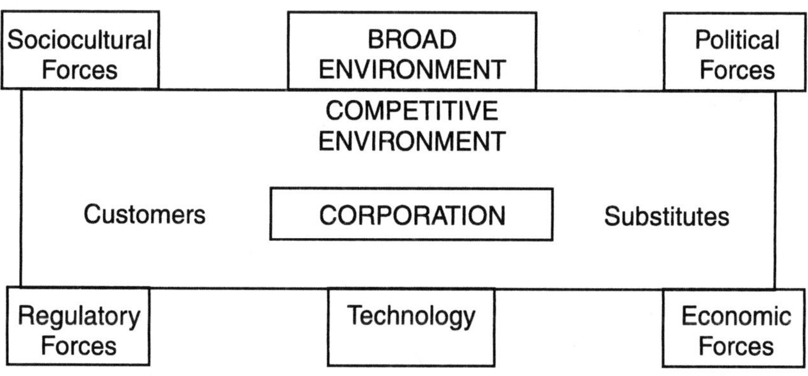

FIGURE 3.3. Forces That Affect a Corporation

conservation must consider both the immediate and the long-term consequences.

International events have profound impact on strategic management. Since World War II, the world has been changing at an accelerating rate. For example, the United States is now one of several large consumers and producers worldwide. The recent changes in the Middle East, Europe, and the Far East have created a whole new market environment. Just one hurdle to be overcome in attacking these new markets is the language and social customs barrier. Not many people predicted the economic difficulties in Japan and the Southeast Asian countries during 1998. Their impact on U.S. business was not well understood by many people, including Congress. Richard Armey, then Republican House Majority Leader from Texas argued against bailing out some of these countries.[25]

In the legal environment, because of product liabilities, no major aircraft manufacturer is producing private aircraft in the United States. Today twice as many aircraft are made in people's basements than in factories. Piper Aircraft moved its operations to Canada.[26]

The emergence of new global competition has resulted in a significant competitive threat for many U.S. companies. At the same time, developing nations offer enormous opportunities for U.S. companies to expand their global operations.

ENVIRONMENTAL SCANNING

Scanning the corporation's external environment prevents surprises and helps ensure a corporation's long-term health. Both the societal and task environments must be monitored to detect strategic factors that are likely to have strong impacts on corporate success or failure. Scanning the external environment supports strategic planning activities in many ways.

1. Data can be used to measure the marketplace by surveying changing tastes and needs, assessing buyers' intentions and perspectives, and evaluating the characteristics of the market.
2. Information is critical for keeping tabs on the competition and staying knowledgeable about developments in new products, changes in market share, individual company performance, and overall industry trends.
3. Information helps managers predict changes in the legal and political environments, including the effect of stipulations, tax laws, and import regulations.

4. Environmental scanning is required to stay knowledgeable about economic conditions in the United States and abroad, including interest rates, foreign exchange rates, and economic growth.
5. Intelligence data can give answers to two key business questions: "How is the business doing?" and "Where is it going?"
6. In decision making, information thwarts uncertainty and indecision. In strategic planning, it decreases skepticism about an unknown future.

Valuable as it is, information carries with it numerous problems and costs:

1. Information is limited by time, cost, and availability; no one can obtain all the information needed. The sheer mass of obtainable data makes research a disheartening task.
2. Much information discovered in analyzing the environment is not pertinent to the user's needs, and such information may be fragmented, disassociated, and rarely found in precisely the required form.
3. Few companies have the luxury of unlimited time frames for research; the range of a search is invariably limited by an established deadline.
4. Planners often do not know what information is lacking until it is actually needed, at which point it may be too late.

Costs involved in acquiring information can be either direct or indirect. Whether the company hires a consultant, purchases expensive publications, or merely uses its own time to track down the answers, each method has a direct cost. Information also has such indirect costs as delayed decisions, wrong decisions, and lost opportunities.

Estimated costs can often be misleading. People frequently believe that insignificant questions will be simple to research, when the exact opposite is usually true. "Big questions" are often easiest to answer because someone else has already taken the time to research them.

The most difficult aspect of business research is determining at what point the benefits of the information justify the cost. Benefits may be hard to assess, or may accrue long after the information is first obtained. Perfect information is obviously preferable to imperfect: yet in the real world, perfect information is rarely found. Imperfect information thus is preferable to no information. Researchers must assess the reliability and accuracy of what they uncover and decide whether to accept it or pursue additional facts.

The following are factors to consider when determining whether continued searching is no longer prudent.

1. Time constraints can determine when further research is unwarranted for the researcher.
2. When time is not a crucial factor, however, a good indicator is the importance of the consequences of the decisions. The potential size of the profit or loss to the organization is an excellent standard of the importance of the information.
3. Another consideration is whether the information addresses a recurring problem or can be applied to other situations in the future.
4. The knowledge, skills, and interest of the researcher also determine the route an investigation will take.

In the final analysis, all these factors help determine how much research will be done. Each researcher regularly weighs the costs and benefits of information, if only on an unconscious level. Information can be categorized as internal or external. Internal information is generated within the organization, while external information is gathered from the outside. External information is classified as either primary or secondary. Primary information is produced specifically for the problem at hand. Secondary information is a by-product of some other task that is then applied to the matter under consideration.

Forms and Sources of Information

The strategic purpose of obtaining information on internal strengths and weaknesses is to compare them with perceived external environmental threats and opportunities and to make decisions on the basis of these comparisons.

F. J. Aquilar has described four modes of scanning the external environment for information about threats and opportunities.[27]

1. Undirected viewing—general exposure to information with no purpose other than exploration
2. Conditioned viewing—directed exposure to, but not an active search for, specific kinds of information, which will be evaluated as they are encountered
3. Informal search—search for specific information carried out in a limited and relatively unstructured fashion
4. Formal search—active, deliberate, structured search for specific information undertaken with a purpose in mind

Most organizations use all four types of scanning, depending on the cost benefit of each. These four approaches form a continuum from general exposure to information to active and deliberate search for specific information. Every firm must remain alert to the general environment (external) and to its own operations (internal environment) in order to continue to gather available data.

Another source of information is the profit impact of market strategy (PIMS). A program was developed by General Electric to assist in evaluating the performance of its business units in a formal and systematic way during the 1960s. Other companies were invited to join by sharing their quantitative and qualitative information. Interested members provide information about market share, the quality of products and services, new products or services introduced, prices, and market expenses. Some of these data are provided as a percentage of sales along with two profitability measures, return on sales (ROS, net operating income before taxes divided by total sales) and return on investment (ROI, net operating income before taxes divided by total investment or total assets).

Information related to the internal strengths and weaknesses of the organization should be available in the organization's management information system (MIS). This information may be gathered through informal sources:

1. Cost analyses
2. Quality of products and services
3. Annual, quarterly, and monthly financial reports
4. Cost-benefit analyses
5. Capital budget statements
6. Marketing reports on sales and related information
7. Personnel report on major human resource concerns
8. Long-term investment
9. Environmental responsibility

Most information systems, however, contain only limited data on human resources and cultural matters. Organizations are only beginning to recognize the need for and application of this type of information. Although organizations usually collect data on absenteeism, tardiness, turnover, and so forth, they can seldom measure organizational climates, satisfaction, leadership style, etc., since these are basically nonquantifiable, yet they are important ingredients in productivity.

A formal search is desirable any time specific information is needed for strategy formulation. Information on environmental factors can be obtained through various sources, such as *The Wall Street Journal, Fortune, BusinessWeek,*

Harvard Business Review, and numerous other scholarly, popular, or trade journals and newspapers. Any number of government, industry, news media, research, and reporting services provide additional information. These various information sources vary in validity, reliability, accessibility, and timeliness.

A danger exists when a corporation monitors its own industry too closely in environmental scanning. Although information about competitors may be readily available, a company may get superfluous information about competitors at the expense of critical information about other important groups in the environment. Figure 3.4 shows the sources of data for industry analysis. External environmental information that should be actively sought includes the following areas:

The economy
Competition
Society
Technology
Government
The industry
Suppliers
Substitutes
Organized labor
Creditors
Pressure groups
International events
New entrants
Customers/clients
Natural resources
Other factors

Trade Journals/ Internet
EXTERNAL SOURCES
Government Reports

Marketing Reports
Personal Reports
Cost Analysis
INTERNAL SOURCES
Cost-Benefit Analysis
Financial Reports

Financial Publications (e.g., *Moody's*)
Financial Reports
Business Magazines (e.g., *The Wall Street Journal, BusinessWeek*)

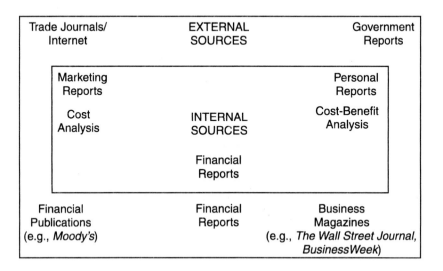

FIGURE 3.4. Forms and Sources of Information

Most corporations rely on outside organizations to provide them with environmental data. Firms such as A. C. Nielsen Co. provide subscribers with bimonthly data on brand items and percentages of stock-out stores. This data can be used to spot regional and national trends as well as government regulations, competitors, and new products that can be bought from "information brokers." Such firms as FIND/SVP, a New York company, get their data from periodicals, reference books, computer data banks, directors, and experts in the area.[28] In addition, advertising agencies and public relation firms often research for their clients.

Making Use of the Data: Analytical and Forecasting Techniques

Once a business corporation has collected data about its current environment, it must analyze present trends to learn if they will continue into the future. The strategic planning horizon for many large corporations is five to ten years in the future. A long-term planning horizon is especially necessary for large, capital-intensive corporations such as automobile or heavy-machinery manufacturers. These corporations require many years to move from an accepted proposal to a finished product. As a result, most corporations must make future plans on the basis of a forecast, a set of assumptions about what the future will look like. Assumptions about the future may be derived from the vision of an entrepreneur, from a head-in-the-sand hope that the future will be similar to the present, or from the opinions of experts.

The basis of successful strategic action is information. What types of information does scanning the corporation's internal environment provide? What should the corporation's goals be in regard to information? A forecast is nothing more than an educated guess. Environmental scanning provides reasonably hard data on the present situation, but intuition and luck are needed to predict the future. Nevertheless, many firms formulate and implement strategic plans with little or no realization that their success is based on a series of assumptions. Many long-range plans are simply based on projections of the current situation; this can be dangerous. Examples of assumptions for sectors of the broad environment follow.

To appropriately use all of the gathered environmental data, descriptive and forecasting techniques are used. Forecasting techniques involve inferences about future conditions. Descriptive techniques involve current data analysis. These techniques require a familiarity with analytical statistical processes such as correlation, regression, and probability. Forecasting through descriptive techniques has become more useful as factors not easily quantified gain in importance. Both forecasting and descriptive techniques are necessary as areas of uncertainty grow and the economic environment becomes more volatile.

Computers and specialized software can be of great benefit in assimilating all of the information gathered about the environment. To do a simulation of a company within a particular economy, many "what if" questions must be asked. Simulations became possible in the 1970s due to advances in hardware and software. Proper simulations for large organizations are very expensive and complex because of the many variables involved. For smaller companies, spreadsheet-type programs can be used on personal computers. While computers aid the strategist, they cannot make decisions. Therefore, computer simulation output must be constrained by the strategist's experience and intuition.

Corporations, when forecasting the future, are faced with pressures from the external environment. Creditors want to be paid on time. Unions exert pressure for comparable wages and employment security. Governments and interest groups demand social responsibility. Stockholders want dividends. All of these pressures must be considered in the selection of the best alternative. Strategy makers will often attempt to satisfy pressures from groups in their corporation's task environment in the following order:

1. Suppliers
2. Government
3. Society in general
4. Local community
5. Employees
6. Customers
7. Stockholders

In attempting to assess the importance to the corporation of these pressures, planners may ask the following questions:

1. Which groups are most critical for corporate success?
2. How much of what they want are they likely to get under this alternative?
3. What are they likely to do if they do not get what they want?

By ranking the key elements in a corporation's environment and asking these questions, strategy makers should be better able to choose strategic alternatives that minimize external pressures.

REVIEW QUESTIONS

1. What is a dynamic environment? How does it affect larger companies versus smaller companies? What is critical to an organization's survival in a dynamic environment?
2. Name and describe three internal variables that affect strategy formulation.
3. State and define the key internal variables that affect strategy formulation.
4. Why is information important to the strategic process?
5. Distinguish between managerial functions and roles.
6. Describe the importance of operational planning and control.
7. Describe what an organization's external environment is.
8. Name the four major forces of the macroenvironment.
9. How does each of these external forces affect an organization's strategies and management?
10. List the ways in which scanning the external environment supports strategic planning.
11. List the problems and costs associated with obtaining information.
12. Distinguish between internal and external information and between primary and secondary information.
13. Describe the four modes of external scanning for threats and opportunities.
14. List the major pressure groups that influence organizational strategies. What questions should be asked to assess the influence of each?

APPENDIX: THE USE OF FINANCIAL RATIO ANALYSES

Financial statements are a foundation upon which financial managers can base their estimates for the firm. With financial statements, management can utilize ratio analysis to help formulate a strategic plan. The four statements used most often are the statements of financial position, income, cash flows, and retained earnings. These are measures of a firm's performance, which can be used to predict the future.

Basically, there are six frequently used ratios on which financial managers can base an analysis. *Liquidity ratios* measure the firm's ability to meet its short-term obligations. *Leverage ratios* measure to what extent the firm has been financed by debt. *Activity ratios* measure how well a firm has been watching its resources. *Profitability ratios* reflect management's effectiveness as shown by the returns generated on sales and investment. *Growth ra-*

tios measure the ability of a firm to maintain its position in the industry and the economy. Finally, *valuation ratios* measure the extent to which a firm creates market value in excess of investment cost outlays.

Ratios alone do not reveal a firm's strengths and weaknesses. A financial manager must look at the situation as a whole in order to establish a coherent, viable strategic plan. Some of the most popular ratios in use today are the following: current ratio, quick ratio, accounts receivable turnover, days sales uncollected, inventory turnover, debt ratio, equity ratio, debt to equity ratio, sales growth rate, and asset turnover. Each of these ratios gives an organization a viewpoint concerning a different phase of the operation. For example, *inventory turnover* tells an organization how much inventory it has built up and whether the product is moving at a particular pace. *Equity* and *asset ratios* are used to determine how much capital an organization has, how much of that capital is tied up in other areas, and whether the organization can handle certain situations such as expansion or takeover. In the past decade, takeovers have been occurring again, especially in the banking industry. One way a company can manage to avoid takeover is to keep its assets and capital availability higher than what is locked up in inventory and research.

Management is always concerned with these ratios so that they can change operations as needed to enhance profitability. Banks and lending companies examine an organization's financial ratios when deciding whether to lend money to an organization. A bank will not lend money to a company if it is considered a high risk. An organization with poor financial ratios stands to be at a higher risk than one with favorable ratios.

An organization will usually set up a timetable of where it wants to be at certain points in time, and it usually uses financial ratios to determine its success in achieving these goals. If an organization wants to make a strategy that requires using a certain proportion of the company's assets, and the financial ratios indicate that such a strategy is not feasible with the company's current situation, then the company should devise another strategy to reach its objectives. Ratios can be used for decision making regarding expansion, strategy formulation, and bankruptcy. The ratios reveal information about inventory, production, management, and turnover. So, as one can see, financial ratios have an array of uses in the corporate world today.

Interpreting Financial Statements

Ratio analysis studies the relationships among different components of a single financial statement. Every financial statement analyst has a preferred system of ratio analysis, but most agree on the usefulness of several ratios.

The ratios are developed from a firm's balance sheet and the income statement. They are usually compared to other firms' ratios in the same industry. They are also compared to the firm's own historical ratios. The financial ratios must be analyzed on a competitive basis. Comparing one company to similar companies and industry standards over time is crucial. The comparisons help determine the firm's SWOT.

Understanding the Industry

It is important to compare the company and its competitors in the same industry (benchmarking). Sources of industry information include published articles and annual reports, such as *Standard and Poor's, Moody's, Robert Morris and Associates,* and other financial reports available on corporate Web sites. Hoover's online provides information about forty-nine industries with selected specific industry links to quick overviews of what is happening in the industry and companies within the industry <www.hoovers.com/industry/snapshot/index>. Also, the SEC provides information about companies' financial positions. In addition, the Annual Report Gallery is a Web site with links to more than 2,000 annual reports and numerous databases. Keep in mind that what is good for one industry may not necessarily be good for another. The company must evaluate its competitive advantages and how they could be used as an opportunity in the future. Benchmarking is always important. This process of comparing the company's products or process to those of industry leaders and the changes and developments required to build similar or better practices keeps the company's competitive advantages alive. Comparing one company to similar companies and industry standards over time is crucial. A company can benchmark with other companies in different industries.

It is important for any company to know whether its industry is sensitive to the economy and how it is measured in the different industry life cycle. While the airline industry suffered from 1991 to 1993 with losses close to $7 billion, a few companies actually did better than others. For example, Southwest Airlines made about $1.68 billion in revenues and about $105 million in profits during 1992. On the other hand, the auto industry did very well in the late 1980s. However, Ford Motor Company saw its operating margin decline from 20 percent to 9 percent, and its net margin decline from 6.5 percent to 1.4 percent. In addition, return on equity went from 25 percent to less than 4 percent.

It is important to understand how company market share changes over the years in comparison to the industry as a whole. The percentages might change and thus a change of strategy might be required.

In many cases, the prices of products and services provided in one industry are directly related to the prices of the products and services in another industry. For example, an increase in oil prices will lead to an increase in prices in the transportation industry.

Understanding the Income Statement

To understand the income statement, we need to look at the following items:

1. Revenue from sales and earnings growth over time.
2. Trends in margins or return on sales. We need to look at the following margins:
   a. Gross profit margin (sales – cost of goods sold = gross profit)
   b. Operating profit margin (gross profit – selling and administrative expenses = operating profit)
   c. Before-tax profit margin (operating profit – other expenses = before-tax profit)
   d. Net profit margin (before-tax profit – income taxes = net profit)
3. Growth in cost of goods sold (COGS). It is important to determine if the growth in COGS has exceeded the growth in sales. If so, the company will experience gross profit margin pressure.
4. Rate of change in selling & administrative expenses (S&A). If S&A expenses are accelerating, the operating margin will come under pressure.
5. Behavior in the tax rate over time. A company can experience pressure above the before-tax profit line with a declining tax rate.
6. Are the patterns in sales and earnings cyclical or has the company exhibited stable growth over time? This will impact the debt levels firms can assume. Companies with stable earnings are better able to service debt during economic downturns.

Understanding the Balance Sheet

To understand the balance sheet, we need to look for the following items:

1. The first measure that needs to be considered is the *working capital,* the amount by which total current assets exceed total current liabilities. Current liabilities are debts that must be paid within a year. Cur-

rent assets should cover liabilities by a comfortable margin. Lack of working capital can lead to a company's failure. Many companies have been forced to file for bankruptcy when they ran out of short-term liquidity.

2. Behavior of accounts receivable. An increase in receivables relative to sales may indicate that the company is using easier credit terms to stimulate current sales. This could lead to reduced future sales and increased bad debt expenses.
3. Recent behavior in inventory and type of inventory valuation (LIFO [last in first out] versus FIFO [first in first out]). In general, LIFO will understate inventories in times of significantly increasing prices. The company should make sure that inventories are not building to excessive levels, which may indicate a future problem with sales.
4. Financial leverage and ability of the company to add more debt. The analyst needs to look at total debt as a percentage of total capital (total debt plus stockholders' equity). If the balance sheet is healthy, a company can survive. The analyst also needs to consider the company's ability to service debt. Have financial leverage and debt been improving or deteriorating?
5. Return on total assets, total capital, and stockholders' equity (net worth). A firm needs to generate adequate returns or assets should be deployed elsewhere.

Ratio analysis gives an accurate, up-to-date picture of how the firm can best utilize its resources to accomplish and develop future objectives successfully. This information allows the firm to take full advantage of strategic opportunities. It must be noted that financial ratios by themselves do not mean much. At best, they are ballpark figures. To be meaningful, they must be compared with those of other similar companies or appropriate industry averages. Other parties interested in the information gathered through ratio analysis are bankers, creditors, and investors. Bankers and creditors are interested in forecasting the firm's future performance. Likewise, investors would be interested in sound investments based on these ratios.

Examples of Ratio Analysis

Strategic and management control techniques are identical measures of strategic and management performance. Among them are the strategic plan, budget, performance appraisals, policies and procedures, and statistical reports. Some of the ratios are discussed in this section. For further review of a complete list of these ratios, review managerial finance books.

$$\text{Current Ratio} = \frac{\text{Current Assets}}{\text{Current Liabilities}}$$

- Best when used as a comparison
- Low ratio indicates risky investment
- If it is too high, indicates too many assets on hand, which could be used to earn better returns
- Overall, it shows the ability of a business to pay its bills and repay outstanding loans
- Measures the company's short-term debt paying ability

$$\text{Quick Ratio} = \frac{\text{C.A. - Inventory \& Prepaid}}{\text{Current Liabilities}}$$

- Shows the short-term liquidity of the company
- Indicates the ability of the business to quickly meet unexpected demands from assets readily convertible to cash

$$\text{Accounts Receivable Ratio} = \frac{\text{Net Sales}}{\text{Average Receivables}}$$

- Measures the effectiveness of collecting receivables and the effectiveness of credit policies
- Shows the number of times AR are cycled during a year
- Measures the liquidity of receivables

$$\text{Days Sales Uncollected} = \frac{\text{Days in Year}}{\text{Receivable Turnover}}$$

- Shows whether the customers pay on credit or take advantage of cash discounts
- The average number of days elapsing from the time of sale to the time of payment; average time taken to collect receivables
- Also shows the average length of time the company must wait after making a sale before receiving cash

$$\text{Inventory Turnover} = \frac{\text{COGS}}{\text{Average Inventory}}$$

- Measures the relative size of inventory
- Measures the liquidity of the inventory
- Measures the number of times the merchandise inventory was replenished during the period or the number of dollars in the COGS for each dollar of inventory

$$\text{Number of Days Supply in Inventory} = \frac{365}{\text{Inventory Turnover}}$$

- Shows the number of days taken to sell inventory

$$\text{Debt Ratio} = \frac{\text{Total Liabilities}}{\text{Total Assets}}$$

- Calculate the percentage of assets used through borrowing

$$\text{Equity Ratio} = \frac{\text{Total Stockholders' Equity}}{\text{Total Assets}}$$

- Shows the percentage of assets financed by the stockholders

$$\text{Debt to Equity Ratio} = \frac{\text{Total Liabilities}}{\text{Total Stockholders' Equity}}$$

- Shows the debt in proportion to equity and the proportion of the company financed by creditors in comparison to that financed by stockholders

$$\text{Book Value of Purchase of Common Stock} = \frac{\text{Common Stock Equity}}{\text{Shares of Stock Outstanding}}$$

- Shows the value of the net assets behind each share of stock

Profitability

$$\text{Profit Margin on Sales} = \frac{\text{Net Income}}{\text{Net Sales}}$$

- Measures net income generated by each dollar of sales

$$\text{Return on Total Assets} = \frac{\text{Net Income}}{\text{Total Assets}}$$

- Measures net income generated by each dollar of assets
- Shows the overall profitability of assets used

$$\text{Return on Net Worth} = \frac{\text{Net Income}}{\text{Net Worth}}$$

$$\text{Return on Investment} = \frac{\text{Net Income}}{\text{Total Assets}}$$

$$\text{Asset Turnover} = \frac{\text{Net Sales}}{\text{Average Assets}}$$

- Measures how efficiently assets are used to generate sales

$$\text{Return on Common Stockholders' Equity} = \frac{\text{Net Income}}{\text{Average Common Stockholders' Equity}}$$

- Measures the profitability of owners' investment

$$\text{Earnings per Share} = \frac{\text{Net Income}}{\text{Weighted Average of Common Stock}}$$

- Measures net income earned on each share

NOTES

1. Kumar, V., Simon, A., and Kimberley, N. (2000). Strategic capabilities which lead to management consulting success in Australia. *Management Decision*, 38(1), 25.
2. Katz, D. and Kahn, R. L. (1978). *The Social Psychology of Organizations*, Second Edition. New York: Wiley and Sons, Chapter 2.
3. Bridges, J. F. (1972). *Management Decisions and Organizational Policy*. Boston: Allyn and Bacon, pp. 25-51.
4. Corcoran, E. (2001). Reinventing INTEL. *Management*, Ninth edition. Guilford, CT: McGraw-Hill/Dushkin, pp. 56-57.

5. Hickman, C. R. and Silva, M. A. (1985). Creating Excellence. *Ad Forum,* 6 (March), 81.

6. Kaplan, R. S. and Norton, D. P. (1992). The balanced scorecard: Measures that drive performance. *Harvard Business Review,* 70(1), 71-79.

7. The Conference Board (1970). *A Survey by the Conference Board.* New York: National Industrial Conference Board Inc., Surveys 9, 11, 15.

8. Ibid.

9. Walton, M. (1986). *The Deming Management Method.* New York: The Putnam Publishing Group, p. 90.

10. Gimein, M. (2002). You Bought They Sold. *Fortune,* September 2, pp. 64-68.

11. Bourgeois, L. J. (1996). *Strategic Management from Concept to Implementation.* Fort Worth, TX: Dryden Press, p. 56.

12. Strickland, T. (1996). *Strategic Management: Concepts and Cases.* Chicago: Robert D. Irwin, Inc., pp. 61-62.

13. Porter, M. E. (1979). How competitive forces shape strategy. *Harvard Business Review,* 57(2), 137-145.

14. Ibid.

15. Byars, L. L. (1991). *Strategic Management,* Third Edition. New York: HarperCollins, p. 42.

16. Taylor, B. and Hawkins, K. (1972). *A Handbook of Strategic Planning.* London: Longman Group Ltd., p. 138.

17. Ibid., p. 142.

18. Byars, *Strategic Management,* p. 43.

19. Ibid., p. 28.

20. Drucker, P. F. (1980). *Management in Turbulent Times.* New York: Harper & Row, p. 62.

21. Bryson, J. H. (1988). *Strategic Planning for Public and Non-Profit Organizations.* San Francisco: Jossey-Bass Ltd., p. 122.

22. Hagen, A., Emmanual, T., and Alkhafaji, A. (2002). Major challenges facing diverse workforce in American corporations and proposed solutions. *Business Research Yearbook,* Volume IX, p. 813.

23. Byars, *Strategic Management,* p. 44.

24. ABC, *NightLine* and CNN, *Crossfire* (1991). November 22.

25. *ABC News* (1998). Interview with Richard Armey, Republican House Majority Leader, July 1.

26. Mckenna, J. T. (1991). United 10 top US international airlines with winning bid for Pan American's Latin division. *Aviation Week and Space Technology,* 135(24, 25), 23.

27. Aquilar, F. J. (1967). *Scanning the Business Environment.* New York: Macmillan, p. 45.

28. Nag, A. (1981). Information brokers thrive by helping firms get facts. *Wall Street Journal* (July 7), A3.

Chapter 4

Corporate Strategy

INTRODUCTION

Today's firms are continually confronted with the need to develop and effectively implement strategies to achieve success in the world's competitive markets. Corporate strategy is the organization's field of endeavor and how it chooses the business in which to compete. It answers the question, "What business areas should we be in to maximize the long-run profit of the organization?" For many organizations, competing successfully often involves vertical integration. Vertical integration refers to the expansion of the company in its related businesses either to acquire the source of raw materials (backward integration) or to acquire the retailers to be closer to the consumer (forward integration). It could also involve diversification into new business areas. Strategic alliances are an alternative to vertical integration and diversification. More specifically, corporate strategy answers these questions:

- Does the organization have a specific interest or a definite strategic advantage in some business?
- Does the organization desire competition, or choose to find a niche?
- Does the organization wish to focus on one particular product line, or does it seek multiple products or product lines?
- Will the corporation be innovative or intimidating?
- Is it necessary for the organization to expand, stabilize, defend itself, turn around, or reduce its investments?

Corporate strategies are needed to manage diversified enterprises or conglomerates whose activities cut across several lines of business. These business activities, or holdings, make up the corporate portfolio. Corporate strategy focuses on two major areas: (1) molding and shaping what an organization does and does not do, and (2) selecting the emphasis to be placed upon each of the organization's chosen business activities and the role each business is to have in the makeup of the corporate portfolio.

There are four major types of corporate strategies (specialization, diversification, strategic alliance, and retrenchment). Each of these has specific applications and, if used incorrectly, will have a negative effect. Therefore, the application of these corporate strategies requires careful analysis to determine the best fit in relation to the corporate goals.

Developing an appropriate and effective corporate strategy requires practice. Once developed, strategies must be evaluated. Several matrices have proven successful in evaluating diversified portfolios, including these:

1. The four-cell BCG (Boston Consultant Group) Growth-Share Matrix, which plots industry growth rate and relative market share. This analysis relies on the learning curve effect and the experience curve, which result from learning effects, economies of scale, substitution, innovation, and value engineering.
2. The nine-cell GE Matrix, which plots long-term attractiveness against business strength/competitive position. Like the BCG model, the GE model yields only general prescriptions as opposed to specific strategies.

CORPORATE STRATEGIC ALTERNATIVES

Several corporate strategies exist to meet the needs of different types of businesses.

Specialization

A *specialization strategy* focuses on a single market or a single technology. In fact, most organizations begin with one or two products or services such as selling only ice cream or only hamburgers. A company marketing one product or service, or a set of related products or services, is usually considered a single-focus business. Some of the reasons for a focus or specialized strategy are:

1. the company attempts to uphold its size and current line of business;
2. the costs of modifying such a strategy far exceed the benefits;
3. the economies of scale are manageable;
4. quality is to improve by concentrating on one product or service;
5. the company operates in a low-growth market; and
6. there is limited capital to diversify.

A company can specialize in a particular market segment, geographical area, or channel of distribution. An example of specialization is Candella Laser Corporation, which focuses solely on producing tunable by-lasers for medical, scientific, and defense applications.

Internal Growth

Some companies prefer to expand internally through increased sales, production, location, and workforce. Internal growth allows for incremental decision making that can accommodate changing environmental conditions.[1] Management concentrates on increasing production capacity and not on acquiring or merging with another company. Such a strategy is used to preserve the company's image, culture, quality, and efficiency. For example, McDonald's chose to grow internally and not through acquiring new businesses. McDonald's, Pizza Hut, and many other fast-food restaurants prefer to expand internally by increasing production capacity, selecting good geographic locations, and making new franchise agreements.

Diversification

A *diversification strategy* is suitable for organizations seeking to add new products that have technological and/or marketing synergies with the existing product lines. Most large companies in the United States have typically diversified beyond a single focus. A company may diversify in several ways.

1. *Vertical integration* is one type of diversification that moves forward or backward on the vertical chain from raw material supplier to end consumer. *Backward vertical integration* occurs when an organization seeks ownership or increased control of its supply systems to secure the flow of raw materials. In recent years, this strategy was pursued to ensure the quality of the raw material for companies adopting total quality management. *Forward vertical integration* occurs when an organization seeks ownership of, or increased control over, competitors by securing more channels of distribution or more activities in the delivery of goods to the ultimate consumer. In recent years, companies have adopted this strategy to be closer to the customers to better assess their needs.

Some companies are wholly integrated (forward and backward), such as oil corporations who explore, produce, transport, refine, and market their own products. This usually happens with *related-product diversification*. Companies choose such a strategy to have more control over their needed raw materials and to be close to their customers in order to better assess customers' needs and wants and to eliminate the market cost involved. For example, GM heavily depends on material produced from within. IBM spent $3.5 billion trying to vertically integrate into personal computer software by acquiring Lotus Development Corporation. Disney's $20 billion acquisition of Capital Cities/ABC can be considered as a vertical integration move into the entertainment industry.

2. *Horizontal-growth integration* involves expanding the existing business within its current product-market structure, e.g., adding more outlets in additional geographic areas. A corporation can further increase its sales volume by penetrating both domestically and internationally. A company can also increase the range of products or services offered to current markets. The primary goal is to increase market share. The company will also benefit from synergy, a situation in which the combination of two or more business units or product lines results in greater efficiency than the total yielded by those businesses or products when they are operated separately.[2] A problem with this approach is rising administrative costs. An example of this is Philip Morris's acquisitions in the brewing industry. Coca-Cola tried to acquire Dr. Pepper Company; however, the Federal Trade Commission concluded that such a merger could have led to oligopoly power for Coca-Cola.

3. *Conglomerate or unrelated diversification* involves the addition of new products or businesses that have no relationship to the company's current technology, products, or markets. This type of diversification also tends to be less profitable in the long run than the other types. Critics think that unrelated diversification is inspired by top management's attempt to enhance their power base. Peter Lynch, the manager of the stellar Magellan Mutual Fund, calls diversification such because managers' energies are dissipated in too many directions. He prefers enterprises that are close to their core.[3] Examples of this type are Xerox Financial Services Activities, Sears Financial Network, and Coca-Cola Company's acquisition of Columbia Motion Pictures.

4. *Acquisition* occurs when one company buys another company. The process takes place by acquiring an inefficient and poorly managed business and attempting to improve its efficiency. A study on major U.S. companies conducted by Michael Porter for the period between 1956 and 1986 indicated that most of the companies had diverted many more diversified acquisitions than they had kept.[4]

5. *Geographical diversification* involves expanding the business to other regions of the country or going overseas. This is related to globalization.

Strategic Alliance

A *strategic alliance* is a long-term association between two or more companies in order to share the costs, risks, and benefits resulting from developing new business opportunities. Such arrangements include joint ventures, joint marketing agreements, franchises, license agreements, and joint research and development. These alliances create an arrangement whereby companies provide resources and skills to produce a new range of products for a new business and thus minimize risk. Many of these alliances are established to participate in R&D projects. It is an important operational response to international business. For example: Texas Instruments and Hitachi have an agreement to collaborate on a super computer chip development. TI's previous policies discouraged cooperation with all but U.S. firms. General Motors and Mitsubishi have formed a partnership, which proves that you can have an alliance with your competitor. Another good example is GE providing IBM with semiconductor chips.

Joint Venture

A *joint venture* strategy entails two or more businesses entering into an agreement or partnership to temporarily combine strengths to overcome obstacles in carrying out a project or cooperating in a selected business area that would prohibit a single entity from entering the market. Each company contributes assets, owns equity, and shares risk. Each company maintains its own identity as before the venture. The companies involved will share technology, market expertise, and risk. This is also called a consortium. A joint venture allows firms to spread development costs.

Retrenchment

A *retrenchment* strategy involves a firm falling back and regrouping by getting rid of any holdings that are inefficient and that negatively affect the organization's financial well-being. Cost cutting, eliminating weaknesses, and building on strengths are also appropriate. When survival is at stake, extreme measures are warranted. Reasons for retrenchment are the desire to focus on an organization's profitable ventures; limit the size, scope, and exposure to risk; or to survive. Retrenchment is usually a temporary effort. Three main strategies are used.

Divestiture involves a firm either selling a business unit or spinning it off into another company. This usually occurs when a unit is performing poorly or no longer fits the company profile. Other reasons for divestiture include having too small of a market share to be competitive, the need to increase investments, or a legal action that requires it.

A *liquidation* strategy is employed when a multiproduct organization suspends a unit's operations or when a single-business organization terminates its existence and sells off the assets. This usually happens after the company exhausts its efforts to find a buyer for its assets. Liquidation is the most extreme of the retrenchment strategies, and is usually the last alternative because of the large number of stakeholders affected.

Turnaround occurs when a company is transformed into a leaner and more efficient business. This can be accomplished by eliminating unprofitable outputs, reducing the number of employees, cutting the costs of distribution, and reworking market strategy. A good example of this strategy is Chrysler's comeback after its 1970s problems.

A *combination* strategy is needed when two or more types of businesses are used in combination, i.e., using more than one strategy at the same time in different segments of the business. Organizations must always be alert to the possibility of redefining their business strategies. Businesses and their environments change over time, and therefore strategic variables change as well. They also must continually reconsider the basic actions in which they engage to create value for customers in order to be competitive.

To be competitive, business portfolios need to be managed better and given the necessary autonomy. Studies indicate the probability that had SBUs been left independent, their individual profitability would have been greater. Therefore, strategies should include measures for autonomy. Managers need to bring skills and assets to acquisitions to increase the probability of reaching greater heights than they would have achieved had the SBU remained independent.[5]

With leaner corporate staffs, linking pay to strategy is extremely necessary. High levels of employee participation and profit sharing can generate great benefits. Pay is usually determined by both short-term and long-term performance. Whereas bonuses and merit pay work best in some situations, employee stock option plans and contingency raises prove valuable in others. Corporate strategy should specify the reward plans. Regardless of the organization or circumstance, it is important that objectives and associated timetables are stated clearly, as well as the rewards for such efforts.

ANALYSIS OF CORPORATE STRATEGIES

Specialization Strategies

A large number of organizations specialize in a single-product, single-market, or single-technology business. Companies such as McDonald's, Holiday Inn, Campbell Soup Company, and Anheuser-Busch have made their marks by concentrating on a single business at the right time.

Numerous strengths and advantages come with the concentration strategy. With a single focus, management can develop in-depth knowledge of the business, the market, the organization, the organization's competitors, and its customers. Several advantages to using a concentration strategy are as follows:

1. Focuses on doing one thing very well
2. More clearly identifies specific needs of specific customers
3. More readily anticipates changes and trends in customer needs and is ready to respond when they occur
4. Achieves proficiency in developing new approaches to customer needs, in meeting stiff competition, and in reacting to industry trends and developments
5. Creates a strategic advantage through market reputation and gains competitive strength by developing distinctive competence
6. Gains an experience curve much sooner

There are, however, major risks in choosing a specialization strategy. By specializing, an organization puts all its eggs in one basket. Changing customer needs, technological innovations, or new substitute products can undermine, or virtually destroy, a single business firm. Also, by concentrating in a specialized market, an organization may eventually lose the expertise to diversify. Invariably, all products, services, and technologies are someday faced with declining market share; therefore, a single business should guard against this prospect by always keeping open some options.

Diversification Strategies

As already mentioned, there are several types of diversification strategies. A discussion of vertical integration, related diversification (adding new products and services similar to those currently provided), and conglomerate diversification follows.

Vertical Integration Strategy

Two factors trigger the consideration of a vertical integration strategy:

1. Diminished profit potential from further expansion of the main product line into new geographic markets
2. Inability to realize economies of scale and performance potential from inadequate organization size

The first item, diminishing profits, results from market saturation and the impracticalities of oversized market coverage. The second factor has a variety of underlying causes, but there are warning signs that are easily spotted. For instance, if one, or a few, of the organization's products or distribution activities are disproportionate, it may be difficult for the organization to support the volume, product line, or the market standing required for economical operation and long-run competitive survival.

Vertical integration is a good strategy for dealing with these two factors. Backward integration, whereby an organization seeks ownership or control of its supply system, offers the potential for converting a cost center into a profit producer. This is especially attractive when suppliers have wide profit margins. Backward vertical integration also has the potential to reduce dependency upon suppliers and to permit the organization to coordinate and routinize its operating cycle. It helps insulate the manufacturer against runaway costs of supplies during heated inflationary periods. Backward vertical integration will help ensure the quality of the raw materials. This is especially important for companies adopting total quality management. In addition, backward integration may be the best and most practical way to obtain a workable degree of commitment from suppliers.

Forward integration, where the organization seeks control of its channels of distribution or financing operations, e.g., GMAC for General Motors, has much the same roots as backward integration. Undependable sales and distribution channels can result in costly inventory pileups or production shutdowns, and an undermining of the economies of a stable production operation. These three factors may force an organization to gain stronger market access through forward integration in order to remain competitive. Companies that adopt TQM utilize the forward integration strategies to be closer to customers so that they can better assess their needs and expectations.

There are disadvantages to vertical integration. The large capital requirements sometimes accompanying a vertical strategy may strain an organization's financial resources. Integration also introduces more complexity into the management process since integration requires new skills and the assumption of new risks. Integration requires learning a new business. In times of scarce raw-material supplies, it may be advantageous; or if quality is of concern, then integration becomes an organizational strength.

Whether an organization chooses forward or backward vertical integration depends on several factors:

1. Its compatibility with the organization's long-term strategic interests and performance objectives
2. Its ability to strengthen an organization's position in its primary business

3. The extent of its ability to permit fuller exploitation of an organization's technical talents
4. How regulatory bodies view such structuring

These issues must be addressed to ensure that vertical integration is the appropriate corporate strategy to adopt.

Conglomerate Diversification Strategy

There is one simple criterion for conglomerate diversification: "Will it meet our minimum standard for expected profitability?" Organizations choose to adopt this strategy when their distinctive competencies are too narrow or lacking depth. When an organization's distinctive competencies are too narrow, it may find little commonality with other businesses. If they lack depth, indications are that any type of diversification will inherently take the organization into something completely new. Some view conglomerate diversification as a way to escape a declining industry or alleviate overdependence on a single product-market area. This strategy is aimed at reducing risk. There are six alternative scenarios where conglomerate diversification strategies are appropriate, including the following:

1. Seeking a match between a cash-rich and a cash-poor firm
2. Diversifying into areas with a counterseasonal or countercyclical sales pattern to smooth out sales and profit fluctuations
3. Attempting to merge an opportunity-poor, skill-rich company with an opportunity-rich, skill-poor enterprise
4. Seeking out a strategic alliance of a highly leveraged, opportunity-rich firm and a debt-free firm to balance the capital structure of the former and increase its borrowing capacity
5. Gaining entry into new product markets via licensing agreements or the purchase of manufacturing or distribution rights
6. Acquiring any firm in any line of business so long as the projected profit opportunities equal or exceed minimum criteria

There are some important limitations on conglomerate diversification. First, while unrelated diversification can lead to improved sales, profits, and growth, an organization should be skeptical of "promising opportunities" in businesses where it has no skills or prior experience. So, when a firm contemplates diversifying into new, unrelated areas, it should ask, "If the new business got into trouble, would we know how to bail it out?" Second, despite the fact that performance may improve, the price a conglomerate pays to place itself in a growth industry may impair stockholder earnings. Third, unless there is some kind of effective strategic fit, a conglomerate enterprise will tend to perform no better than if its divisions were independent firms, and performance may even be worse to the extent that centralized management policies hamstring the operating divisions. Finally, if the diversification attempts to combine one cash-rich business with another business that has large cash requirements, the desired financial synergy may not be realized if the two businesses do not fit well together in expertise or other key areas. Thus, financial synergy, rather than product-market synergy, is the emphasis.[6]

Joint Venture Strategy

Entering into a consortium arrangement is a means of making a workable whole out of otherwise undersized levels of activity. Joint venturing carries the advantage of sharing, and therefore reducing, the risk of each of the participating firms. Joint ventures may involve two or more independent organizations forming a separate jointly owned business. In this case, each parent organization may contribute factors the other lacks, and when these factors are combined, they create a new enterprise much different than either parent. Joint ventures may also be created chiefly to surmount political and cultural obstacles. In these cases, the political realities of nationalism may require a nonnational company to form a joint venture with a national one to gain government approval to operate inside national boundaries.

Retrenchment Strategy

Retrenchment at the corporate level can assume either of two variations:

1. Stringent, across-the-board, internal economies aimed at wringing out organizational slack and improving efficiency
2. Selective pruning and revamping of the weakest-performing businesses in a corporate portfolio

Corporate retrenchment is a typical reaction to internal or external adversity. Ordinarily, it is a temporary or short-run strategy for coping with economic downturns. Retrenchment takes one of the following forms: divestment, liquidation, turnaround, or a combination of any of the three.

Divestiture Strategy

Market potentials change over time. An initially rewarding diversification may cease to perform to expectations, thus requiring a reevaluation of its suitability for the organization. Additionally, several diverse operating units may not complement the overall organization as planned. In these cases a particular line of business may become unsuitable, leaving divestiture of that business as the most attractive corporate strategy.

There are three options when considering divestiture:

1. *The outright sale*. This is best accomplished by identifying companies already in the business, or companies wishing to enter.

2. *The spin-off with declining equity*. A company usually considers the spin-off when faced with inadequate financial resources or inadequate net worth of the business. The spin-off creates a separate company and the parent company sells a share to the (potential) purchaser. With the spin-off, there is a gradual transition of ownership. A spin-off allows the purchaser added time and/or use of generated profits to fund the purchase as well as a gradual transition of ownership. Barron's defines a spin-off with declining equity as

> a form of divestiture that results in a subsidiary or division becoming an independent company. In a traditional spin-off, shares in the new entity are distributed to the parent corporation's shareholders of record on a prorated basis. Spin-offs can also be accomplished through a leveraged buyout by the subsidiary or division's management, or through an employee stock ownership plan (ESOP).[7]

3. *Sale to employees*. Employees have the greatest stake in the business, and many times the employees are capable of turning a low-profit business into a more profitable one. Health Care Agency (HCA) followed this strategy when it sold its underperforming hospitals to the employees by using their retirement fund.

Liquidation Strategy

Liquidation means terminating the organization's existence. Liquidation is the most unpleasant and painful corporate strategy, more so for a single-business enterprise than a multibusiness firm. In the multibusiness firm, liquidation of a failing business unit can be a positive move by leaving the remaining organization more viable. Another possibility is to seek relief from creditors by filing for Chapter 11 bankruptcy. This may give the corporation enough time to turn around its operations to reach profitability. Recently, many airlines and retail-store chains have adopted this strategy. Bankruptcy has the primary benefits of organizational survival and asset preservation.

Turnaround Strategy

Turnaround best occurs when a corporation's problems are pervasive, but not yet critical. Two phases of turnaround strategy are (1) contraction, which is a quick fix through an across-the-board cutback in size and costs; and (2) consolidation, the implementation of a program to stabilize the now-leaner corporation. Reducing overhead and justifying functional activities are the main goals.

The economic environment and competitive pressures force corporations into this strategy of looking at internal business processes and assessing the alignment of these processes to achieve new competitive advantages. One such corporation is John Deere, among the world's largest farm, industrial, and lawn-care equipment companies. The crisis of the early 1980s' disastrous downturn in the farm economy and the parallel downturn in construction forced John Deere to change its internal business processes to survive. The difference in John Deere's approach was not to take the quick-fix approach, but to look at long-term solutions. A new strategic vision was developed at the corporate level. The vision focus was on downsizing, cost cutting, and fundamental business-process changes. The corporate office allowed the decentralized product divisions the latitude to find their own ways to meet the corporate vision. The primary challenge was to do away with the step-by-step functional approach to new product development. Design teams across functional groups were put in place. These teams began to have a stake in the product development effort, with employees who were never asked before contributing to the design. Subteams grew out of the team concept. Much of the hierarchical organization was eliminated with the managers now playing the roles of strategic guides and facilitators. Strategy bridged the gap between traditional, technically driven product development and the more inclusive, integrated-team approach to developing products. The integration process not only broke down functional walls but also smoothed production startups and shortened the turnaround time needed to make changes in tooling or in part design. A sense of ownership by employees was born along with a feeling of participation in the flow of products from concept to customer. The integrated approach provided better technical performance and buy-in and commitment to continuous improvement of the product line.[8]

Combination Strategy

As the name implies, a combination strategy is any mixture of the individual strategies. Hence, an organization can create its own individualized strategy to match a particular situation. Usually, the firm's market position and competitive strength indicate that one particular corporate strategy is more logical than the others. Figure 4.1 depicts a firm's competitive position on a market growth/competitive position matrix.

A firm in quadrant I is clearly in an excellent strategic position. Related strategy has appeal, and vertical integration is desirable for undergirding the firm's market standing and protecting profit margins. Related diversification is a means of spreading business risks and capitalizing on the firm's distinctive competence.

Firms in quadrant II have ample opportunity to carve out a viable market niche using a concentration strategy, provided strategic and organizational shortcomings can be overcome and the needed resource base can be developed. Other alternatives in this quadrant are a horizontal merger with another company, which has the necessary cash and other resources to support additional development. If all else fails, divestiture for a multiproduct firm or liquidation for a single-product firm must be considered.

Organizations in quadrant III should consider retrenchment to free unproductive resources for possible redeployment. Another alternative in this quadrant is either concentric or conglomerate diversification, depending upon what opportunities exist elsewhere. Finally, divestiture or liquidation can be considered as a last resort.

Firms in quadrant IV should consider concentric diversification, based upon the distinctive competence that allowed the initial dominant position. Conglomerate diversification could be contemplated when concentric di-

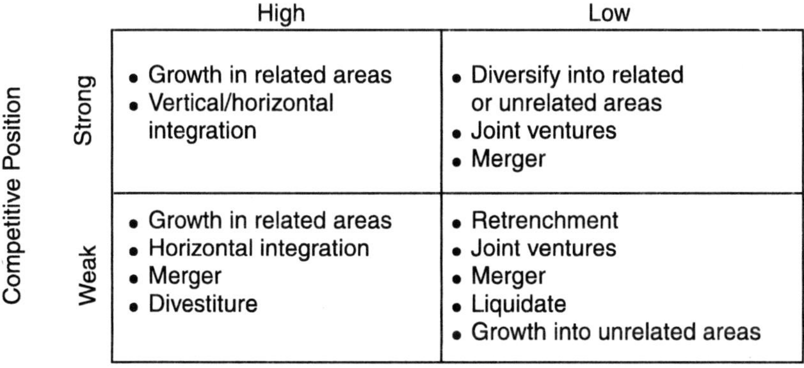

Market Growth Potential
High
Low
Competitive Position
Strong
Weak
• Growth in related areas
• Vertical/horizontal integration
• Diversify into related or unrelated areas
• Joint ventures
• Merger
• Growth in related areas
• Horizontal integration
• Merger
• Divestiture
• Retrenchment
• Joint ventures
• Merger
• Liquidate
• Growth into unrelated areas

FIGURE 4.1. Competitive Position on a Market Growth and Competitive Position Matrix

versification is not attractive. Joint ventures are a viable alternative when the firm wants to minimize new investments or risks.

STRATEGY IN MULTIPLE-SBU FIRMS

This section focuses on ways multiple-SBU organizations can achieve their business objectives. Strategy for multiple-SBU organizations is commonly referred to as corporate strategy or grand strategy. Such strategy concentrates on portfolio management techniques and policy guidelines. After the Industrial Revolution, the market witnessed the emergence of fierce competitors that resulted in many new products and technologies. This level of competition and increasing demand forced companies to evaluate how and where to invest. More scientific strategic approaches emerged in the late 1960s and 1970s. These strategies granted companies new methods to evaluate the market and their resources. The use of SBUs was established, initiated by the Boston Consulting Group (BCG) and enhanced later by General Electric Corporation. These methods described the strength of product businesses by the attractiveness of the market and the strength of the firm. Both approaches worked well for basic markets with limited competition and less diversified product technologies. During the 1980s and 1990s, information technology developed more rapidly, which invited many new competitors and created access to new markets. In such markets the static approach of SBU analysis proved to be insufficient as a sole guide to performance.

Corporate strategy is mainly concerned with the management of a portfolio of businesses, and with providing each SBU proper direction and corporate service. Corporate strategy is the primary concern of multiple-SBU headquarters where corporate strategists are responsible for ensuring that all SBUs of an organization function in harmony. Corporate headquarters also provide functional services and related policies for marketing, manufacturing, finance, personnel, and planning. Corporate strategists must answer the following questions in relation to the overall organization: "Where are we now?"; "Where do we want to be?"; and "How do we get there?"

A typical grand strategy for many corporations is to grow through diversification. In multiple-SBU firms, each SBU usually operates independently with little guidance from higher levels. The principal tasks of the corporate strategists in multiple-SBU firms are:

1. to establish strategic objectives,
2. to determine whether current businesses are helping to achieve those objectives and what the appropriate actions are in regard to those businesses,

3. to determine the remaining objectives left to be accomplished, and
4. to determine the appropriate actions to achieve the remaining objectives.

A *portfolio matrix* is one of the most important of several portfolio-management techniques used by multiple-SBU firms. Several of the more commonly used matrices are the (1) BCG Business Portfolio Matrix, (2) the GE Business Screen, and (3) the Product/Market/Industry Matrix. Strategists will utilize a specific matrix depending upon the circumstances encountered. The BCG matrix has been, for the most part, superseded by more advanced techniques. The GE-style matrix is primarily used when the products and market segments are diverse. The Product/Market/Industry Portfolio Evolution Matrix is used when the products and market segments are limited in type. The following is a description of the first two matrices mentioned above.

The BCG Matrix

The most publicized matrix is a four-square grid developed by the Boston Consulting Group (see Figure 4.2). It treats the development of corporate strategy as a problem that can be researched, mainly by examining economic, financial, and marketing data.[9] The BCG matrix evaluates two variables: (1) the growth rate of the industry on the vertical axis, and (2) the firm's relative competitive position in the industry, or its market share, on the horizontal axis.[10] The market-share leadership is directly related to profitability. Based upon these two criteria, a business is plotted on the matrix by drawing a circle in one of four possible quadrants, or cells. Hence, a specific function for each product or market segment is represented on the finished matrix allowing the strategists to integrate each unit's position into a total company strategy.

The matrix is divided into four cells, with each cell representing the desirability of the combination of competitive position and growth. The four cells are labeled stars, cash cows, question marks, and dogs. Strategists will plot their SBU in one of the four cells, and then pursue the appropriate strategic action.

1. The "stars" cell (upper left) represents businesses in a high-growth industry, with a high market share. Businesses in this quadrant offer excellent profit and growth opportunities. A good strategy for a firm in this position would be to continue its current course of action and make every effort to maintain the status quo even though this may require substantial investment. Stars usually require considerable cash to support expansion of production

		Relative Market Share (Strengths and Weaknesses)	
		H	L
Market	H	Stars	Question Marks
Growth	L	Cash Cows	Dogs

FIGURE 4.2. The Boston Consulting Group (BCG) Matrix

facilities and working capital needs. They also tend to generate a large internal cash flow. These businesses are the ones the corporation will depend upon to boost performance of the overall portfolio.

2. The "cash cows" cell (lower left) represents businesses in a low-growth industry, but that have a relatively good competitive position in that industry. These businesses are able to generate good cash flow with relatively little investment. A typical strategy for these businesses is to maintain them as cash cows for as long as possible, using the profits to finance other endeavors. Thus, a business in this cell will be "milked" of its cash to support other SBUs within the organization. A firm must guard against a cash cow turning into a dog. The suggested strategy for an organization with an SBU in this cell is to acquire cash cows, if possible.

3. The "dogs" cell (lower right) represents the least desirable position of low industry growth and low market share. These businesses produce low, if any, profits. Businesses in the dog quadrant should be harvested, divested, or liquidated, depending on which alternative gives the most positive cash flow. Occasionally, a turnaround strategy can be used to make these businesses profitable. They are in weak competitive positions and have low profit potential associated with slow growth or impending market decline. Dogs usually cannot generate cash flows on a long-term basis.

4. The "question mark" or "problem child" cell (upper right) represents businesses with high growth potential but low market share. Profit potential in this quadrant is questionable. A company can move to either star or dog status from this tenuous position; but creating a star may require considerable investment. However, the potential reward may be well worth the investment risk. Businesses in this cell must be carefully monitored. These businesses are usually "cash hogs" because they require high investment

levels to ensure rapid growth and product development. Their internal cash generation is low because their low market share gives less access to experience-curve effects and economies of scale, thus resulting in thinner margins than the market leader. The corporation has to decide whether it is worthwhile to invest in the question-mark business. The BCG matrix was designed to draw attention to various business units' cash flows and investment levels, and to aid in the allocation of overall financial resources. The goal of using the BCG matrix is to enhance the entire portfolio. Two disastrous sequences in the BCG scheme can occur: (a) a business in the star quadrant can decline into a question-mark position and then into a dog position, or (b) a cash cow business can lose market share and eventually become a dog (see Figure 4.1).[11]

The most stringent BCG standard calls for the dividing line between high and low relative market share to be placed at 1.0. Relative market share is the ratio of a business's market share to the market share held by the largest rival firm in the industry, with market share being measured in terms of unit volume, not dollars. Business units that fall to the left of this line are leaders in their industries, while those falling to the right trail the market share leader. A less stringent criterion is to fix the boundary so that businesses to the left enjoy positions as market leaders (but not necessarily the leader), while those to the right are considered in underdog market-share positions.

Relative market share is used rather than actual market share because the relative position is a better indicator of comparative market strength and competitive position. An actual market share of 10 percent can be very good if the market leader has only 12 percent, but the same 10 percent actual share can be bad if the market leader has 50 percent. The basic assumption of the BCG analysis is the learning-curve effect: total cost per unit will decline (perhaps by 20 to 30 percent) every time total production is doubled.

The BCG approach is seen to have several strengths, but it also poses a number of weaknesses. First, the strengths: The BCG approach allows the organization's various businesses to be viewed as a collection of cash flows, and it is a major step forward in understanding the financial aspects of corporate strategy. The matrix highlights the financial interactions in a corporate portfolio to show the kinds of considerations with which an organization must deal. This explains why the priorities for corporate-resource allocations can be different from business to business. The matrix also provides good rationalization for both investment and divestitures.[12]

The BCG also has a number of weaknesses. First, the matrix works better in a growing economy than in a declining economy. Second, a four-cell matrix hides the fact that many businesses are in average growth markets or average share positions. Third, although the categories can be useful, they can lead to oversimplification. Not all businesses with low relative market share

are truly dogs or question marks—some have proven track records for growth and profitability. Fourth, the matrix is not a reliable indicator of relative investment opportunities across business units. The matrix does not show whether a question-mark business is a potential winner or a potential loser.

Thompson and Strickland provided a matrix that looks very much like the BCG matrix.[13] The intention of the new matrix is to overcome some of the limitations of the BCG model. The *vertical axis* represents the company's competitive strength, and the *horizontal axis* represents the industry market growth potential. Substituting competitive position for market share provides more flexibility and better representation of companies with low market share but strong competitive position.

The GE Business Screen

The GE Business Screen is an advanced portfolio matrix developed by General Electric for its use in determining which SBUs or major products to keep in GE's portfolio and which to delete. The GE matrix can also be used to evaluate possible acquisitions, mergers, and/or new product development (see Figure 4.3).

The GE matrix eliminates the majority of the inherent weaknesses of the BCG matrix by employing composite measures of business strengths and industry attractiveness. With the GE matrix, a strategist may plot a business in any of nine positions, as opposed to the BCG's four positions. GE's matrix also includes a corresponding increase in the number of advisable strategies identified. The GE matrix consists of nine cells of different colors that indicate appropriate strategies for different businesses or products. The vertical axis represents industry attractiveness while the horizontal axis represents the strength of the business or product. Both axes have high, medium, and low locations.

Within the GE matrix, there are three grids labeled G, R, and Y. If a firm or product under analysis falls in an intersection within Grid G, or a "green" cell, then an invest-and-grow strategy should be used. An organization or product falling in an intersection within Grid R, or a "red" cell, should either (1) be harvested and ultimately divested or (2) employ a retrenchment and turnaround strategy, curtail or reduce investment in the business, and extract as much as possible before the business is divested. Grid Y portrays a firm that intersects in a "yellow" cell, where the firm or product has low business strengths but high industry attractiveness. Here, the organization should employ a selectivity/earnings strategy. If this demonstrates good earning potential for the business, it should receive an invest-and-grow strategy and be

Business strength (controllable dimensions):
The ability of the company to compete effectively in its industry or market includes knowledge about industry, customers, market share, financial performance, quality of its marketing personnel, and production capacity.

Market or industry attractiveness (uncontrollable dimension):
These include market growth rate, competitive industry factors, legal constraints, plus opportunities and threats from the SBU's external environment.

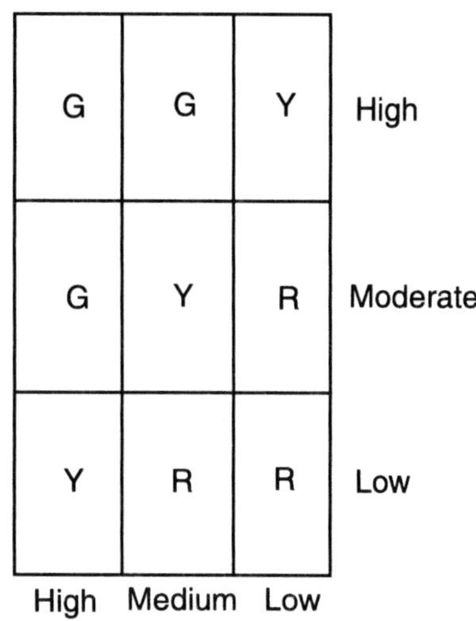

G = High Priority for Investment
Y = Moderate Priority for Investment
R = Low Priority for Investment

FIGURE 4.3. General Electric (GE) Matrix

monitored continually. If it does not prove worthwhile, it should be divested.

The GE model has several advantages over the BCG matrix. First, it allows for intermediate rankings between high and low. Second, it incorporates a variety of strategically relevant variables. Third, it emphasizes channeling corporate resources to those businesses that combine market attractiveness with business strength.

The GE model shares some weaknesses with the BCG model. It yields only general prescriptions as opposed to specific strategies. Although a strategy such as "hold and maintain" may be useful as a starting point, specific approaches to implement the strategy remain wide open. Further, the model fails to show when businesses are about to emerge as winners because the product is entering the takeoff stage. It is therefore recommended to utilize more than one model to overcome some of these problems. Using one model might help managers to solve a particular problem but overlook other possibilities.

EVALUATING CORPORATE STRATEGY: BEYOND THE BUSINESS PORTFOLIO MATRIX

Evaluate the Firm's Competitive Position

A competitive position analysis lets a firm measure its ability to take advantage of opportunities in industries in which it has a stake. All of a firm's business units should be in attractive industries, although an attractive industry does not automatically make the firm's business unit attractive. The business unit must also be a viable competitor in its industry.

Two considerations are involved in assessing the firm's competitive position and competitive strength. The first involves finding where the firm stands versus its rivals on market share, prices, breadth and quality of product line, profit margins, technology and cost differentials, facility locations, proprietary know-how, key accounts advantages, and overall image/reputation with buyers. The second consideration entails defining the key success factors for the industry and assessing how well the firm ranks on these key factors. Key success factors can be thought of as answers to the question, "How does one make money in this industry?"

Identify Opportunities and Threats in Each Business

A corporation should concentrate on how opportunities and threats in the industry affect the firm's portfolio. Explicitly assessing the firm's ability to cope with industry opportunities and threats helps to size up the risk associated with each business in the portfolio. This assessment helps both in determining the company's overall strength and in setting funding priorities for various businesses in the portfolio.

Opportunities and threats are present in every industry that might significantly strengthen or weaken the competitive position of each business in a corporation's portfolio. In making strategic decisions, risk-oriented managers lean toward opportunistic strategies with higher payoffs.[14]

Build Corporate-Level Competitive Advantage in Diversified Companies

Corporate-level general managers coordinate the strategies of the various business units in ways that produce a corporate-driven contribution to the competitive advantage of business units. Performing this task makes corporate managers more than portfolio managers, and makes the corporation more than a holding company. In fact, this is the chief way for corporate managers to add value to a diversified organization.

Building a competitive advantage at the corporate level results from managing the relationships in the firm's business units. In looking for relationships to build upon, one must carefully examine opportunities where sharing appears to be a benefit. Sometimes the degree of relatedness disappears when the opportunity is carefully scrutinized.

Once the relationships among business units are identified, it is necessary to identify important relationships among a firm's present business units and other industries not represented in the firm's portfolio. Shared relationships with businesses not currently in the portfolio can indicate interesting acquisition possibilities.

Assess the relationships found to build a corporate-based advantage. Although there are many actual and potential business unit relationships and linkages, only a few of these will have enough strategic importance to generate a competitive advantage. Develop a corporate action plan to coordinate the targeted business unit relationships. Coordination can be pursued in several different ways:

1. Implement sharing of the related activities in the cost chain.
2. Coordinate the strategies of the related business units.
3. Formulate a corporate-level game plan for attacking and/or defending against multipoint competitors.
4. Diversify into new businesses.
5. Divest units that do not have strategic fit.
6. Establish incentives to work together.

Compare Short-Run Profit Potential and Risk with Long-Term Profit Potential and Risk for Each Business Unit

When a company is protected from industry competition, it could decide to exploit its competitive advantage by engaging in a strategy to maximize profits. A company adopting this approach will attempt to pump up the present returns from its previous investments. Only a slight portion will be reinvested, with the remaining profits being returned to stockholders. The strategy works well as long as the competitive forces remain relatively constant; therefore, the company can retain its profit margins. The company, however, must remain alert for threats from the environment and must take care not to become complacent and unresponsive to changes in the competitive environment.[15] Long-term profit potential would, therefore, appear to be extremely high.

A company willing to reinvest in its business for the long term will find a higher potential for profits. It should be positioned to handle future peaks and valleys by investing in the company's future.

Examine the Overall Portfolio

When evaluating corporate strategy, the final phase involves determining (1) whether the performance of businesses in the portfolio will achieve corporate objectives, and (2) what kind of strategy changes should be devised if objectives seem nonachievable. Management has five alternatives to stimulate the businesses to achieve corporate objectives. First, management can alter various business-level strategies of some, or all, of its businesses. Second, the corporate portfolio can be altered by adding new business units or, third, by deleting current business units. Fourth, the corporation could use political action through lobbying and public relations to alter the conditions that may be responsible for the business's (substandard) performance levels, e.g., unfair foreign trade practices. Finally, management could reevaluate established performance objectives.

Although formal analysis is undertaken, most corporate strategy emerges incrementally from the unfolding of different internal and external events, and not necessarily from the application of one or two of the analytical tools.

The effectiveness of managing corporate strategy can be improved in several ways. One way is for the firm to remain proactive and to anticipate changes. Also, formal strategic analysis is more likely to contribute to the management of significant environmental changes. In addition, management should make final strategic commitments as late as possible, consistent with the information available. Last, portfolio analysis and corporate strategy formulation and evaluation must be an ongoing process with continuing reappraisals.

To be successful, strategic management must be applied through successful change programs that make a positive difference in corporate performance. Strategic management is the coming together of planning, decisions, actions, and strategic thinking.[16] A strategic-agenda management team and CEO must be dedicated to the strategic plan and be willing to implement it. This often takes exceptional leadership, even courage.

Choosing a corporate strategy is key to the early success of a company. This chapter discusses many options from which a company can choose when deciding what strategy is the best. Flexibility and alternatives have to be taken into consideration. The model approach is conceptually appropriate, but difficult to put into practice because of the numerous variables involved. Models offer the opportunity to improve strategy formulation by relating strategy to the factors that influence it, but because of their complexity, models are most often oversimplified.

As the strategic manager determines objectives and implements strategy, he or she also will have to review the seven dimensions of managerial action that the management consultants McKinsey & Company call the Seven S Model.

McKinsey & Company, a consulting firm, developed the Seven S Model to facilitate the implementation of its strategy. (McKinsey & Company is one of the largest and most successful strategy consultant companies.) The company discovered that many of its clients failed to effectively implement the strategies it had suggested. Newly suggested strategies cannot succeed within old organizational structures, shared values, systems, etc. These older elements of the organization were incompatible with the new strategies. Following are the seven S's that constitute the McKinsey model:

- Strategy: the direction or the course of action that leads to the allocation of organizational resources to achieve the predetermined goals and objectives.
- Structure: the method used to group people, tasks, and equipment in the organization. How the organization is divided into separate entities and how they are linked to work toward same goals.
- Systems: these include the formal processes and procedures of the organization. It also includes the planning, organizing, influencing, and control systems, and the performance measurement and reward system, as well as how people relate to these systems.
- Shared values: the guiding concepts that give purpose and meaning to the people in the organization.
- Skills: the competencies that include individual experiences and expertise, as well as management practices, technological abilities, and other capabilities that exist in the organization.
- Style: the type of leadership in the organization and the overall style of management of operations. It also refers to the norms people act upon and how they work and interact with one another.
- Staff: How to recruit, select, develop, and advance people in the organization.

The McKinsey framework emphasizes that although each of the seven areas is important, it is the congruence and fit among them that is crucial. The key to successful strategy implementation requires the development of an internal organization that is consistent with and supportive of the strategy. After designing the strategy, the structure must be in a position to facilitate the timely exchange of information among the various entities. Successful implementation also requires the organizational members to share information and work as a team. Policies and procedures must facilitate the implementation process. A compensation system must reward people who work together and share information effectively. Information sharing involves data gathering, use of technology, appropriate analysis, and distribution of skills. Staff members with the best information skills should be placed in key positions in which information is gathered and transferred. Finally, the leadership style of senior managers must be consistent with other aspects of the framework.[17]

In strategic implementation, these seven dimensions of managerial action are common to all levels of strategy.

REVIEW QUESTIONS

1. What key areas does corporate strategy focus on?
2. What are the reasons for a focus or specialized strategy?
3. What are the major risks in choosing a specialization strategy?
4. An organization chooses forward or backward vertical integration based on what factors?
5. What are the two phases of the turnaround strategy?
6. What are the strengths of the BCG approach?
7. What advantages does the GE matrix model have over the BCG matrix?
8. What are the disadvantages of vertical integration?
9. What are the principle tasks of corporate strategists in multiple SBU firms?

NOTES

1. Montgomery, C. (1997). *Corporate Strategy: Resources and the Scope of the Firm.* Chicago: Irwin, p. 94.

2. Wright, P., Pringle, C. D., and Kroll, M. J. (1992). *Strategic Management.* Needham Heights, MA: Allyn and Bacon, p. 90.

3. Cited in Kotler, P. (1983). *Principles of Marketing,* Second Edition. Englewood Cliffs, NJ: Prentice-Hall, Inc., pp. 651-653.

4. Cited in Kenyon, A. and Mathur, S. S. (1993). Strategies for corporate success. *Accountancy,* 111(1194), 44-45.

5. Downes, J. and Goodman, J. E. (1986). *Barron's Finance and Investment Handbook.* New York: Barron's, p. 19.

6. Moulton, W. N. and Thomas, H. (1993). Bankruptcy as a deliberate strategy: Theoretical considerations and empirical evidence. *Strategic Management Journal,* 14(2), 125-127.

7. Cited in Anderson, R. E. (1992). Strategic integration: How John Deere did it. *Journal of Business Strategy,* 13(4), 21-26.

8. Bourgeois, L. J. (1996). *Strategic Management from Concept to Implementation.* Fort Worth, TX: Dryden Press, p. 415.

9. Thompson, A. A. and Strickland, A. J. (1995). *Strategic Management: Concepts and Cases,* Eighth Edition. Chicago: Irwin, p. 189.

10. Bourgeois, *Strategic Management from Concept to Implementation,* p. 415.

11. Rowe, A. J., Mason, R. O., and Dickel, K. E. (1982). *Strategic Management and Business Policy: A Methodological Approach.* Reading, MA: Addison-Wesley Publishing Company, p. 150.

12. Thompson and Strickland, *Strategic Management: Concepts and Cases,* p. 193.

13. Ibid.

14. Saloner, G., Shepard, A., and Podolny, J. (2001). *Strategic Management.* New York: John Wiley and Sons, Inc., pp. 35-36.

15. Hill, C. W. L. and Jones, G. R. (1992). *Strategic Management.* Boston: Houghton Mifflin Company, pp. 147-158.

16. Waalewijn, P. and Segaar, P. (1993). Strategic management: The key to profitability in small companies. *Long Range Planning,* 26(2), 24-28.

17. Black, S. and Porter, L. (2000). *Management: Meeting New Challenges.* Upper Saddle River, NJ: Prentice-Hall, pp. 219-221.

Chapter 5

Business and Functional Strategies

INTRODUCTION

Business strategies are concerned with producing the desired performance in the competitive marketplace. Thus, business strategies focus on improving the position of products or services within a market segment. The question is how to effectively compete in the chosen industry or business. Three main approaches for choosing a business strategy are discussed in this chapter: (1) the contingency theory approach, (2) the generic theory approach, and (3) the use of descriptive characteristics.

Business strategies, like corporate strategies, should be applied only after careful analysis. Developing an appropriate and effective corporate or business strategy requires practice. Once developed, strategies must be evaluated.

Portfolio matrices are only the initial steps in the evaluation of a strategic situation. Additional steps require identification of the present corporate strategy, evaluation of the firm's competitive position, and an appraisal of the opportunities and threats in the industry.

Functional strategies are more short-term, specific, and action oriented than corporate and business-level strategies. The functional level of the organization is responsible for developing strategies for every major activity, including finance, production, marketing, and human resources. These strategies must be congruent with strategic objectives determined by corporate and business-level managers. Coordinated and mutually supportive strategies are crucial for the overall business strategy to have optimum success.

BUSINESS STRATEGY ALTERNATIVES

Organizations are divided into various units. Each of these units represents a subsystem that provide products or services and operates in an industry. Business strategy deals with the method used by a business unit to compete in that industry. If the organization is a single company that operates within only one industry, the business strategy and corporate strategy are the same. Selecting business strategic alternatives consists primarily of the following:

1. **D**etermining the critical success factors in the particular business.
2. **I**dentifying organizational strengths and weaknesses.
3. Searching for an effective **c**ompetitive advantage.
4. **A**ssessing the opportunities and threats in particular markets and for particular products.
5. Evaluating **r**ival organizations' competitive strategies.
6. Trying to **m**atch specific product market opportunities with the organization's strengths (e.g., internal skills, distinctive competencies, and financial resources).

These can be remembered by using the acronym DICARM.

Depending on the company's situation, the main concern will be to determine an appropriate corporate strategy and its corresponding business strategies. Each strategy should be closely examined for its efficiency before determining which one to use.

FORMULATING BUSINESS STRATEGY

Managerial approaches to strategy formulation can vary with the type of organization. In a multibusiness firm, the central tasks of corporate strategy evaluation usually involve (1) determining whether the company is on target in terms of its planning goals and objectives, (2) determining the attractiveness of the company's current lines, and (3) determining how the performance of its portfolio can be upgraded by better strategic management of its current businesses, diversification, or divestiture. No matter which type of strategy evaluation best fits the company, evaluation begins with monitoring, gathering, and analyzing detailed information about the company's present condition and situation. For a strategy to be successful, it must be in line with the company's environment.

The first obvious step in strategy analysis and evaluation is a determination of the current corporate strategy. To do this, both external and internal factors that affect the present situation must be considered. The *external factors* include:

1. the present diversity of the firm's activities that concern customer groups, needs, technologies, and major products;
2. the nature of any recent acquisitions or divestitures by the firm;

3. the priorities of each of the company's business activities and interests;
4. the opportunities available; and
5. the means by which the company minimizes the impact of external threats.

The *internal factors* include:

1. all of the company's objectives,
2. the method of allocating investment capital and expenses to proposed projects,
3. the company's attitude toward risk as reflected by its current policies, and
4. the focus of the company's research and development costs.

Tools and procedures are also available to help analysts with the formulation of business strategy. There are three main approaches to choosing among alternative business strategies: the contingency theory approach, the generic theory approach, and the use of descriptive characteristics. The profit impact of marketing strategies, or PIMS, study also provides information that may be useful to strategists.

The Contingency Theory Approach

The contingency theory approach to strategy formulation suggests that "for a given set of circumstances, a best strategy exists."[1] Research indicates that certain organizational and/or environmental variables or characteristics greatly influence strategies that would be most appropriate for a certain situation. These recognized variables could be isolated and evaluated to aid in the selection of the best strategic choice for the business. Since it is impossible to consider all possible variables and their resultant combinations, only the most relevant are analyzed. This approach is mainly concerned with the grand strategies, including basic action strategies, manufacturing, marketing, and many other functional strategies. The compromises among all these strategies are what drive the business organization. The contingency approach is most often used in profit-oriented businesses. In the future it may be used more often in nonprofit businesses.

The contingency approach indicates that there are alternative strategies for different situations. In many specific situations, appropriate strategies can be selected. However, one of the important elements in forming strategies is the position of the product in its life cycle. Knowing the stage of the product will assist in better selecting strategies from the contingent strategies available. Such a strategy should also take the impact on the business society into consideration.[2]

An example of this approach is if a company decides to undertake a project with higher future cash inflows than present costs. The next consideration for the company is to analyze the effect of such a decision on the environment, including whether a new plant should be built on land nearby because of cost advantages, even though it is a home to an endangered species, or on other land that will be more expensive but safe to the environment. Bad public relations and possible legislation may persuade the company to build the plant on land acceptable to society.[3]

As stated previously, "a best strategy exists," but finding it may not be as simple as it appears. The process is long and difficult. When the process is completed, the strategy may be good, but not necessarily the best alternative available to the business unit. Many environmental and organizational variables must be dealt with.

The Generic Theory Approach

The generic approach to strategy formulation is based on the fact that successful firms participate in similar, identifiable patterns of behavior. According to the generic theory, if a certain pattern of behavior was successful for one organization, it is likely to be successful for another. Although this approach has been criticized for not considering the complexities of each organization's specific situation, its results have proven to be satisfactory.

In our earlier example, the generic approach would lead the company to build the plant on the same land where the endangered species lived, because their competition had gotten away with a similar action the previous year. They would not see that the other company had different circumstances or reasons.

A number of generic approaches are based upon some particular variables or a combination of variables. Michael Porter's well-known theory indicates that cost leadership, differentiation, and focus (serving a particular target market very well) are the three generic theories.[4] A firm with a successful low-cost strategy has the ability to "design, produce, and market a comparable product more efficiently than its competitors."[5] Covin denotes four business strategy dimensions: commodity-to-specialty products, marketing intensity, cost leadership, and product line breadth.[6] Which of these four approaches should be used depends on the degree of environmental stability.

Although generic approaches are only theories and no single one has been chosen as best, strategists are wise to be aware of, and consider, the possibilities offered by the generic approach.

Sustainable Competitive Advantage

The key to employing a successful competitive strategy is to know which strategy works under what conditions. Each of the three generic competitive strategies has certain risks associated with it. Each requires different skills and resources and different organizational settings to be successfully implemented.

The acid test of a successful business strategy is to position the firm in the marketplace where it can be a winner in the ensuing competitive struggle. The important criterion for strategy selection is the magnitude and duration of any competitive advantage that the various strategic options offer. Cost leadership strategies offer the advantage of being in position to sell at a lower price and still earn acceptable profits. Such strategies are appealing when customers are price sensitive and switching cost is not high. The low-cost strategy is also advisable when the offerings of the various companies in the same industry are essentially standardized or differences are not clear. Such industries include newsprint, sheet steel, fertilizer, plastic pipe, lumber, and bulk commodities.

Focus strategies offer the advantage of being in a position to cater to the special needs of particular types of buyers. Going to a focus strategy has merit when

1. there are distinctly different groups of buyers who either have different needs or utilize the product in different ways;
2. rival firms have not attempted to specialize, preferring instead to try to appeal to all types of buyers; or
3. the firm's resources do not permit it to go after a wide segment of the total market.

Differentiation strategies have the advantage of offering better value to customers than rival firms. Efforts to differentiate products or services typically take one of four forms:

1. Strategies based on technical superiority
2. Strategies based on quality
3. Strategies based on giving customers more supporting services
4. Strategies based on the appeal of a lower price

Differentiation strategies are suited for situations where

1. there are many ways to differentiate the product or service, and these differences are perceived by some buyers to have value;
2. buyer needs and product uses are diverse; and
3. not many rival firms are following a differentiation strategy.

Often, the most attractive avenue for product differentiation is the one least traveled by rival firms. Also, experience indicates that it is hard to excel in more than one of the four approaches to differentiation simultaneously. To attempt to differentiate in too many ways at once tends to deteriorate into trying to be all things to all people, thus blurring the image the firm presents to its target markets. The best advice in formulating a differentiation strategy is to stress one key value and to develop a distinctive competence in delivering it.

Product differentiation creates competitive insulation (and elasticity) by delivering to all or part(s) of the market uniqueness of one or more product dimensions. Differentiation may include advantageous access to distribution (e.g., McDonald's network of prime sites) or be facilitated by distribution (e.g., selective distribution in upscale malls). The assessment of the interaction of these factors is critical to judgments of price elasticity relative to competition. Differentiation creates the opportunity to brand, and branding leverages advertising, merchandising, and promotional effectiveness.

Porter's Generic Strategies

There are many sources of a sustainable competitive advantage, and many ways to achieve one. Porter shows that low cost, differentiation, and focus are three generic strategies available to firms to achieve a sustainable competitive advantage.[7]

The overall cost leadership position can be achieved through a large market share or through other advantages such as favorable access to raw materials or state-of-the-art manufacturing equipment. The differentiation strategy can be implemented by creating a higher quality image through technology, innovation, features, a customer service dealer network, and so on.

The third strategy involves focusing the business upon either a relatively small buyer group or a restricted portion of the product line. Even with the focus strategy, however, the firm still must apply either a differentiation or a low-cost strategy. Thus focusing is not so much a different strategy, but restricting or focusing the business can sometimes be central to success, and it is worth explicitly identifying it as a distinct strategy.

Cost-leadership strategy. This strategy is also known as low-cost strategy. It is designed to outperform competitors by producing goods and services at a lower price than the competitors can. It is an advisable strategy when you are an industry leader or the product differences in the market are not clear to consumers. This strategy will produce larger profits than the competition makes and will put the business in a position to fight off price wars. As development costs go down, the sales volume goes up. For example, Southwest Airlines, which traditionally served a limited market, adopted this strategy. The company uses one type of airplane (Boeing 737) and provides no meals, no assigned seating, and reusable boarding passes. Other company examples are McDonald's, Burger King, Kmart, Lowe's, and Wal-Mart. Some of the high-tech companies adopted low cost strategies because of the continuous changes and breakthroughs in that industry. The prices of semiconductors, computers, and other communication devices (such as satellites) have been dramatically decreasing over the years.

Cost leaders offer to customers only products that are proven to be wanted and therefore the company seeks to gain market share. These businesses do not spend large amounts for development but do develop unique ways to produce the products or services that will result in reduced costs. Examples of such cost reductions are: large sales orders, which would allow for longer production runs and allow for volume buying of materials at discounts; a stable customer base, allowing for planning of production runs; and the use of tight budget controls in the production process. Businesses using this strategy make all efforts to contain their costs in production, marketing, and distinctiveness through a mind-set of cost minimization.[8]

The idea behind an overall cost leadership strategy is to be able to produce and deliver the product or service at a lower cost than the competitors. Cost leadership is usually attained through a combination of experience and efficiency. More specifically, cost leadership requires close attention to production methods, marginal overhead costs, and overall cost minimization in areas such as sales and research and development. A cost leadership strategy is attractive for a number of reasons, including the following:

1. Giving the firm above-average returns even in the face of strong competitive force
2. Defending the firm against rivalry from competitors because it is difficult for competitors to force the firm out on the basis of price
3. Guarding the firm against powerful suppliers by providing flexibility to deal with input cost increases
4. Defending the firm against powerful buyers because buyers can exert pressure only to drive prices down to the level of the next most efficient competitor

5. Providing substantial barriers to entry (such as expensive production equipment)
6. Putting the firm in a favorable position to defend against substitutes from the firm's competitors[9]

Achieving an overall low-cost position usually requires that the company develop some unique advantage or advantages over its competitors. Examples include a high market share, favorable access to raw materials, use of state-of-the-art equipment, or special design features that make the product easy to manufacture.

Differentiation strategy. This strategy attempts to make products or services seem unique in the customer's eyes. This perceived uniqueness will enable the business to charge premium prices when customers are deemed to be satisfied. Premium prices mean that the business should have above-average returns and outperform its competition. The less the product resembles others, the more it is protected from competition and the wider its market appeal is. An example of this strategy is to have the customer perceive that the luxury automobile Lexus is far superior to Honda automobiles. Other examples include the following:

- Superiority brand image (Izod or Polo in sportswear)
- Design image (Tiffany in glassware)
- Technology (Hewlett-Packard in small computers)
- Quality image (Mercedes, BMW, or Rolls-Royce in cars; Maytag quality and dependability; KitchenAid appliances; Coca-Cola and the positive image that firm is associated with; Xerox and its high-quality image)
- Customer service (IBM in office equipment and computers, Sears in home appliances)
- Dealer network (Caterpillar and John Deere)
- Any combination of these

In the differentiation strategy, the company will still attempt to control costs of production, although marketing costs may be significantly higher in order to develop brand loyalty. The main problem for this type of business is to maintain its perceived uniqueness in customers' eyes in an age when uniqueness is imitated and copied by competitors.

Following a differentiation strategy does not imply that the business should have little concern for costs, but rather that the major competitive advantage is sought through differentiation. Differentiation has several potential advantages:

1. It can provide protection against competition because of brand loyalty by customers and their resulting willingness to support higher prices for brand items.
2. It can increase margins because of the ability to charge a higher price.
3. Through higher margins, it can provide flexibility for dealing with supplier power (such as raising the cost of raw materials).
4. It can mitigate buyer power because there are no comparable alternatives.
5. It can provide entry barriers for competitors as a result of customer loyalty and the need for a competitor to overcome product or service uniqueness.
6. Because of customer loyalty, it can put the company in a favorable position to defend against substitutes from competitors.[10]

Depending on what is required to achieve differentiation, a company may or may not find it necessary to incur relatively high costs. For example, if high-quality materials or extensive research is necessary, the resulting product or service will create a willingness on the part of the customers to pay the premium price. While such a strategy can be very profitable, it may or may not preclude gaining a large share of the market. For example, Rolex demands a very high price for its watches and makes a profit, but it has a very small share of the market. In contrast, IBM generally demands some higher prices than its competitors and still maintains a large market share.

Focus strategy. A third generic competitive strategy is to focus on a particular market segment. A particular buyer group, a geographic market segment, or a certain part of the product line may define the segment sought. As opposed to low cost and differentiation strategies, which have an industry-wide appeal, a focus strategy is based on the premise that the firm is able to serve a well-defined but narrow market better than competitors who serve a broader market. The basic idea of a focus strategy is to achieve a least-cost position or differentiation, or both, within a narrow market. The company in this strategy focuses on small-volume custom products or services and leaves the large-volume standardized market to the cost leader. Small specialty companies exploit a gap in the market and develop a product the customers want. These companies may eventually become large companies using the cost leadership strategy.

Gucci has followed a focus strategy by targeting that segment of the ladies' handbag industry that is attracted by exclusivity. In the automobile industry, Lamborghini has focused on the sports car market.

After a company has decided on its market segment, it can use either a differentiation or a low-cost marketing approach. The differentiation approach means that the organization competes on the key differentiation in its industry, but in just one or a few aspects. The focused organization can only compete on a limited number of aspects because competing on numerous aspects would bring it into direct competition with stronger key differentiators.

In the low-cost approach, the focused company competes with the cost leader of the industry in one of two ways. First, the focuser may be able to sell locally produced products to its small segment at a lower cost than the industry's cost leader. The focused company could also compete by offering custom-made products that the cost leader is unable to supply.

Stuck in the Middle

The three generic strategies each provide defenses against forces in the economic environment. The firms that develop one of these strategies will earn higher than average returns in their industries. The implication is that firms that do not develop one of the basic strategies will earn lower than average returns in their industries. Porter calls this being "stuck in the middle." Such a firm lacks the market share, capital investment, and resolve to use the low-cost strategy or the industry-wide differentiation necessary for low-cost position in a more limited sphere.

If some of the firms in an industry follow one of the three basic strategies and earn higher than average returns, then some firms in the industry must be earning lower than average returns (not all firms can perform above average). The in-between firms lose all the high-margin business. They cannot compete well for high-volume business from customers who demand low prices, for the high-margin business of the differentiated firms, nor for the low-cost or focus-differentiated businesses.

The high returns are earned by the industry-wide firms with large market shares (the low cost and differentiated firms) and the firms that are focused with small market shares. Those firms in between, in terms of market share, earn lower than average returns. The result is a U-shaped curve. John Deere is the industry leader and earns high returns. However, small specialty manufacturers such as Hesston and New Holland also earn high returns. Massey Ferguson and J.I Case are trapped in the valley, and International Harvester has a substantial market share, but earns low returns.[11]

Points of Concern

At the conceptual level, Porter's theory of generic strategy can be condensed into two propositions: (1) there are only three generic and comprehensive strategies, and (2) success depends upon using only one of the three generic strategies.[12] Although generic strategy is valuable to many organizations and has provided a real contribution to business literature, several questions arise. First, the generics are viewed as separate and completely distinct from one another (each strategy is mutually exclusive). Second, the framework fails to show techniques that could be employed to shift from one strategy to another.[13] Third, although Porter's generic strategies are based on earlier work, they lack theoretical or empirical substantiation.[14] Fourth, Porter, along with others, believes that competing simultaneously with low cost and differentiation is inconsistent. This means that when a business emphasizes differentiation, it cannot maintain low cost at the same time. Also, a business that keeps costs low cannot produce significantly differentiated outputs.

The fact is that many empirical and theoretical studies demonstrate that a dual emphasis on low costs and differentiation can result in high performance. A low-cost/differentiation strategy can be effective if the company provides an environment in which the strategy begins with an organizational commitment to quality process, products, and services. When a company provides high-quality output, it immediately differentiates itself from its competitors. Inevitably, customers are drawn to high-quality products and services. This will result in a higher demand for the company's output. It follows an increase in market share leading to economies of scale, thereby permitting lower per-unit cost in the company's overall cost structure. The successes of Anheuser-Busch, General Electric, Coca-Cola, and Pepsi-Cola support this scenario. All of these companies have differentiated their outputs through offering high-quality products while simultaneously maintaining low per-unit cost operations.

Use of Descriptive Characteristics

A major approach to the formulation of business strategy is to use descriptive characteristics. Peters and Waterman, authors of *In Search of Excellence,* have studied successful firms and have identified eight descriptive characteristics of those organizations:

1. A bias for action
2. Closeness to the customer
3. A feeling of autonomy and entrepreneurship
4. Productivity through people
5. A hands-on, values-driven approach (especially the value of customer service)
6. "Sticking to the knitting," or concentration on what the firm does best

7. A simple structure form with a lean staff
8. A system of simultaneously loose and tight controls[15]

The descriptive characteristics approach to strategy formulation suggests that emulation of the characteristics of successful firms is an effective strategy. However, criticism of Peters and Waterman's research design suggests that this approach should be used with caution.

COMPETITIVE STRATEGIES AND THE HEALTH CARE INDUSTRY

In recent years, the competitive strategy of low cost has received much attention in the health care industry. Cost control strategy is used to protect from competitive forces in this industry and to cope with regulatory changes. Organizations pursuing a low-cost strategy are expected to stress internal efficiency and protection of their domain. Low-cost strategy is appropriate in a stable and predictable environment.

Hospitals have also used many different approaches, such as differentiating by types of technology, quality of medical support staff, patient support services, and quality of services offered. In general, hospitals pursuing this strategy have tried to offer patients a differentiated service that provides value by satisfying their unique needs. Differentiation strategy is associated with dynamic and uncertain environments. Differentiators also emphasize growth, value innovation, and learning, and will be interested in external expansion to achieve profitability.

Successful execution of strategy requires the appropriate interaction between external factors and internal capabilities. An organization's relationship with its external environment can be measured in terms of six sectors of the environment: *customers, competitors, suppliers, financial/capital, government/regulatory,* and *labor unions.* A study by Kumar Kamalish of 100 hospitals indicates that about 36 percent of the hospitals in the study put primary emphasis on cost leadership. The hospitals placed average emphasis on the differentiation strategy.[16] About 28 percent of the hospitals in the sample showed below-average emphasis on cost-leadership strategy. However, their primary emphasis utilized differentiation as the competitive strategy.

Finally, about 36 percent of the hospitals are characterized by an above-average emphasis on differentiation. Also, the hospitals in this group strongly emphasize cost leadership. Hospitals in this group, therefore, appear to be pursuing a combination of cost leadership and differentiation strategies. Using Porter's terminology, these hospitals are labeled as stuck in the middle.

The study also showed that hospitals in the differentiator group perceived their competitors and governmental/regulatory sectors as being more uncertain than other strategy groups, while hospitals in the cost leadership group perceived the supplier sector as being more uncertain. Hospitals in the stuck-in-the-middle group generally perceived all the environmental sectors, except the labor union sector, as uncertain.

In terms of management philosophy and values, the cost leadership group placed greater emphasis than the other two groups on "formulating effective personnel policies," "minimizing turnover," and "effective grievance resolution," all of which are designed to achieve and promote internal efficiency in operations.

The differentiator group, on the other hand, placed the highest emphasis of all the three groups on "rewarding creativity," "improving employees' attitudes," and providing "employee education," processes that are critical for creating and sustaining advantage over the competitors. Hospitals in the stuck-in-the-middle group, however, placed almost equal emphasis on all of the values, thus indicating absence of a firm belief or clear philosophy.[17]

FUNCTIONAL STRATEGIC ALTERNATIVES

Strategy at the functional level supports the business strategy with more detailed plans. Some functional strategies are discussed here.

Financial Functions

The finance department performs many important functions in a multinational corporation. The activities of the department impact both present and future operations. The finance department is responsible for managing the cash flow of the company as well as securing funds for investment opportunities. The department is also responsible for providing international administrative services to the parent company and arranges many aspects of the risk associated with the company's operations. Finally, the finance department is responsible for evaluating the financial aspects of future investments.

Cash flow management for the firm includes managing the liquidity of the firm and minimizing financial costs. The finance department must also strive to minimize taxes. Multinational firms must deal with the differing monetary, political, and financial aspects of these assignments since they operate in many countries.[18]

The flexibility of a firm to adjust to a changing environment often depends upon its ability to obtain monetary supplies. Multinational firms have increased monetary demands resulting from currency and interest rate fluctuations. However, one of the advantages of being a multinational firm is that various financial markets will be available in which to raise funds. The finance department must coordinate the monetary flows in and out of these markets so that stakeholders such as stockholders and creditors see their required rates of return.

It is the responsibility of the finance department to secure funding for the current and future operations of the company. This requires the department to keep in touch with global interest rates, currency fluctuations, and financial policy decisions. Securing funding also requires the finance department to develop and maintain good relationships with financial institutions and other funding sources.

Because of the stiff global competition that multinational companies face, they often find themselves seeking alternative financial instruments to meet their funding needs. Alternative financing can be used to raise funds for company expansion or operations. Some innovative instruments that have been derived from traditional sources include bond interest and principal payments that have been separated, securities linked to foreign currencies, and variable-rate securities. There are also junk bonds and zero-coupon bonds.

A few other important functions of the finance department are managing growth and risk, evaluating investments, and understanding the importance of the cost of capital. Growth is expensive because it consumes capital and, therefore, must be managed carefully. Collection of all relevant information to evaluate investment opportunities is imperative to avoid bad decisions. Capital budgeting is required of all finance students; this is because money is not free. Finally, risk must be ascertained. All risk needs to be accounted for so the company is never in an unexpected position.

Production Functions

The process of turning raw materials into marketable products is called production. One of the first decisions on the functional level of production management in today's global economy is where to produce the products. The decision to produce overseas can cause both external and internal pressures on the firm. Internal pressures may come from cost-cutting measures. External pressures can come from foreign countries that want access to the technology. The multinational corporation (MNC) cannot produce its product in every country that it serves. Problems arise once it has decided on manufacturing in a certain country. The governments of the host countries want factories to be built in their countries. Factories are visible signs of growth. Some other visible signs are jobs, income, consumption, savings, houses, and tax revenue. More and more pressure is put on the MNC to have more local sourcing.

Since World War II, there has been a decline in the importance of production departments in the United States, so that MNCs are now led by the marketing departments. Now some are turning back to production to improve quality, speed up product development, and invest in equipment. It can be argued that one of the reasons that the United States is no longer the world leader in manufacturing is that the production departments have been ignored for too long. These departments have had very little appeal to most managers. Most of the emphasis has been on R&D and technical services. It can be said that in most corporations the production department manager is not one of the most prestigious positions.

Numerous things can be done to improve the production department. Many have adopted TQM to help them compete. The main idea of TQM is continuous improvement. Along with TQM, a company should also practice benchmarking as a tool for continuous improvement. Benchmarking is a means of searching the world for the best practices and then implementing these practices in a continuous improvement program. Ultimately, functional management must be made responsible for planning and executing the installation of benchmarking practices.

Benchmarking does not need to be contained to the same industry. A world-class leader in one field can help another firm in a different industry. In the field of operations management, Disney is considered the best, while in the field of shipping and warehousing, L.L. Bean is the best.[19]

State and local governments are also becoming involved in quality issues. State programs and the National Chamber of Commerce are teaming up to help businesses compete for the Malcolm Baldrige Award.

The production department has been given the task of improvement, and several innovative strategies have emerged recently to evaluate production in the corporate structure. There have also been attempts to get improvements out of production other than cost cutting, such as General Electric's rule of 40-40-20, whereby only 20 percent of the gains come from cost cuts, efficiency, and workforce enhancements. The first 40 percent of the gains come from technology improvements, and the other 40 percent come from better management strategy, such as global sourcing.

Human Resource Functions

Human resource management strategies, as with the other functional areas, occur at the corporate, business, and functional levels. Human resource activities are primarily executed at the functional level because that is where the workers are.

At the functional level, human resource management includes translating corporate and business unit strategies into specific functional activities. These include setting functional goals, analyzing strengths and weaknesses, determining distinctive competencies and competitive advantages, and developing, evaluating, and communicating functional plans within the organization. Major activities of human resources include planning for future human resource needs, recruiting personnel, placing people in new jobs, compensating them, evaluating their performance, training them, developing them into more efficient employees, and enhancing their work environment.

The most effective strategy for any organization, and particularly large organizations and their business units, is to develop commitment among employees to the organization and to the job. Many organizations consider human resources to be their most important asset and competitive strategic advantage.

In today's global marketplace, to attract and retain competent employees, human resource managers must consider a variety of progressive working conditions and benefits, including customized fringe benefits, child day care, and flexible work hours (including four-day weeks). Also, high performance requires appropriate reward systems to encourage and promote teamwork.

In the past, during growth periods, companies were often able to retain employees through temporary downturns, a paternalistic strategy which created a loyal workforce that worked hard with little turnover. Today's strategies of downsizing, restructuring, outsourcing, and so on have resulted in a reduction of corporate loyalty.

Human resource systems provide support to top management for implementing the organizational strategy by providing the people, skills, and systems to facilitate and reinforce the behavior required. Matching the organization's human assets with its strategy can require changing the individuals assigned to a job or changing the behavior of the individuals in their positions. It is the task of human resource management to provide the means to do either. This is done through systems for planning, staffing, appraisal, compensation, and rewards.

Human resource planning integrates functional plans and activities into strategic plans in a manner consistent with the organization's business plans. Human resource planning includes resource planning and forecasting, career management, work scheduling, and job design.

The contributions of human resource management to strategic planning include knowledge of the corporate culture in assessing the feasibility of the strategy. Knowledge of the organization's available skills as well as skills obtainable in outside labor markets facilitates assessing the costs of the alternatives. Human resource planning greatly enhances environmental scanning by providing external information on education trends, labor markets, laws, and regulations, as well as internal information on productivity, absenteeism, turnover, and other people's problems. Assessing future needs involves both quantitative forecasting (how many managers and other personnel will be required) and qualitative forecasting (what skills these people will need).

Staffing consists of recruiting, selection, and placement of persons with the appropriate competencies. Staffing involves matching the position with the best functional background depending on the strategic direction desired, and identifying individuals that fit the job requirements. Among the factors to be considered are the overall framework of the organization's global philosophy, including ethnocentrism (assignment of key positions to home country executives found in highly centralized firms), polycentrism (assignment of key positions to host country nationals, who bring knowledge of the local market, people, and government policies), regiocentrism (assignment of key positions to a specific region used when products are similar all over the world), and geocentrism (assignment of key positions to qualified people of any background and culture; staffing, manufacturing, and marketing is done on a global basis).[20]

Because the optimum source of talent for the future of any organization is found in its present employees, the staffing aspect of human resource management includes training and development to develop new skills and behaviors that will be needed in the future for strategic implementation. Such activities range from managerial training in cultural values to teaching employees new skills based on new technologies, and include cultivating cultural sensitivity for international assignments. In addition to training, employee development must include individual career path planning aimed at aligning employee aspirations and capabilities with the organization's goals.

Appraisal and reward systems tell the organization's members what is important, therefore providing reinforcement for the proper behavior. It is essential that the relevant behavior is well defined and accurately measured, and the criteria used to appraise performance must reflect strategic goals and plans. Executive compensation must be in sync with strategic direction. Accordingly, a compensation plan should define proper performance behavior, measure results, and tie compensation to performance. The focus of compensation plans should be on organizational strategy; accordingly, multi-year evaluations encourage a long-term perspective.

Compensation arrangements are becoming more complex and include not only pay, but other benefits as well (health care, child daycare, and flexible hours, for example). These benefits can often attract and retain qualified individuals to fill key positions. The appraisal and reward system also involves performance management and control aspects, including: employee outplacement assistance, personnel policy, and program evaluation.

Human resource management also includes handling labor relations, collective bargaining processes, and labor-management cooperation.

Marketing Functions

The marketing segment of the business is the link that brings all the other aspects into a full circle. Marketing generates the revenues that the financial people manage and the production people use in creating products or services. The challenge that faces marketing is to generate those revenues by satisfying customers' wants at a profit and in a socially responsible manner. Whether the consumers are in the domestic market or the international market, the marketing function is basically the same. However, there are many adaptations of key concepts and/or techniques when a business is globalized.

Marketing refers to the collection of activities undertaken by the firm to relate profitably to its market. The firm's ultimate success depends primarily on how well it performs in the marketplace.[21] Marketing is the means to achieve corporate goals and objectives through the process of planning and executing the conception, pricing, promotion, and distribution of ideas, goods, and services. Two concepts are important to note in this definition. The first is how planning and execution relate to ideas and services and are not limited only to products. This emphasizes that marketing is more than just selling goods. The second is that the modern marketing function is indeed a strategic matter in that it contributes to the overall strategic mission of the organization. This is an enormous task in that the internal and external goals of the business must be woven into a strategic marketing plan so that every aspect of the business succeeds.

Public Relations Functions

A common definition of *public relations (PR)* is *the management function that identifies, establishes, and maintains mutually beneficial relationships between an organization and the various publics on whom it depends for success.*

Public relations is utilized by a wide variety of institutions such as businesses, government agencies, medical facilities, educational organizations, trade associations, foundations, religious bodies, and activist groups. To achieve their objectives, these organizations must effectively relate to a variety of audiences such as employees, customers, shareholders, volunteers, community members, and others while also serving some useful social purpose.

If these important people (your publics or stakeholders) do not know about you, they cannot feel good about doing business with you. Countless studies show that in today's "Age of the Consumer," how your customers and others perceive your company can make or break you. A key goal of public relations involves reinforcing credibility to ensure that what you are (or appear to be, i.e., your *reputation* and *image*) adds value to what you do (or say or sell).[22]

Studies also demonstrate that stories about your company that appear in the news carry more weight than straight advertising (i.e., *third-party endorsements*). But seeing public relations as nothing more than product publicity and favorable media coverage is an especially common error. Although very important, media relationships form just one element of a strong PR program. Yet many business executives and leaders of not-for-profits fail to understand the importance of public relations and its broad range of activities to their organization until a crisis hits and instant communication is demanded.

From a practical perspective, PR is closely tied to strategic planning. Although this communication function varies from organization to organization, it involves a range of mostly proactive activities that support the organization's main objectives. Other examples of public relations include management counseling, public opinion research, issues management, media placement of news releases, internal communications and employee training, investor relations, lobbying and other public affairs activities, customer service, community activities, event sponsorships, support of charitable events, fund-raising, and multicultural affairs.[23]

STRATEGY TYPES

Strategy has three forms: globalization, multinationalization, and triadization. The type of strategy a business chooses and becomes committed to is the first step toward a successful marketing plan. The strategy does not have to be independent of other strategies; a business could adopt variations of several strategies.

Globalization defines the world as a homogeneous global village where superficial regional and national differences are ignored. Companies that adopt this type of operation must have a direct investment of more than 10 percent in a foreign country. Convergence is a trend toward uniformity; everything will be similar to everything else. Telecommunications will bring ideas, events, products, lifestyles, working conditions, and life in general from places thousands of miles away into everyone's living room. The result will be a marketing effort to sell a product in Dallas, Texas, that will create demand for the same product in Stuttgart, Germany.

A consequence of this globalization of customers' needs will be standardization of products, manufacturing, and the institutions of trade and commerce. For a business to be a global success, it will have to focus on efficiency in production, distribution, marketing, management, and price. Subsidiaries of a global company are more linked to each other in a complementary manner.

Multinationalization is seen as a number of large and small markets whose differences dictate considerable product and marketing mix adaptation. A company that originates in one country and invests heavily in others is using this strategy. Multinationalization dictates that firms operating in many diverse places must adjust their products and practices in each, which is a costly practice. Subsidiaries of an MNC operate more independently from each other. Managers who practice this philosophy will not benefit from product and technique standardization.

The third strategy is *triadization*. Kenichi Ohmae, the managing director of McKinsey and Company, a well-known consulting firm, claims that "there is an emergence of the Triadians, or the residents of Japan, North America, and the European community."[24] These are the people whose academic backgrounds, income levels, lifestyle, use of leisure time, and aspirations are quite similar. Ohmae believes if firms are to succeed, they must develop products and techniques that will capitalize on the similarities of these markets and accommodate their differences at the same time. The benefit of this strategy is that the cost of adapting to three markets with 600 million customers with large disposable incomes is much less than that of adapting to hundreds of markets with only a few thousand customers in each market.

CONCLUSION

Business strategies depend on the careful planning, execution, and coordination of functional-level activities. One supports the other; neither can function alone. Functional strategies add detail to business strategy and govern how the various functions in the organization will be managed.

The major strategy alternatives can be remembered using the acronym DICARM. These strategies are formulated through a variety of theoretical approaches: contingency, generic, and alternative generic descriptive characteristics. The generic approaches include cost leadership, differentiation, and focus strategies.

Functional strategy formulation can be broken down into financial, human resource, production, marketing, and public relations strategies. The extent that these tasks are coordinated will determine how effectively each strategy is completed. Corporations that are most likely to achieve competitive advantages are those that are best able to achieve functional integration.

REVIEW QUESTIONS

1. Define and differentiate business strategy and functional strategy. Discuss the interrelation of the business and functional strategies of a company in the process of serving the company's long-term goals and objectives.
2. What are the major factors that a manager should take into consideration in selecting a business strategy? Which are most suitable for achieving the company's goals?
3. What is the initial step in the analysis and evaluation of a business strategy? What are the external and internal factors that should be considered by managers during the strategy analysis and evaluation process?
4. Define the contingency approach to strategy formulation.
5. Define the generic approach to strategy formulation. What are the strengths and weaknesses of that approach?
6. What are the most common tactics of differentiation? Under what conditions are differentiation strategies most suitable?
7. According to Porter, what are the three generic strategies available to firms to achieve sustainable competitive advantage? Discuss the strengths of each strategy.
8. What are the criticisms of the three generic strategies offered by Porter?
9. Discuss the use of descriptive characteristics in strategy formulation. What are some of the descriptive characteristics of successful organizations as identified by Peters and Waterman?

NOTES

1. Higgins, J. and Vincze, J. (1996). *Strategic Management: Text and Cases.* Chicago: Dryden Press, p. 173.

2. Hambrick, D. C. and Schecter, S. M. (1983). Turnaround strategies in mature capital goods industries: A contingency approach. *Academy of Management Journal*, 26(2), 231.

3. Govindarajan, V. and Fisher, J. (1990). Strategy, control systems, and resource sharing. *Academy of Management Journal,* 33(2), 259.

4. Porter, M. E. (1985). *Competitive Advantage: Creating and Sustaining Superior Performance.* New York: Free Press, pp. 36-38.

5. Porter, M. E. (1990). *The Competitive Advantage of Nations.* New York: Free Press.

6. Zahra, S. A. and Covin, J. G. (1993). Business strategy, technology policy and firm performance. *Strategic Management Journal,* 14(6), 454-455.

7. Porter, M. E. (1980). *Competitive Strategy.* New York: Free Press.

8. Thain, D. H. (1993). Managing the strategic agenda: The CEO's job 1. *Business Quarterly,* 57(3), 18.

9. Porter, M. *Competitive Strategy,* p. 45.

10. Ibid., p. 46.

11. Miller, D. (1992). The generic strategy trap. *The Journal of Business Strategy,* 13(1), 37-41.

12. Porter, *Competitive Strategy;* Porter, *Competitive Advantage: Creating and Sustaining Superior Performance,* pp. 36-38.

13. Bracker, J. S., Keats, B. W., and Pearson, J. N. (1988). Planning and financial performance among small firms in A G. *Strategic Management Journal,* 9(6), 595.

14. Wright, P., Kroll, M. J., and Parnell, J. (1998). *Strategic Management: Concept and Cases.* Upper Saddle River, NJ: Prentice-Hall, pp. 159-161.

15. Peters, T. and Waterman, R. (1982). *In Search of Excellence: Lessons from America's Best-Run Companies.* New York: Harper and Row, p. 186.

16. Kumar, K. (1996). Examining the role of competitive environment in the market orientation-performance relationship. *Business Research Yearbook,* 3, 854.

17. Ibid., p. 852.

18. Hamel, G. (1991). Competition for competence and inter-partner learning within international strategic alliances. *Strategic Management Journal,* 12, 83-103.

19. Ibid.

20. Alkhafaji, A. (1995). *Competitive Global Management: Principles and Strategies.* Delray Beach, FL: St. Lucie Press, p. 96.

21. Terpstra, V. and Sarathy, R. (1997). *International Marketing,* Seventh Edition. Orlando, FL: Dryden Press, p. 5.

22. Public Relations Society of America (2001). *Careers in Public Relations: An Overview.* New York: PRSA (available online at http://www.prsa.org/prc/).

23. Ibid.

24. Ohmae, K. (1999). *The Borderless World.* New York: HarperCollins, pp. 40-41.

Chapter 6

Strategic Management in the International Environment

INTRODUCTION

Internationalization has become the major trend in business since the 1980s. It allows a firm to expand into new markets in order to seek higher profits and lower-cost resources. In addition, internationalization allows a firm to increase economies of scale and lengthen the life cycle of its products. International trade has continued to increase over the years. As of December 2001, U.S. exports of goods reached $729,100 million, and imports of goods reached $1,140,999 million.[1]

International strategic planning allows a firm to approach internationalization systemically. Scanning the external environment allows a firm to detect opportunities and threats in international markets. Evaluating internal weaknesses and strengths allows a firm to check into utilizing international opportunities and avoiding threats; determining the scope of internationalization makes it possible to formulate international strategic objectives and develop appropriate strategies.

The scope of internationalization includes: (1) home-market oriented; (2) multidomestic; and (3) global market oriented. Strategies for international management are: (1) global high-share strategy; (2) global niche strategy; (3) national high-share strategy; and (4) national niche strategy.

In choosing a foreign market to enter, factors such as the government, economy, demographics, and business situation have to be considered. Ways of entering a foreign country include exporting, licensing/franchising, strategic alliance, joint ventures, and full ownership of overseas subsidiaries. Multinational corporations have to face many challenges that are unique to them, including coordination between headquarters and the overseas subsidiaries and the relationship between MNCs and the host country.

TRENDS TOWARD INTERNATIONALIZATION

If we open a national newspaper or magazine, it is not difficult to find some news that may look like the following:

> The Hungarian Ministry of Transport, Telecommunications and Water Management has accepted an $875 million joint bid from Ameritech and Germany's Deutsche Telekom for a 30 percent stake in Matav, Hungary's national operator.[2]

> Turner, who helped cable TV mature in the U.S., is looking to leverage his company's programming assets into an international empire by creating its own satellite-delivered entertainment channels worldwide.[3]

> The Japanese and South Korean economies dominate one of the world's most vital regions.[4]

> The Daimler-Chrysler merger in 1998 is affecting the U.S. auto market by getting more competition from Japanese and European auto markets.[5]

These are just a few examples that show the abundant opportunities existing outside of the United States. Although doing business with foreign countries in the forms of importing and exporting already existed thousands of years ago in China, the Middle East, and India, the process of globalization started only about three decades ago.

During the 1970s and 1980s, American companies lost ground to international companies, and competition from abroad continued to increase. Businesses responded swiftly to protect their market shares and regain their competitive edge. For example, in 1994, fifty of the world's one hundred largest companies were Japanese, and only thirty-five were American businesses. By the year 2000, fifty of the world's one hundred largest companies were American.

With the world economy and trade increasing rapidly, global changes and competition affect companies large and small. The 1990s, however, provided new challenges and opportunities for companies and their employees that are carrying over into the new century. Some challenges that have resulted in the global shift are:

1. Changes in technology and the availability of information.
2. Increases in the level of competition domestically and internationally. An important reason for such expansion is because the domestic market has become saturated.

3. Demands for products in foreign markets have increased tremendously. The competition became global and intense.
4. Changes in communist countries (the former Soviet Union and Eastern European countries) and the movement from controlled economies to more free enterprise economies.
5. While the United States and the Soviet Union were engaged in an arms race, the nations of the Pacific Rim (Japan, Singapore, Hong Kong, Taiwan, and South Korea) and Western Europe were successful in gaining a global economic advantage.
6. Attempts by emerging countries to improve their standards of living through inviting world markets.

Key reasons for such sudden development of international businesses include advances in technology and changes in government attitudes. Today's technological improvements have made the process of internationalization much easier than before. Global communication through satellites, telephones, fax machines, e-mail, and computer networks such as the Internet is linking headquarters with their overseas subsidiaries to make the planning and implementation of global strategy possible. In addition, the availability of more efficient transportation has greatly reduced the cost of delivery and improved the flow of raw materials, products, capital, and human resources.

The change in attitude of many governments also facilitates global business. Tariffs on imports and restriction on foreign ownership and capital, which discouraged multinational corporations in the past, are now gradually being reduced. Many countries have joined the World Trade Organization (WTO) since its creation in 1995. The WTO promotes reducing tariffs and other trade restrictions between countries. Proposals to harmonize monetary policy across national borders are becoming popular as global trade becomes increasingly concentrated.[6] These changes create new opportunities for business firms and allow them to reap the benefits of internationalization.

ADVANTAGES OF INTERNATIONALIZATION

The benefits of internationalization to a business firm depend on its objectives and resource constraints. In general, internationalization allows a business firm to expand into larger and more profitable markets, exploit economies of scale, utilize foreign countries' strengths, etc. The following explains the benefits in some detail.

New Markets

Expanding into the international market extends a firm's opportunity to the world. Although the United States is a big country with more than 280 million people, its population constitutes only 5 percent of the world's total population. If one looks at the United States as the only market, one will miss the other 5 billion consumers outside America. Large multinational corporations such as Coca-Cola may have operations in as many as 200 countries, reaching about 95 percent of the world's population that lives outside the United States.[7] Interestingly, although the United States is the home of Coca-Cola, its highest per capita market is American Samoa, where a person drinks an average of 500 eight-ounce servings of Coca-Cola products a year. The second highest per capita market is Iceland, with an average consumption of 397. In the United States, the figure is only 296.[8]

Although many MNCs have traditionally concentrated on industrialized countries, which can provide relatively more stable markets and better infrastructures, today's greatest opportunities indeed come from emerging markets such as China, the Middle East, Mexico, and other economies with rapid development. The reforms in many former communist countries in Eastern Europe and Asia have created consumers with strong appetites for Western products and capital, as well as technology.

One example is China. The World Bank named it as the third largest economy after America and Japan. China's ten-year reform has brought many changes to its 1.2 billion people, as well as enormous opportunities for MNCs. In 1992, the U.S. exported $7.5 billion of goods to China while it imported over $25 billion of goods, much of which were actually manufactured by Hong Kong, Japanese, and American factories in China.[9] Today, China, with an annual growth of about 9 percent, has emerged as a major economic power and a significant market in the world.[10]

A recent trend toward trading blocs has also changed the way business firms look at international markets. Instead of viewing countries as many individual markets, firms now can view those with free-trade treaties as a big market. Not only is the new market larger than any individual member country but it also facilitates the flow of capital, raw materials, and human resources across borders. The European Union (EU), which currently consists of fifteen member countries in Western Europe, has made substantial progress toward an integrated economy after many regulations and standards were integrated and harmonized at the end of 1992. The total population of this new giant market is 320 million people and growing. In the future, the joining of some Eastern European countries and further integration of economic policies will make this market larger and easier for business resources to move within.

The largest trading bloc, however, is the North American Free Trade Agreement (NAFTA), which consists of Canada, the United States, and Mexico. Other existing trading blocs include the European Free Trade Association (EFTA), Latin-American Integration Association (LAIA), Caribbean Community and Common Market (CARICOM), Andean Common Market (ANCOM), Association of South East Asian Nations (ASEAN), and some smaller groupings in Africa.

Economies of Scale

Larger markets resulting from internationalization implies greater demand for a company's products, which in turn leads to a larger scale of production. The result is usually economies of scale, which allow a business firm to lower its operating costs and strengthen its competitiveness among domestic as well as international competitors.

Utilize Foreign Countries' Strength

Beside opportunities and economies of scale, internationalization also allows a firm to take advantage of a foreign country's competitive advantages, including low-cost resources and high technology. For example, China's abundance of low-cost laborers ($374 per worker per year[11]), land, and raw materials has attracted over $25 billion in foreign direct investment (FDI). Similarly, Mexico also encourages many American manufacturers to shift their plants across the southern border.

In the late 1950s, over 80 percent of the world's major innovations were first introduced in the United States. However, nowadays, France has made strong advances in electric traction, nuclear power, and aviation. West Germany became a leader in chemicals, pharmaceuticals, machinery, electrical goods, metallurgy, and surface transport equipment. Japan now leads in automobiles, computers, and home appliances. The changes indicate that the United States is not the only place with high technology and innovations. Having production facilities in a foreign country allows a firm to take advantage of high technology in that country.

MNCs utilizing foreign countries' competitive advantages will ultimately build specialized plants in different countries. For example, the design of Ford's automobile may come from Japan, where technology in engine design may be the highest. The production of major parts may then occur in the United States where the highest productivity can be found. Other minor and less sophisticated parts may come from Ford's plants in Southeast Asia where low-cost labor is abundant. Finally, the whole automobile may be assembled in Mexico and distributed to other parts of the world or supplied directly to the local market.

The term *export platform* vividly describes the strategy of using a third country for the last process of production and exporting the final products from that country to the target country. Mexico, in this case, becomes the export platform for Ford's automobiles. The use of an export platform is not new to the Japanese. Between 1987 and 1996, the appreciation of the yen against other currencies has more than doubled the cost of production in Japan and forced many Japanese firms to move their plants to Asian countries such as China, Korea, and Malaysia. These places, not surprisingly, are the main export platforms for many Japanese products.

Lengthen Product Life Cycle

Entering international markets also allows a business to lengthen its product life cycle. Fast-food restaurants such as McDonald's, having been in existence in the United States since the 1950s, have expanded almost to the point of saturation in the domestic market. However, in countries such as Russia and China, the demand for McDonald's fast food is so large that the first McDonald's store in Shenzhen, China, ran out of hamburger after the first few hours of operation. It had to send trucks immediately to neighboring Hong Kong to pick up hamburgers to satisfy curious customers.

Diversification

With so many countries as choices, business firms now do not have to concentrate only on the domestic market, putting all their eggs in one basket. Internationalization allows a firm to spread the risk of doing business, making it less sensitive to the changes within a single country. Due to differences of economic situation, the returns of business from different countries may vary. Diversification may offset declines in the domestic market and smooth out the profits for a company.

Bring Back New Products and Ideas

As with traveling to new places, extending business overseas can bring back products or ideas that may not be discovered if the operation is limited to the home region. Power Rangers, the TV characters that have driven tens of thousands of children crazy all over the United States, are actually what most Japanese young people were familiar with ten years ago. Haim Saban, the founder of Saban Entertainment, discovered them on Japanese TV and brought them to the United States after obtaining the exclusive rights for using the Power Rangers outside the Pacific Rim.[12]

Drain Competitors' Cash Flows

Direct penetration of foreign markets can drain vital cash flows from foreign competitors' operations. The resulting reduced income can impair competitors' ability to compete domestically. As a case in point, IBM established a strong position in the Japanese mainframe computer market before two key competitors, Fujitsu and Hitachi, could become dominant. Once it gained enough market share, IBM worked to deny these competitors vital cash and production experience needed for them to compete in U.S. markets.

Following Customers

The expansion of many firms into international markets has created chances for their suppliers to also go into the foreign environment to continue serving their customers. For example, driven by demand from U.S. multinationals, advertising agencies are increasingly seeking business beyond national borders. According to industrial statistics, in the mid-1990s advertising billing increased by 7.5 percent in Europe, 7.7 percent in the Pacific Basin, and 14.9 percent in Latin America, while U.S. billing dropped by 2.6 percent. At McCann-Erickson, an advertising agency handling more global accounts than any other, about 75 percent of billing comes from global marketers such as Coca-Cola, General Motors, Goodyear, Exxon, McDonald's, and L'Oreal.[13]

Even though a company may choose not to invest globally, that choice does not exempt the business from foreign competition. Foreign firms conduct business in virtually every industry represented in the United States. In most cases, they directly compete with the American domestic firms. Therefore, virtually every top manager must have an understanding of the issues involved in international strategic management.[14]

INTERNATIONAL STRATEGIC MANAGEMENT

The term international, in the context of international strategic management, refers to anything that deals with, or affects, two or more countries.[15] Therefore, the concept of international strategic management refers to the effect of strategic management on the interaction of organizations in two or more nations.

MNCs are likely the most complex form of organization in widespread existence today. Operating across products, markets, nations, and cultures, MNCs face problems and situations much more diverse than even the largest domestic firms. Because of this, the planning of strategic management becomes the first, most important step in the process of internationalization.

Planning is crucial at all levels of management, especially when an organization competes in a different country where the operating variables change. A business firm not only has to plan which foreign country to enter and how to enter, it also has to have plans for meeting foreign competition, adapting to foreign markets, complying with foreign regulations, etc. An example of unsuccessful strategic planning occurred in the 1970s, when KFC was aggressively expanding its overseas markets. Described as "throwing some mud against the map on the wall and hoping some of it would stick" by its own management, KFC opened its first store in Japan after only two weeks' preparation in 1970. The result? The store threw out more chicken than it sold and lost $400,000, KFC's whole amount of starting capital in Japan.[16]

International strategic planning starts with the analysis of the international environment. Then comes the examination of an MNC's internal condition to match a firm's weaknesses and strengths to the opportunities and threats in international markets. Based on the availability of international opportunities and company resources, a firm can decide on the scope of internationalization and formulate objectives. The next step of the planning process is the development of international corporate strategies. The steps in international strategic planning can be summarized as follows:

1. Evaluate international opportunities, threats, problems, and risks.
2. Evaluate internal strengths and weaknesses.
3. Define the firm's scope relative to international business involvement.
4. Formulate the firm's international corporate objectives.
5. Develop specific corporate strategies for the firm as a whole, an international corporate strategy.

Because of the change in operating variables, international strategic planning is different from domestic planning. The *transnational management support system* (TMSS) is emerging as a tool for global decision making and strategic management at MNCs. A TMSS is an integrated system of decision support systems, expert systems, and executive information systems that supports the operational, tactical, and strategic decision-making processes of MNCs. TMSS is a viable weapon for improving the effectiveness of global strategic and tactical management processes by analyzing the multinational, multifunctional, and multibusiness consequences of decisions. It evaluates the trade-off between the long- and short-term effects of a decision. TMSS attempts to balance the conflicting goals of long- and short-range planning and facilitate the interactive and iterative flow of the MNC strategic decision-making process.[17]

Evaluation of the International Environment

The analysis of the international environment is the first step of internationalization. It is also the most important one, because it allows MNCs to detect opportunities in the international market and helps to determine the feasibility of capitalizing on these opportunities. To thoroughly analyze the international environment, evaluation can be made on three levels: the multinational, the regional, and the country level.

1. *Multinational.* Multinational environmental analysis consists of very broad identifying, forecasting, and monitoring of critical factors in the world environment. It involves knowledge of global technological developments, various trends in government intervention in economies, and overall value and lifestyle changes. These factors are evaluated according to their perceived degree of impact, both now and in the future.
2. *Regional.* Regional environmental analysis focuses on a more detailed study of the critical factors within a particular geographic area, such as Western Europe, the Middle East, etc. Efforts would be directed toward identifying the market opportunities for a company's products, services, or technologies in the chosen region.
3. *Country.* A country environmental analysis involves an even more refined examination of the critical environmental factors. This level of analysis continues to focus on the economic, legal, political, and cultural factors, but in a small number of countries. However, to achieve successful planning, this analysis must be oriented to each of the individual market entry strategies involved.

In collecting data for analyzing the foreign environment, the following suggestions can be followed:

1. *Scan the international situation.* This includes reading patent reports and journals as well as attending scientific and technical conferences and seminars to meet people.

2. *Make connections with academia and research organizations.* Firms engaging in R&D overseas sometimes form consulting agreements with foreign academics and faculty members.
3. *Increase the company's international visibility.* Some methods include booths at trade fairs and circulating brochures about the company and its products. Countries with strong appetites for foreign investment usually distribute information about themselves at trade fairs, too. Sometimes preliminary contracts can be signed at these fairs.

Data collection should be followed by careful analysis of the foreign environment, including economic, political, technological, societal, ecological analysis, etc.

Economic Environment

The analysis of the economic environment will help the firm to detect opportunities such as potential markets and low-cost resources. If, in another case, a firm views the foreign country as a place for manufacturing its products, economic analysis can help to determine whether the country has competitive advantages in manufacturing.

The economic environment is probably the most critical and most difficult to analyze, requiring a firm to predict what will occur on the national economic scene. A number of economic issues are the projected growth of the gross domestic product, the expected growth in the consumer price index, and the stability of the U.S. dollar and other currencies.

The appearance of many emerging markets further reinforces the need for the analysis of the economic environment. An example of analysis is the economic cycle. Many Eastern European countries are experiencing high inflation during economic development. Annual inflation has exceeded 20 percent in Poland, Hungary, and the former Czechoslovakia, jumping to over 1,000 percent in some former Soviet and Yugoslav republics. Meanwhile, collapsing output, shrinking price controls, and falling exchange rates are becoming common. As these countries pass this early stage, medium-term prospects will become more positive.[18] Eastern European countries that made the transition from communist to market economies have recorded some growth since 1996. Inflation has declined tremendously in the region. For example, in Russia inflation declined from 200 percent in 1995 to about 50 percent in 1996. U.S. exports to Eastern Europe and Russia have also increased in recent years.[19]

Political Environment

Even under an ideal economic environment with abundant opportunities, foreign investment cannot promise a good return without a stable political environment. Frequent changes of government, social upheaval, and other political instability can damage all the efforts of a multinational corporation.

The company must find reasonable and acceptable conditions to conduct business overseas. It is advisable that companies ignore insignificant or risky markets. *Political risk* is defined as the uncertainty of the political environment MNCs have to face when operating in foreign countries. Although a political risk assessment (PRA) is an integral part of environmental scanning, unfortunately, a number of European- and U.S.-based MNCs have discontinued the PRA function because of declining profits, as found by a study done in 1992.[20]

PRA is meaningless if the strategy development of MNCs does not include ways of handling political risk. A way to exit from a foreign market becomes necessary when the political situation in a foreign country threatens the operations of subsidiaries. This happens when there is war, severe social upheavals, or a change in attitude toward MNCs because of new government officials or new regulations. Possible exit alternatives are a management buyout, the temporary suspension of activities, the closing down of operations, or sale to a local company, another MNC, or a trust. In any case, an exit strategy should take into account the objectives of the firm in relation to present and anticipated competitive environments.[21]

Government regulation. A stable political environment does not, however, imply favorable government regulations. Some countries, such as China and Mexico, in their rapid economic development stage have exhibited friendly attitudes toward MNCs while others may be less interested or even hold hostile attitudes at the prospect of MNCs operating in their countries. There are few countries that impose no restrictions on MNCs doing business in their territories.

Some governments in developing countries impose heavy taxes, quotas, or administrative red tape on imports in order to reserve foreign exchange. Such a policy would limit an MNC's choice of industrial parts to local suppliers if MNCs have production facilities in those countries. Other possible restrictions include foreign exchange rules, local content requirements, employment quotas, ownership limitations, and permit controls for those who wish to operate in certain industries.

U.S. MNCs have often complained that some countries discriminate against outsiders. In Malaysia and the Philippines, foreigners cannot own land. In some other places, MNCs cannot make certain local investments that are open to their domestic rivals. In some countries, having a local partner is mandatory. For example, in Indonesia, at least 70 percent of any project must be held locally. Australia requires a company to invest locally if it wants to sell locally.[22]

The recent trend toward regional cooperation has harmonized some of the different regulations across borders. The Association of Southeast Asian Nations (ASEAN), an economic cooperation group, has begun drafting an investment code which consists of a set of common rules to be applied uniformly by eighteen nations around the Pacific rim. The increased consistency in regulations is expected to enhance the overall commerce in that region.

Technological Environment

In many cases, the technological environment may be the deciding factor for expansion, as a firm's survival often depends on its ability to stay on the cutting edge of technology. Some countries, such as Singapore, offer high technology in telecommunications and computers. MNCs should choose the countries that can provide adequate technology in the industries they operate.

Social Environment

MNCs may face great difficulty if they do not pay attention to local societies and cultures. Sociocultural forces include values, religions, traditions, attitudes, languages, lifestyles, and other basic foundations of social behavior. To be successful in international business, managers of MNCs must be knowledgeable and comfortable in the culture of the host country. By acknowledging and indicating cultural importance through strategic planning, intercultural relationships can be greatly enhanced and human capital more effectively utilized.

Value systems determine the way people treat each other and thus the way of doing business. Westerners value individualism and entrepreneurial initiative, and believe that the best leaders are those who quickly communicate clear goals and delegate decisions about how to implement them. However, Asians believe that a good organization is like a caring family, where leaders are like fathers who accept responsibility for the development and well-being of employees in return for their obedience and personal loyalty.[23]

Lifestyles can vary across countries. A survey conducted by Eugene Fram found that there are large differences between dual-income and single-income families in the United States, Jordan, Singapore, and Turkey.[24] Despite the recent shortage of rice, the Japanese are reluctant to import foreign rice. The Japanese contend that their rice is simply the best in the world, and they may be right. In a blind taste test for six kinds of rice, including American and Australian rice, some thirty Japanese housewives rated Japanese rice first, followed by two Chinese rices. The American rice ranked fourth.[25]

Ecological Environment

As people increasingly seek to preserve and protect the earth, the ecological environment is a critical area of concern. Today, firms must carefully assess their impact on the environment and include ecological costs in their calculation of profit. Although environmental laws may be less strict in many developing countries, taking advantage of the leniency of these laws may put the ethics of MNCs in question. Moreover, environmentalists have been pushing many governments to tighten their environmental laws.

In 1994, trade ministers from around the world gathered in Marrakech, Morocco, in an attempt to sign a world trade pact. One year later the World Trade Organization (WTO) was established. The United States sought to create a world environmental organization as well. Although an agreement has not been reached, proponents hope that the committee will ensure that trade laws do not violate the environmental treaties governing ozone-depleting chemicals and endangered species. Environmentalists in the United States and Europe want to bar imports of tropical wood unless logging is conducted in a way that preserves the rain forests. These changes mean that U.S. MNCs must comply with tough pollution laws and higher expenses for environmental protection.[26]

When determining which foreign country to enter, additional factors should be considered.

Economies:

1. Size of GNP per capita, and their projected growth rates
2. Current and potential inflation, employment, interest rates
3. Prevailing wage levels and expected growth rate
4. Foreign exchange position
5. Size of market for the company's products and the rate of growth
6. Demographics such as age distribution and population

Politics:

1. Form and stability of government
2. Attitude toward private and foreign investment by government, customers, and competition

3. Practice of favorable treatment to state-owned firms
4. Degree of anti-foreign discrimination

Government Regulations:

1. Restriction on size, location, or ownership of foreign investment
2. Restriction on profit repatriation
3. Tax rate trends (corporate and personal income, capital, withholding, turnover, excise, payroll, capital gains, customs, and other indirect and local taxes)
4. Special tax treatment for foreign investment
5. Tariffs on imported goods

Geography:

1. Efficiency of transports (railways, waterways, highways)
2. Proximity of site to export markets
3. Availability of local raw materials
4. Availability of power, water, gas

Labor:

1. Availability of managerial, technical and office personnel able to speak the language of the parent company
2. Degree of skill and discipline at all levels
3. Degree of unionization
4. Degree and nature of labor voice in management

Capital source factors:

1. Cost of local borrowing
2. Local availability of convertible currencies
3. Modern banking and accounting systems
4. Government credit aids to new businesses

Business factors:

1. State of marketing and distribution system
2. Normal profit margins in the company's industry
3. Competitive situations in the firm's industry; do cartels exist?
4. Availability of amenities for expatriate executives and families

Analysis of Internal Situation

Determining the degree to which the firm has the resources to successfully exploit potential opportunities in foreign markets, the second step of international strategic planning is to evaluate the strengths and weaknesses of the firm's managerial, material, technical, and functional (finance, marketing, etc.) capabilities. This step focuses on the business as opposed to the environment. The primary purpose of this audit is to appropriately match the company's managerial, technical, material, and financial resources with those required for successful international business. The audit concentrates on key factors essential to success in a particular business. This audit is considered country related because the amount of resources needed varies from country to country.

Scope of Internationalization

After detecting opportunities in international markets, the firm can determine the degree of internationalization. Different firms may make different decisions, depending on corporate objectives and resource availability. There are generally three levels of internationalization.

1. *The Home-Market-Oriented Mode.* Firms just entering the global marketplace use this mode. This usually occurs when a firm produces a product in a foreign environment and exports it to the home environment. The purpose of producing the product overseas may be lower production costs there, but the product remains geared to the home market. Companies may select to enter the international market through indirect operations at a minimal level of involvement. Some of the indirect strategies applied for entering international markets are: direct exporting and importing, countertrading, foreign licensing, franchising, establishing joint ventures, and entering strategic alliances.

2. *The Multidomestic (Multinational) Mode.* As we have seen earlier, an MNC is a firm that originates in one country and conducts business (production and marketing activities) in one or more foreign countries. The more spread out the company is, the more multinational it is. These companies do more business outside the home country than at home. They are usually involved through direct investment, by either buying an existing company or starting their own subsidiary with complete ownership. The firms competing in several different international markets usually use the multidomestic mode. The firm develops a strategy to fit each country's market. They do not transfer the products and services geared to a particular country's market to another country's market. In a multidomestic industry, the subsidiaries of an

MNC are managed as distinct entities. Each subsidiary is relatively autonomous, with room to make decisions and respond to local market conditions. Factors determining the degree to which a market is multidomestic include:

a. the need for customized products for each locale;
b. a very fragmented industry with many competitors in each national market;
c. the lack of economies of scale;
d. distribution channels unique in each country; and
e. a low technological dependence on corporate R&D.

Firms using the multidomestic mode usually compete globally. Examples include retailing, insurance, and consumer finance.

3. *The Global Market Mode.* In the global market mode, a firm pursues an integrated strategy in major world markets. There are no national boundaries limiting where their products can be sold. At this point, the company will have a worldwide approach to production, sales, finance, and control. Firms using this mode compete in the world market. Although a global company is very similar to the MNCs in entering through direct investment, its subsidiaries operate more interdependently. They complement each other as a company-coordinated system. Examples are commercial aircraft, cars, mainframe computers, and electronic consumer equipment. In such industries, a multinational firm must link its subsidiaries together, maximizing its capabilities through a worldwide strategy. This means that more decision-making power must be concentrated at the corporate level so that trade-off decisions can be made. Factors influencing the creation of global markets include:

a. economies of scale;
b. a high level of R&D expenditures;
c. a level of dominance by multinational companies in the industry;
d. homogeneous product needs;
e. a small group of global competitors in the industry; and
f. a low level of trade and foreign direct investment regulation.

Although the global and multidomestic distinction is convenient, few pure examples of either exist. Most MNCs blend the two approaches. An MNC competing in a global industry must, to some degree, also be responsive to local market conditions. Similarly, the multinational firm competing in a multidomestic industry cannot totally ignore opportunities to use intracorporate resources in competitive positioning.

The question becomes, which activities should be performed at which level, and what degree of coordination is needed? Typical functional activities of a business include purchasing input resources, operations, research, marketing, and sales. An MNC has many possible location options for each of these activities and must decide which set of activities will be performed in how many and which locations. Some activities may be best performed at every location, while others may be best performed in only one location. Centralizing R&D work at one location is a good example.

The degree of coordination between headquarters and overseas subsidiaries depends on the scope of internationalization. In a multidomestic industry, competition occurs within each country; consequently, little coordination of functional activities across countries may be necessary. However, as the industry becomes increasingly global, the firm must begin to coordinate an increasing number of functional activities in order to effectively compete across countries.

With respect to the function and scope of international production, MNCs may employ one of the three strategies. With a standalone strategy, MNCs establish foreign affiliates that largely replicate the home company; with a simple integration strategy, MNCs outsource specific operations to subcontractors in other countries; and with a complex integration strategy, MNCs set up independent affiliates abroad.[27]

Therefore, a global approach to business is the key to future success. The United States has felt pressure to move into foreign markets for reasons of survival and the need to expand markets, leading to more exporting and importing. Many emerging nations are attempting to improve their standards of living through world markets. This represents new opportunities for businesses to sell their goods and services in new and expanding international markets. Some elements of success in this global market include the following:

1. Continuously improving quality and innovation
2. Creating more efficient organizations
3. Careful hiring of people who are motivated and multilingual
4. Better understanding of foreign cultures and foreign markets

Formulation of International Corporate Objectives

The decision to internationalize brings radical change to a company's existing direction and operations. Multinationalization subjects a company to a radically redefined and challenging set of environmentally determined opportunities, constraints, and risks. To prevent the company's direction from being dictated by these external factors, top management must reassess the corporation's mission, philosophy, and strategic intentions prior to multinationalization, thus ensuring that these basic values will continue as decision criteria in proactive planning.

Because of the differences in cultures and value systems, the missions of many U.S. firms may not be acceptable in foreign countries. For example, maximizing the profit of shareholders has been traditionally the mission of many U.S. corporations. In some countries, however, profit maximization may be less important than employment stability and social harmony. It could even be viewed as exploiting the host country exclusively for the benefit of the parent's home country. Therefore, the mission statement needs to reflect the bidirectional flows of benefits between the MNC and the host country.

International corporate objectives further define the corporate mission. If the mission is thought of as the direction, objectives can be viewed as the road toward this direction. Constructing this road allows a firm to head in the direction without wandering around in darkness. Similar to corporate strategies, the formulation of an international corporation requires the establishment of figures and time frames such as "obtaining 10 percent of market share in China within five years." Of course, cultural differences should be taken into account in setting up international corporate objectives.

Development of International Corporate Strategies

Depending on a company's desired level of internationalization, there are two basic types of strategies. The first, developed by Leontiades, considers the global or national scope of the organization and its market share objectives, whether they are high or low. Under this strategy, there are four basic strategic orientations.[28]

1. *The Global High-Share Strategy.* Using this strategy, firms seek to obtain high world market share through pricing, promotions, and products. Usually very large MNCs apply this approach. For example, IBM uses this type of strategy through expansion into new areas such as the former Soviet Union. AT&T, which is grappling with slow growth in the United States, is setting up foreign units in Asia, Europe, and Latin America. While its U.S. business grows at less than 5 percent a year, these foreign countries are modernizing archaic phone systems and promising big orders.[29]
2. *The Global Niche Strategy.* The global niche strategy is used by organizations that operate in the world market but only want to achieve low market share. Usually, small firms competing in global markets use

this strategy to gain a small market share by trying to pursue a specialty. For example, the Brunswick Corporation sells fun and games, such as bowling. Bowling centers are going up in several countries and they plan to cash in on the market. Brunswick has contracts for five bowling centers in China and is closing in on deals in Asia, Japan, and South Korea.[30]

3. *The National High-Share Strategy.* Companies that want high volume and low cost in a competitive national market typically use this strategy. It prevents a firm from having to pay tariffs and quotas, as global firms must. Therefore, they are also able to take advantage of government subsidies and tax breaks.
4. *The National Niche Strategy.* Firms using this strategy specialize in a national market where the competitors are few. They survive on the hope that large international corporations will find these markets unattractive and choose not to pursue them.[31]

For a company to adopt a successful global strategy, it is necessary for it to assess its strengths and weaknesses before setting its overall objectives. Benchmarking with competitors can be beneficial to future strategies. It is advisable that if the early assessment of the international market is not significant, the company should ignore that market. The company should consider only those markets or regions where the political and economic conditions are considered reasonable.

The organization needs to assess the environment of a particular region (foreign environment) to test the suitability of expanding there. This assessment requires relevant and reliable information. It is advisable to avoid countries with undesirable or unpredictable environments. Once the company selects a suitable market, it must design the strategy to enter that market. The company must respond to the following questions: Can we compete effectively in this market? What type of entry strategy should we apply? What types of modifications of our current products or services are needed? The availability of suppliers, human resources, and the infrastructure are all-important elements of corporate composition. See the model in Figure 6.1, which a firm's management can use in determining a global strategy.

ENTERING A FOREIGN MARKET

A business does not have to physically invest in a foreign country to enter the international market. Some of the indirect ways include export/import, licensing, franchising, etc.

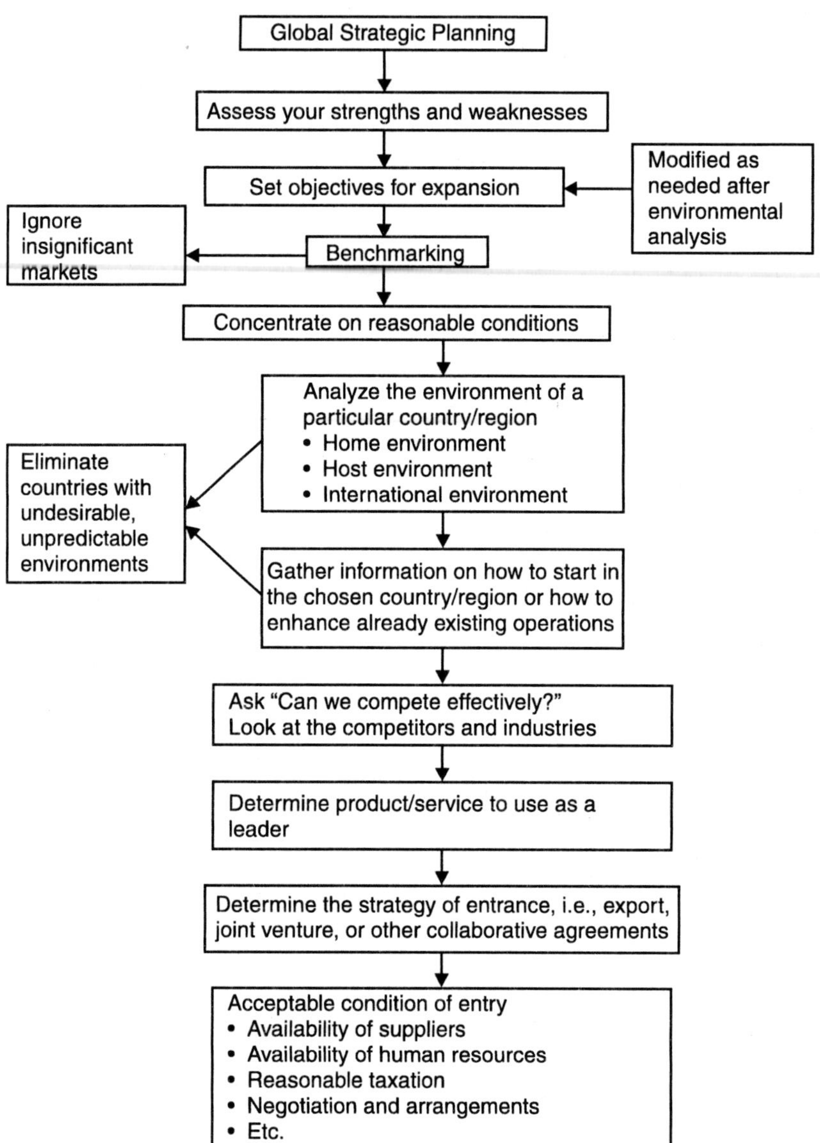

FIGURE 6.1. Global Strategic Planning

Export/Import

The simplest way to get into a foreign market is perhaps by exporting products. Exports are the products and services produced in one country and sold in another. Usually, business firms export their products to countries where greater demand and profits are found. However, some firms export their products to other countries because their domestic demand is not large enough to sustain their operation. Industries such as chemicals, computers, and aerospace depend heavily upon exports for sales and profits. The largest U.S. export category is farm products, accounting for about 18 percent of exports.

Imports are goods and services sold in one country that were produced in another country. In the United States, more services are exported than imported, and more goods are imported than exported. The United States is heavily dependent on imports of petroleum, toys, and coffee.

The difference in value between a country's total exports and its total imports is called the *balance of trade*. When exports exceed imports, a favorable balance of trade exists. When imports exceed exports, this is an unfavorable balance of trade. The United States has had an unfavorable balance of trade every year since 1971, except for 1973.

The ratio of one currency to another is called *foreign exchange rate*. This shows how much a unit of one currency is worth in terms of another. The supply and demand for a certain currency determines its value on foreign exchange markets. Fluctuating exchange rates add another element of risk to international businesses.

It is important to know that the higher the value of the U.S. dollar against foreign currencies, the harder it is for international business to export goods and services. The weaker the value of the dollar against foreign currencies, the easier it is for exporters to sell goods and services on the international market. This is because much of world trade is conducted in dollars, which serves as a convenient measure of worth across the globe.

Licensing and Franchising

Licensing in the international context is defined as an agreement in which a licensor gives the right (license) to a foreign company to sell its products in return for royalty fees or other compensation. For example, Yoplait is a French yogurt licensed for production in the United States. The U.S. producer pays a percentage of its income to the French company. The licensor's patent, trademark, copyright, and the rights to use certain technology or production processes can be granted to a foreign licensee in return for a stated percentage of the licensee's sales revenues or profits.

The use of licensing varies from country to country. For example, Korean firms exceeded $4 billion in 1995, with 75 percent of that going to U.S. or Japanese licensors. Most international licensing occurs between industrialized companies. However, some international licensing does occur in companies that are not as technologically advanced.[32]

Franchising is a form of licensing in which a franchisee can operate a store much like a branch of the original franchising company but retain its own profit. In return for the common promotion, internal design, and a common brand name and products, each franchisee has to pay a fee to the franchiser or agree to return the store to the original company after a certain period of operation. Franchising is similar to licensing. It grants the right to distribute a company's product or service in a particular geographic territory.

The advantages of licensing and franchising are obvious:

1. The licenser/franchiser does not have to invest physically in a foreign country, so less effort and resources are required.
2. As licensees or franchisees are to bear the risk of investment, there is limited risk to the licensor or franchisers.
3. A company can grow rapidly within a short time with a minimum outlay of cash.

However, there are disadvantages with licensing and franchising, too. For example, the company has to maintain the consistency of the products for all the franchisees or licensees. This requires much coordination between headquarters and individual licensees and franchisers. In addition, franchisers and licensers do not receive as much profit as owners of overseas branches, since each licensee or franchiser retains their own profit. Finally, franchising may create competitors.

Foreign Direct Investment

Exporting and importing usually incur additional costs such as tariff and transportation costs. Having a production facility located directly in the overseas market, the so-called *foreign direct investment* (FDI), can solve the problem. The best example is Coca-Cola, which has bottling plants in almost all its major markets. Sometimes, MNCs may choose to use a third country as an export platform and export their products to the target country so as to avoid import tariffs incurred when products are directly imported from the home country. In the case of trading blocs, which may have more favorable import treatment of bloc members, placing production facilities in one of the member countries can avoid the potential threat of tariffs.

Direct investment in overseas operations and manufacturing plants demands substantial capital outlays and requires managers to develop international skills. FDI gives management some kind of control over international subsidiaries.

Strategic Alliances

If complete ownership of a foreign company is not desirable, strategic alliance is a way to make foreign direct investment possible. Under a *strategic alliance,* a firm contracts with another firm to work on a specific project. The life of an alliance is limited only to the life of the project. Strategic alliance, therefore, is very flexible and less risky.

The 1980s saw a jump in cooperative agreements and alliances between MNCs. These alliances primarily involve high technology industry MNCs in Europe, North America, and Asia. Such alliances can provide benefits such as access to complementary resources, the sharing of large research and development expenses, and the spreading of risk. Possible disadvantages include loss of competitive strength through cultural misunderstandings, poor communication, and the sharing of technology. Both parties must avoid such problems through correct management of the alliance. As strategic alliances gain importance, competitive advantage is increasingly determined by a firm's ability to create, acquire, and coordinate the use of resources across national boundaries rather than the exclusive appropriation of strategic assets.[33]

According to a survey conducted by management consulting firm McKinsey and Co. of 150 large cross-border alliances established over the past two decades, only half of the alliances were economically advantageous for both partners. The survey found that the average life expectancy of the alliances was only seven years. Firms are generally entering into cross-border alliances in order to penetrate markets otherwise closed to them; to acquire new technology, management skills, or entrepreneurial strength; and to achieve economies of scale to meet specific marketing challenges. Experts say that firms considering alliances should engage in active joint venture projects, carefully examine the extent of cross-holdings, and negotiate a way to unwind the venture before entering into it.[34]

Joint Ventures

In a *joint venture,* two or more different firms come together and establish a new third firm in a foreign country. Similar to strategic alliance, each firm supplies its expertise and shares the profits of the new firm. Unlike strategic alliance, the life of a joint venture can last as long as the life of the new firm. In some developing countries such as China, regulations make joint ventures the only way to gain entrance into the market. Laws may prohibit foreign investment unless local companies or the government own a portion. Therefore, a joint venture with a local firm in such a country is a must. It is important to mention that in a joint venture two or more firms come together as partners in a business, sharing the costs and risks of investing in an international project.

A joint venture may be between an upstream input supplier (local company) and a downstream final goods producer (MNC). The upstream firm benefits from the MNC's ability to produce an input that is not available locally. Similarly, the MNC benefits from the local firm's entrepreneurial knowledge of local conditions, cheaper inputs, and ties to important buyers and the government.[35]

Joint ventures have become increasingly popular. For example, by 1995 the number of airline alliances rose from 324 to 389. They are the mode of choice for approximately 35 percent of U.S. multinationals and in 40 to 45 percent of foreign subsidiaries formed by Japanese multinationals.[36]

A very successful example of joint venture is Caterpillar and Mitsubishi in Japan. Japan is the largest market for Caterpillar's heavy machines such as bulldozers. With Mitsubishi's welding technology, which it developed in shipbuilding, Caterpillar is able to redesign its models to fit Japan's small construction sites and sell them through Mitsubishi's network, called a *keiretsu.*

Similar to strategic alliances, joint ventures are subject to the problems of communication, cultural differences, and sharing of technology and profits. Since in most cases MNCs' partners are local companies that may differ substantially in terms of business practices and cultures, it takes more effort for both parties to resolve problems.

Complete Ownership of Overseas Subsidiaries

Owning an overseas subsidiary gives the firm complete control of its overseas operation. Besides, it allows the firm to take 100 percent of the profit. However, the firm has to bear 100 percent of the risk and make a substantial effort to penetrate a foreign market without help from local firms.

Degree of Control Over Foreign Environment

The more a corporation can impact and influence the host country, the more easily it can pursue its own objectives. Large corporations have a greater effect on developing countries than smaller ones for several reasons:

1. *Size.* According to Ball and McCulloch, the total sales of General Motors Corporation were less than the gross national product of only twenty-one nations.[37] GM sales exceeded the GNP of all other nations.[38]
2. *Geographic diversification.* Large corporations are generally geographically diversified in their operations and are minimally dependent on any single location. This increases their bargaining power in their relationship with host countries. The power differential between two parties determines which will be most influential. The greater the MNC's power, the more likely it can affect the environment of the host country.
3. *MNC's flexibility.* The MNC's flexibility refers to its ability to adapt to changing environments. MNCs have diversified in many ways (products, processes, locations, etc.), which enable them to respond to any kind of threat or opportunity in the environment.

International Organizations

MNCs can obtain assistance from various international organizations that set regulations for multicountry business. Some of these international organizations are the United Nations (UN), the World Bank, the International Monetary Fund (IMF), and the International Organization for Standardization (ISO), as well as entities that enforce treaties of different countries and set exchange rates. The main purposes of the multinational organizations are to facilitate, encourage, and provide security for the international exchange of products, services, and money. Therefore, these multinational organizations and their available resources must be considered and integrated in the strategic planning process of an MNC.

The World Bank is especially important and consists of the International Bank for Reconstruction and Development, the International Finance Corporation (IFC), and the International Development Association.[39] The World Bank mainly supplies the less-developed countries (LDCs) with loans and credit. For example, the IMF and the World Bank considered financing a "social safety net" for Russians to cushion the blow of factory closings and layoffs.[40] Because the LDCs spend millions of borrowed dollars on products and services to realize greater development and self-sufficiency, an

MNC should explore these potential markets. Knowledge of the activities of the World Bank can be a valuable means of contacting potential buyers in the LDCs.

Another way the World Bank (as an example) can facilitate a business relation is to bring attention to the money needs of business partners in an LDC. The World Bank can also serve as an arbitrator, helping to resolve difficulties encountered by businesses in foreign countries. Just the fact that the World Bank exists and provides this function radically impacts the international environment and generally contributes to an atmosphere of fair play. Further, when MNCs and foreign governments are mutually supported by one of the multinational organizations, such as the World Bank, it will probably result in an improved infrastructure for the developing host country. This facilitates business relations when transportation of products and good communication networks are crucial.

The World Bank facilitates enormous projects between nations and huge MNCs. The International Organization for Standardization, on the other hand, facilitates business relations of all different sizes, since it standardizes measurements. Both organizations are representative of all multinational organizations in facilitating international business by giving pertinent information and providing security.

However, the most challenging international economic variables for strategic planners are interest rates, inflation rates, and currency exchange rates. For example, the cost of borrowing money is very high in Latin American countries and can exceed 100 percent. High interest rates are often accompanied by excessive rates of inflation. Countries such as Brazil have experienced inflation rates of 2,700 percent. Common decisions such as pricing products or estimating costs become almost impossible to make under such conditions.[41]

Multinational organizations are catalysts of international business and have to be integrated in the strategic planning process from the beginning. Multinational organizations can even further impact the implementation and control of the chosen strategy. For example, if the World Bank has a major interest in a project and provides financing, it will support that project and help ensure success. Therefore, a company which chooses a strategic alternative that involves one of the international organizations will probably gain support from one of the most powerful forces in the world.

Barriers to International Trade

The barriers to international trade can be divided into the following types. The first type is the natural barriers such as the distance between countries and the physical features represented by the mountains and oceans that prevent trade. The second type is the tariff barrier. A *tariff* is a duty or tax that a government puts on products that are imported into or exported from a particular country. Revenues from tariffs are set at low rates because the purpose is to raise money, not to reduce imports. However, protective tariffs are set at a higher rate to discourage imports of foreign products that are priced lower than domestic products. They are usually imposed to protect home industries, especially the infant ones. The third type of barrier includes the nontariff controls such as the quota and the embargo. *Quota* is the maximum amount of a product that can be imported to a country. The *embargo* is a prohibition or suspension of foreign trade of specific imports or exports. Another type of trade barrier is dumping of products in a foreign market at prices that are below either the home-market price or the full cost of producing it. U.S. firms often complain about dumping by foreign firms in the domestic market. In addition, cultural barriers that include language differences, the role of religion, and values and attitudes are among the most important challenges to international managers.

Many attempts have been made to promote trade between different countries. Nations enter into agreements with each other to promote trade. Many of these nations have succeeded in removing barriers to trade, as in NAFTA, EEC, Pacific Rim, and many other similar agreements. The General Agreement on Tariffs and Trade is a multilateral treaty through which member nations act jointly to reduce trade barriers. This agreement has been in operation since January 1, 1948. The Uruguay Round started in 1986 to extend trade liberalization and to widen the GATT treaty. In January 1995, the World Trade Organization (WTO) was established by GATT to oversee the provisions of the Uruguay Round and any resulting trade disputes.

The European Economic Community (EEC) established a single, unified market in the beginning of 1993 called the European Union (EU) that promotes trade and reduces barriers. U.S. exporters now face a uniform set of rules, regulations, and standards when they deal with European Union countries.

The Pacific Rim, on the other hand, has been growing at a tremendous pace. It includes Japan, Singapore, Hong Kong, Taiwan, and South Korea. Other growing markets are in China, Eastern Europe, and the former Soviet Union. These represent yet another challenge to U.S. companies.

Attempts are also made on the country level. The U.S. Department of Commerce, Bureau of International Commerce organizes trade missions, operates permanent trade centers abroad, and sponsors district export expansion councils. The U.S. Department of State also helps U.S. firms promote their products in foreign markets. Moreover, state and local governments and private groups promote trade for their interests.

MULTINATIONAL CHALLENGES

As a firm expands globally, having subsidiaries abroad is almost unavoidable. Unlike domestic ones, overseas subsidiaries are subjected to dual pressures from the need to adapt to the local environment and the need to maintain consistency within the organization.[42] Beside this trade-off, MNCs have to face the problem of sending expatriate managers overseas to supervise the operations there.

Conflicts Between MNCs and the Local Environment

MNCs' operations in foreign countries often give rise to conflicts between the MNC and the host country with regard to business, developmental, environmental, health, and safety protection issues. MNCs have been frequently subject to charges of exploitation and colonization in third world countries. The sources of these conflicts are mainly the divergence of goals and the abuse of power both by MNCs and the host countries.[43] For instance, increased automation aimed at promoting safety may run counter to host policies for promoting local employment; location in a densely populated area with a large pool of potential workers may be incompatible with safety; and reliance on trained foreign experts may conflict with the desire for local control.

Organizational routines that differ across national cultures also contribute to the conflicts between MNCs and host countries. For example, the expatriate Japanese practice of tapping inattentive American factory workers on the head with long wooden sticks led to escalating resentment and violence before Mazda stopped the practice. To lessen the conflicts, role-based routines must be painstakingly taught to workers.[44] Unfortunately, many MNC managers are often insulated from clearly seeing potential in understanding the cultures of nations, too. Rather than imposing their will on company units overseas, leaders of MNCs should give up the mind-set and adapt to the different environment.[45]

To maintain a lasting, harmonized relationship with the local environment, MNCs should have an ethical commitment to providing the host country workforce with adequate training to prepare expatriate managers for their new assignment.[46] Others suggest MNCs should allow the local population greater access to ownership and control of productive assets, sharing surpluses with local employees and impacted communities, and decentralizing decision making concerning activities that affect the local quality of life.[47]

Multinational corporations must operate in a two-way open system. This means it welcomes inputs from the host government and provides information about its operation to the public. The expectation from the MNC abroad is to act ethically and in a socially responsible way. Ethical practices can enhance overall corporate health and improve relationships with the stakeholders. Therefore, cooperation between the MNC and the host country's government is highly recommended.

> MNCs share information based on global experiences, provide input into host-government developmental policies, and aid in their implementation; the government, in turn, would provide a reasonable regulatory environment. Such a relationship calls for ongoing interactions among officials at all levels of both parties, with the local corporate subsidiary playing a critical role.[48]

The host government has a responsibility to set rules that are clear, consistent, and economically and technically feasible.

Coordination Between Headquarters and Overseas Subsidiaries

The second challenge facing MNCs is how to coordinate the relationship between headquarters and overseas subsidiaries. There are usually two different approaches to managing this relationship. Under the *differentiated fit approach,* the greater the extent to which an MNC differentiates the formal structure of its headquarters-subsidiary relationship to fit the contexts of its various subsidiaries, the better the performance of the organization as a whole. Under the *shared values approach,* a high degree of shared values between the headquarters and subsidiaries also enhances the MNC's performance. Although these two approaches are alternatives, they are not mutually exclusive. In fact, MNCs that are able to simultaneously implement the two approaches have the best performance.[49]

Coca-Cola, for example, tightly coordinates R&D and marketing worldwide to maintain a consistent brand name, concentrate formula, market positioning, and advertising theme. Its manufacturing, however, is adapted to each location. The blending of the two approaches makes Coke the most famous brand in the world.

Studies have found that there are differences in managing headquarters-subsidiary relations across countries. In one study, Japanese MNCs are found to empower subsidiaries in decision making to a high degree. U.S. MNCs, in contrast, are found to give lower degrees of decision-making autonomy to subsidiaries.[50] Another study found that subsidiaries pursuing strategies with a high degree of integration with their corporate parent make much more extensive use of "formal" and "subtle" coordination mechanisms. The same study also found that the subtle mechanisms of coordination appear to play a serious role once the formal ones have been put in place, as the need for coordination escalates. These findings indicate that MNCs that are trying to integrate their activities more closely must achieve a higher level of coordination.[51]

In terms of localization, a study found that Japanese overseas subsidiaries adopted a localization policy closely following the personnel practices of local companies that had similar organizational characteristics. In comparison, American personnel practices reflected greater sensitivity to variations in organizational characteristics, as well as greater headquarters influence.[52]

Regarding human resource practices in a foreign environment, MNCs often face decisions about whether to use expatriates or nationals in management positions. An expatriate is an employee that is assigned to work in a subsidiary abroad. Among the issues that must be considered are the appropriate length of time for an expatriate assignment, compensation and benefits for expatriate managers, recruitment for international positions, and the reentry of transferred managers.[53]

In general, it is essential that subsidiaries have independent international experience, strength in upstream activities, and broad-based managerial expertise. It is also important that subsidiaries continually assess the competitive environment and subsidiary strengths and build organizational and managerial skills.[54]

Other Challenges

Because different safety standards prevail in various countries, business firms should be very careful about the products they import from an unfamiliar foreign country. According to S. Joe Bhatia, Vice President of External Affairs at Underwriters Laboratories, it is becoming increasingly difficult to be certain that materials approved by some testing organizations are in fact safe. There is a risk that some new players in the international safety testing marketplace are looking at product certification as a commercial activity, without due concer for a complete risk assessment.[55]

Doing business overseas means that U.S. dollars must be converted to a foreign currency for investment and back to U.S. dollars for profit repatriation. Due to fluctuating exchange rates, the amount of capital will change. The uncertainty resulting from the fluctuation of exchange rates is an exchange rate risk that can be hedged with financial derivatives such as futures and forward contracts, interest rate swaps, options, etc.

Terrorism is another threat to overseas operation. MNCs' overseas subsidiaries often become the target of terrorists who are usually working against MNCs' home governments. Despite such a threat, a survey conducted in 1993 found that fewer than half of Fortune 500 companies had formal programs to reduce the effect of terrorism. For those with antiterrorist programs, the survey found that they spend money on security equipment and not on training executives and their families. The training that did happen focused on handling weapons and avoiding being kidnapped. In addition, the respondents in the survey pointed out that there was lack of federal government assistance in dealing with terrorists.[56] This situation has changed since September 11, 2001. Many companies have improved their security measures, especially those in the airline industry. The government has also enacted new regulations concerning security in an attempt to prevent future terrorist attacks.[57]

HOW TO COMPETE GLOBALLY

Many American companies, such as Hewlett-Packard, have significantly improved their positions in the market by adopting many of the tactics used by Japanese firms.[58]

According to an article by the originator of the total quality control concept, three new forces are combining to create a competitive crisis for today's international companies, and the most powerful competitive growth strategy for meeting the challenge is total quality. The three critical forces are (1) the formation of a global marketplace that is increasingly open to competitors from all types and sizes of businesses, (2) buyers' growing focus on quality, and (3) the huge economic pressure on firms that results from the new international market and the drive for affordable quality. In these chaotic times, total quality is the ultimate competitive connector to customers, employees, and suppliers. The discipline rigorously integrates the business's resources with best-in-class management processes in the areas of customer satisfaction, operating cost, leadership, and human resource effectiveness.[59]

U.S. COMPETITIVENESS

A business firm's competitiveness depends on its productivity, which in turn depends on technology. Similarly, a country's competitiveness also depends on its abundance in resources, productivity, and technology. A country's competitiveness includes the following:

1. Availability of infrastructure
2. Availability of educated labor force
3. Availability of other resources and technology
4. Political stability
5. Economic conditions that are conducive to trade and development
6. Flexible government policies that will encourage investment

U.S. businesses' massive investment in information technology over the past twenty to twenty-five years may finally be paying off in the form of increased productivity and greater global competitiveness.

The United States has overtaken Japan to become the world's most competitive economy for the first time since 1985, according to the 1994 *World Competitiveness Report* issued by the International Institute for Management and Development and the World Economic Forum. The report attributes the United States' achievement to the strength of the country's economic recovery, entrepreneurship, and almost a decade of economic restructuring. It warns, however, that low savings rates and poor secondary-school education and work attitudes are cause for concern and could lead to a longer-term decline if left uncorrected.[60]

Research by economist Frank Lichtenberg of the Columbia Business School indicates that computer equipment and employment jointly contribute some 21 percent of the output of the companies studied, even though they only account for about 10 percent of labor costs and 10 to 15 percent of total capital expenditures. Moreover, information technology investment and radical restructuring among U.S. businesses should leave them well positioned once the global economy enters a new broad cyclical expansion phase. Several studies have shown that the United States already has a big productivity lead over Europe and Asia in the manufacturing, services, and technology sectors. Much of this success stems from computer investment.[61]

The United States, however, can no longer rely on its corporations to automatically retain global competitiveness. Despite the decline of trade unions, the reduction of corporate taxes, and greater concessions from state and local governments, many indicators of American competitiveness abroad have not yet turned around. These strategies have failed because it is unclear that U.S. businesses have shown a willingness to compete in ways similar to those of their Japanese rivals. Where Japanese companies have cut prices to expand future sales and market shares, U.S. companies have a strong preference for short-term profits and a strong aversion to price cutting. In addition, U.S. firms have come to rely upon corporate expansion strategies such as mergers to expand business while avoiding competition. Thus, firms have not translated the savings from lower labor costs and taxes into lower, more competitive prices. As a result, a serious reassessment of U.S. corporate tax policy and labor law is needed.[62]

American capitalism is due to decline because the American system is built around competitiveness, a highly dysfunctional and destructive quality in an age when firms most need cooperative teamwork inside their organization and collaborative partners outside them to prevail in global markets. According to business historian Alfred D. Chandler, the dynamics of industrial capitalism that the U.S. practices emphasizes a competitive managerial-style capitalism in which companies run by a professional managerial class compete fiercely with one another for market share. In contrast, Germany has cooperative managerial capitalism, in which managers often prefer to negotiate with one another to maintain market share. If the post-2000 period is indeed the era of strategic alliances, a company's ability to compete will depend far more on its cooperative skills than on its competitive zeal. Germany's version of capitalism appears far more suited for success in global markets.[63]

TOMORROW'S ORGANIZATIONS

Historically, organizations have been designed around largely autonomous, self-contained, and traditional functions such as accounting, finance, human resources, strategic planning, law, and marketing. Although these functions remain important, today's business environment calls for organizational structures that also address crisis management, issues management, environmentalism, and ethics. Tomorrow's organizations should be structured around five new organizational entities: a leadership institute, a knowledge/learning center, a recovery/development center, a world service/spiritual center, and a world-class operations center. The centers contribute uniquely to the wisdom of the leadership institute and, therefore, to the organization as a whole.[64]

REVIEW QUESTIONS

1. What are the advantages of internationalization?
2. What is international strategic management? Describe the importance of planning in internationalization.
3. What are the factors affecting foreign environments?
4. What are the three modes of internationalization?
5. What are the four basic international corporate strategies formulated by Leontiades?

6. What are the different ways to enter a foreign market?
7. What are the conflicts that arise between MNCs and the local environment? How can relations be harmonized?
8. What is the position of the United States in the global competitive market?

NOTES

1. Bureau of Economic Analysis, available online at: <http://www.bea.doc.gov/bea/international/bp_web/simple.cfm>; accessed September 6, 2002.

2. O'Shea, D. (1994). Ameritech, Deutsche Telekom win slice of Hungarian telco. *Telephony,* 226(1), 4-5.

3. Amdur, M. (1994). The boundless Ted Turner: Road to globalization. *Broadcasting and Cable,* 124(15), 34-36.

4. Gibney, F. (1997). Stumbling giants. *Time,* 235(22), 75.

5. Anonymous (2000). End of merger. *Wall Street Journal,* July 24, A1.

6. Salinas-Leon, R. (1994). Economic stability and monetary policy. *Business Mexico,* 4(1,2), 70-72. Globalization special issue.

7. Coca-Cola Web site available online at <www2.coca-cola.com/>; accessed August 20, 2002.

8. Huey, J. (1993). The world's best brand. *Fortune,* 127(11), 44-54.

9. Bowles, R. (1997). Food for thought. *The China Business Review,* Volume 7, pp. 8-11.

10. Liu, Y. and Sullivan, R. (1999). Anatomy of the Greater China market. *Business Research Yearbook,* Volume VI, pp. 237-238.

11. Statistics (1994). *China-Hong Kong Economic Monthly,* February, p. 84.

12. Byrnes, N. (1994). Stars of stage, screen, and Toys 'R' Us. *BusinessWeek,* December 5, p. 46.

13. Kaplan, R. (1994). Ad agencies take on the world. *International Management* (Europe Edition), 49(3), 50-52.

14. Thompson, A. A. and Strickland, A. J. III (1996). *Strategic Management: Concepts and Cases,* Ninth Edition. Homewood, IL: Richard D. Irwin, Inc., p. 221.

15. Rue, L. W. and Byars, L. L. (1989). *Management: Theory and Application,* Fifth Edition. Homewood, IL: Richard D. Irwin, Inc., pp. 211-213.

16. Bartlett, C. A. and Randan, U. S. (1986). Case: Kentucky Fried Chicken (Japan) Ltd. *Harvard Business School Case,* 387-443.

17. Eom, S. B. (1994). Transnational management systems: An emerging tool for global strategic management. S.A.M. *Advanced Management Journal,* 59(2), 22-27.

18. Vazzana, G. S., Zbib, I. J., and Nelson, W. E. (1991). Unified European market: Opportunities and threats for small businesses. In Macrae, N., Eurotrends. *International Management,* March, pp. 14-15.

19. Pride, W. M., Hughes, R. J., and Kapoor, J. R. (1999). *Business,* Sixth edition. Boston: Houghton Mifflin Co., p. 67.

20. Stapenhurst, F. (1992). The rise and fall of political risk assessment? *Management Decision,* 30(5), 54-57.

21. Akhter, S. H. (1993). Forced withdrawal from a country market: Managing political risk. *Business Horizons,* 36(3), 47-54.

22. Keatley, R. (1994). APEC may finally draft rules to level playing field for foreign investment. *The Wall Street Journal,* January 28, A4.

23. McRae Watts, R. (2001). Commercializing discontinuous innovations. *Research Technology Management,* 44(6), 27.

24. Fram, E. H. (1994). Globalization of markets and shopping stress: Cross-country comparisons. *Business Horizons,* 37(1), 17-23.

25. Ono, Y. (1994). The Japanese public keeps a wary eye on grains of truth. *The Wall Street Journal,* January 12, A 1,4.

26. Davis, B. (1994). U.S. is hoping to blend environmental world trade issues at Morocco meeting. *The Wall Street Journal,* January 10, A9.

27. Campbell, D. (1994). Foreign investment, labor immobility and the quality of employment. *International Labor Review,* 133(2), 185-204.

28. Leontiades, M. (1982). The confusing words of business policy. *Academy of Management Review,* 7(1), 46.

29. Keller, J. (1993). AT&T to give foreign units more autonomy. *The Wall Street Journal,* December 13, A 3,4.

30. Gibson, R. (1993). Brunswick pins hopes on expanding bowling business. *The Wall Street Journal,* December 13, B 4,3.

31. Ball, D. A., and McCulloch, W. H. Jr. (2001). *International Business: The Challenge of Global Competition* (Seventh Edition). New York: Irvin McGraw-Hill.

32. Beamish, P., Morrison, A., and Rosenzweig, P. M. (1997). *International Management: Text and Cases.* Burr Ridge, IL: Richard D. Irwin, Inc.

33. Gugler, P. (1992). Building transnational alliances to create competitive advantage. *Long Range Planning,* 25(1), 90-92.

34. McIntyre, F. S., Young, J. A., and Gilbert, F. W. (1994). Domestic versus cross-border alliances: An exploratory study of relationalism. *Institutional Investor,* 28(5), 113-116.

35. Purkayastha, D. (1993). Firm-specific advantages, multinational joint ventures and host country tariff policy. *Southern Economic Journal,* 60(1), 89-95.

36. Beamish, Morrison, and Rosenzweig, *International Management: Text and Cases.*

37. Ball and McCulloch, *International Business,* pp. 11-12.

38. Ibid., p. 281.

39. Whittaker, J. (1978). *Strategic Planning in a Rapidly Changing Environment.* Washington, DC: Lexington Books, p. 21.

40. More aid to Russia could come from international institutions (1994). *The Wall Street Journal,* January 21, A 1,5.

41. Wheelen, T. L. and Hunger, D. (2000). *Strategic Management and Business Policy.* Upper Saddle River, NJ: Prentice-Hall, p. 156.

42. Rosenzweig, P. M. (1991). Organizational environments and the multinational enterprise. *The Academy of Management Review,* 16(3), 340-361.

43. Aldaeaj, H. (1991). A power model of multinational corporation–Nation-state relationships. *S.A.M. Advanced Management Journal,* 56(3), 11-17.

44. Kilduff, M. (1992). Performance and interaction routines in multinational corporations. *Journal of International Business Studies,* 23(1), 133-145.

45. Chan, C. (1994). Whose empire is this, anyway? Reflections on the empire state of multinational corporations. *Business Horizons,* 37(4), 51-54.

46. Vance, C. M. (1993). An ethical argument for host country workforce training and development in the expatriate management assignment. *Journal of Business Ethics,* 12(8), 635-641.

47. Sethi, S. P. (1993). Operational modes for multinational corporations in post-apartheid South Africa: A proposal for a code of affirmative action in the market place. *Journal of Business Ethics,* 12(1), 1-12.

48. Amba-Rao, S. C. (1993). Multinational corporate social responsibility, ethics, interactions and third world governments: An agenda for the 1990s. *Journal of Business Ethics,* 12(7), 553-572.

49. Nohria, N. (1994). Differentiated fit and shared values: Alternatives for managing headquarter relations. *Strategic Management Journal,* 15(6), 491-502.

50. Kriger, M. (1992). Strategic mindsets and decision-making autonomy in U.S. and Japanese MNCs. *Management International Review,* 32(4), 327-343.

51. Martinez, J. I. (1991). Coordination demands of international strategies. *Journal of International Business Studies,* 22(4), 429-444.

52. Headquarters, host-culture and organizational influences on HRM policies and practices (1993). *Management International Review,* 33(4), 361-383.

53. Alternative policies for international transfers of managers (1994). *Management International Review,* 34(1), 71-82. International Management special issue.

54. Morrison, A. J. (1993). Developing global subsidiary mandates. *Business Quarterly,* 57(4), 104-105.

55. Mulcahy, C. (1994). Globalization expands product risk. *National Underwriter* (Property and Casualty/Risk and Benefits Management Edition), 98(16), 3.

56. Harvey, M. G. (1993). A survey of corporate programs for managing terrorist threats. *Journal of International Business Studies,* 24(3), 465-478.

57. Siegel, D. (2002). Airport focus. *Attache* (US Airways publication), July, p. 8.

58. How HP used tactics of the Japanese to beat them at their game (1994). *The Wall Street Journal* (Eastern Edition), September 8, A1.

59. Feigenbaum, A. (1994). How total quality counters three forces of international competitiveness. *National Productivity Review,* 13(3), 327-330.

60. Global report finds U.S. has replaced Japan as most competitive economy (1994). *The Wall Street Journal* (Eastern Edition), September 7, A3.

61. Korentz, G. (1994). Computers may really be paying off—And they're giving the U.S. a nice competitive edge. *BusinessWeek,* 20(3358), 33-38.

62. Karier, T. (1994). Competitiveness and American enterprise. *Challenge* (Armonk, NY), 37(1), 40-44.

63. Maital, S. (1994). The bug in U.S. capitalism. *Across the Board,* 31(1), 53-54.

64. Mitroff, I. I. (1994). Radical surgery: What will tomorrow's organizations look like? *Academy of Management Executive,* 8(2), 11-21.

Chapter 7

Corporate Structure and Implementation

INTRODUCTION

The implementation process of strategic management requires putting strategies into action. Successful strategy formulation alone does not guarantee success. If the strategy cannot be translated into action, then the resources and the energies put forth are worthless. *Strategy implementation* refers to the way a company structures itself in order to execute its strategic plan efficiently and achieve its objectives.

In the first section of this chapter, we investigate the general manager's role in the implementation process and the relationship between strategy formulation and strategy implementation. Then we examine key managerial tools that are commonly used to implement chosen strategies. In addition to functional strategies, we look at organizational structure, resources, culture, policy, reward systems, and leadership as key tools in implementation and control. We are able to conclude that the impact of the strategy control is a feedback mechanism for adjusting or changing strategy formulation and strategy implementation.

STRATEGY IMPLEMENTATION

Strategy implementation is accomplished through organizational design and structure. It is the way the company chooses to create its arrangements and design that will help it to achieve the formulated strategy efficiently and effectively. Strategic implementation is how to assign tasks and responsibilities to members of the organization and how to group them into departments or divisions. Then the task is finding the best way to connect the activities of different people in various divisions.

Organizational design deals with the selection of organizational structures and control systems that will assure the application of the company's strategy effectively and create or sustain its competitive advantage. The organization should adopt a combination of structure and control systems that improve quality, create value, reduce cost, and improve communication.

Management should find out how to motivate corporate employees and provide them with the incentives to achieve efficiency, quality, innovation, and customer satisfaction. Management must also learn how to coordinate employee activities so that they work together effectively to implement strategy that increases the company's competitive position. Organizational design and control shape the way people behave and determine how they will act in the organizational setting.

Strategy implementation is the action that converts the strategic plan into reality and accomplishment. Creating a company climate and structure that forces planning and encourages participation is essential in the implementation process. Top management must communicate the end result of strategy formulation (the plan) to all those involved in the implementation stages. In order to avoid any confusion in the implementation stages, policies and appropriate assumptions must be developed and communicated. A contingency plan must be developed, and this can help implementation proceed smoothly when the unexpected occurs. It will be troublesome for the organization to carry out strategy implementation according to personal assumptions and preferences. Action and emergent plans must reflect and directly relate to the major objectives of the organization. During implementation, strategies must be regularly reviewed to more appropriately reflect the new information about changes in the environment.

Boseman and colleagues suggest that effective strategy implementation should focus on four critical factors. These elements are the organizational structure, the corporate culture, human resources, and organizational rewards. The relationship between these four factors and organization strategy has a great impact on the outcome of strategy implementation.[1]

Corporate Structure and Strategy Implementation

Strategy outlines the tasks that must be performed and structure coordinates the people who perform those tasks. Therefore, strategy and structure must have a proper fit. The right type of employee at an appropriate number ensures that tasks can be carried out in a manner consistent with overall strategy if situated in the proper place within an organization. One of the most important aspects of organizational structure is the way the company decides to divide itself into different divisions or departments. This division is based on people skills and experience as well as the match between the human resources, the task, and the equipment available. The next important aspect of the structuring is how to create an environment for all those divisions or departments so that they can work together efficiently and achieve the company's objectives.

In the first aspect, the company tries to allocate people and resources to organizational tasks. This requires management to decide how to delegate decision-making authority in the organization. (Management chooses the appropriate number of hierarchical levels and the correct span of controls.) It also requires management to decide the way labor should be divided in the organization and the appropriate matching with organizational tasks. Management must decide how much authority should be delegated to managers at the divisional or functional level as well as how to divide up people and tasks into functions and divisions to ensure their ability to create value for the organization. For example, should there be separate R&D and marketing departments or should they be combined?

In the second aspect, management attempts to obtain an acceptable level of coordination between human resources and their functions to accomplish the required assignment. These two aspects of implementation determine how an organizational structure operates and assists in the mechanism of organizational control.

Essentially, both strategy and structure should vary according to the type of organization being studied. For a single-SBU firm, both strategy and structure might be very simple. In a conglomerate corporation, both should reflect the complexity of the situation.

The process of structuring an organization begins with the manager's preference for the appropriate number of hierarchical levels in the company and the appropriate span of control for each manager. The *span of control* is the number of subordinates a manager directly manages. The primary decision is between (1) a *flat structure* with few hierarchical levels, and thus a relatively wide span of control; or (2) a *tall structure* with many levels and a small span of control. The type of structure a company chooses depends heavily on the number of employees and the type of business. In general, most companies have fewer than nine levels. Too many levels in the hierarchy may create some problems. For example, the tall structure is very expensive because it requires more managers. Managers' salaries, expenses, and other benefits cost a great deal of resources. Communication between different levels in the hierarchy and integration become difficult.

Integration is the way in which the different divisions and departments are combined with the methods the company follows to coordinate people and functions to accomplish organizational tasks. This might lead to misinterpretation of messages and slows down the implementation process. Usually, managers in flat structures have greater areas of autonomy. Therefore, a certain level of accountability is expected.

Some companies have adopted total quality management. This concept promotes teamwork and encourages employees to exercise meaningful authority and responsibility over resources. Other companies leave less room for employees to participate. In tall structures, managers with few subordinates may have limited authority and responsibility. The appropriate authority structure in the company is an organizational strength, while a rigid one is a weakness. The company needs to choose the proper level of organizational centralization to avoid the difficulties. When managers at the top decide to keep control over all the major decisions, it is called *centralization of authority.* Decentralization, on the other hand, exists when the authority to make decisions is delegated to other managers and employees in the hierarchy. Applying a *decentralization structure* may cut down many of the communications problems, grants operating managers responsibility, and frees top managers' time for strategic decision making. Also, information can be conveyed more smoothly, decreasing the transmission of information up and down the hierarchy. Most large companies and international organizations are decentralized.

It is important that the company chooses the type of structure that matches the needs of its strategy. When the company's strategy changes over time, the structure used must be changed or modified. Seven structures, appropriate for seven different organizational situations, are discussed here. The first four, credited to Higgins and Vincze, among others, are the following:[2]

1. *Simple structure*—found in small organizations in the early stages of their existence. Usually, they involve one person, often the owner, performing all of the responsibilities needed to produce and market a product. When the company starts to expand, this structure must be changed (see Figure 7.1).
2. *Economic functional structure*—adopted as the organization grows, through the marketing of its product and as the supervisory needs of staying in control of the business increase. This situation requires a more complex structure, to meet the new position of the company. This structure requires that people with certain expertise and experience be grouped together based on their job responsibilities. Sometimes the grouping takes place according to the use of the same resources. The functional structure divides the company into various functions or subunits such as: purchasing, sales, production, finance, engineering, and so on (see Figure 7.2).
3. *Product structure*—occurs when the firm reaches an appropriate size such that two or more products are making a significant contribution to its operations. In this structure, operations are grouped according to the demand for the company's products. Sometimes, the various functions are broken down into different product lines on the basis of similarities between the products produced (see Figure 7.3).

4. *SBU structure*—sells either one product or a few to mostly a single industry and occurs when the organization becomes large, complex, and diversified. The company combines divisions based on their similarities and differences. Such a combination of operating divisions will result in a self-contained SBU. Each SBU is managed by its own management team, which acts as a liaison between the corporate management team and the management in each of the different divisions inside the SBU (see Figure 7.4).

These four structures are also described in Chandler's book *Strategy and Structure* and his organization growth model.[3] The remaining three structures include the following:

5. *Geographical structure*—used when a certain geographic region is the basis for forming departments. In this structure, each of the product lines can be listed under different geographic regions and the activities and personnel are grouped by geographic location. For example, a company can divide its operation into Northeastern, Western, and Central regions. Regional managers control operations at the regional level; however, top managers at the center continue to control the overall activities. Companies such as large department stores apply this structure extensively (see Figure 7.5).
6. *Matrix structure*—authority over staff employees is organized by project/product and functional managers at the same time. This structure is based on two principles of grouping people and resources: (a) the vertical axis operations are grouped by a functional logic, so the advantages that accrue to a functional structure are obtained; and (b) the horizontal axis operations are organized by a product or project logic, so the benefits from a product structure are obtained. The result is a complex design of reporting relationships that is distinctly different from all the structures mentioned previously (see Figure 7.6).
7. *Project structure*—falls under team management and divides certain projects among different groups which all perform the same jobs, such as marketing, finance, operations, and human resources.

FIGURE 7.1. The Simple Structure

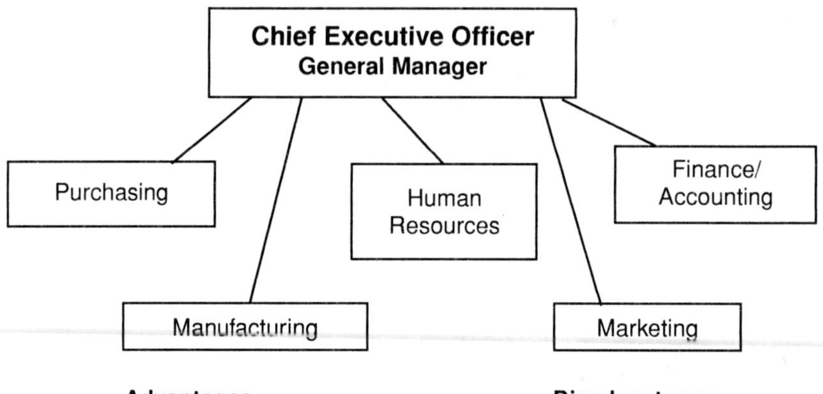

Advantages

- Takes advantage of the learning and experience curves and reaches the economic scale
- Promotes key activities within functional departments and in-depth functional expertise

Disadvantages

- Possibilities of internal conflict rather than team play
- Slower response times
- Excessive fragmentation of the company

FIGURE 7.2. Economic Functional Structure

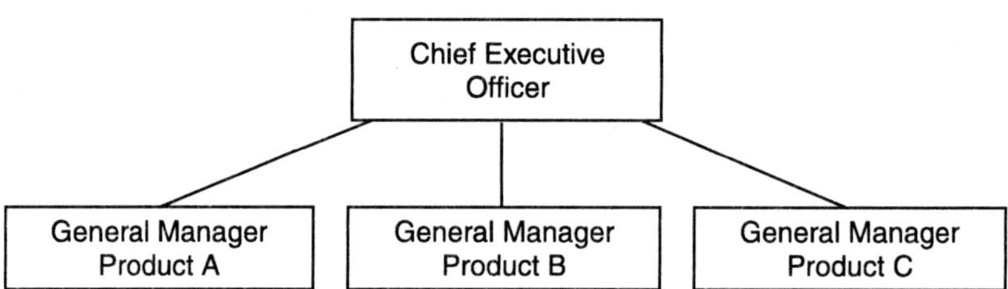

FIGURE 7.3. Product Structure

When determining which structure to use, there is no single factor that stands out or influences the decision made by management. In general, the following factors are considered important in determining the type of structure the organization chooses:

1. Size and growth
2. Technology
3. Environment

4. Top-management philosophy
5. Geographic considerations
6. Type of strategy

All of these have been mentioned and discussed in great detail, but it is necessary to remember the key factors in strategy implementation.

Corporate Culture and Strategy Implementation

The corporate culture is a pattern of norms, attitudes, values, beliefs, and customs that governs the behavior of people within the organization. It is pervasive and refers to how people within the corporation think and act as members of the organization. Culture, by its very nature, is (1) intertwined in the fabric of the organization, (2) passed on from year to year, and (3) very resistant to change.

When organizational strategy is compatible with corporate culture, strategy implementation is facilitated. However, when strategy and culture are incompatible, implementation often suffers from "strategy sabotage." In

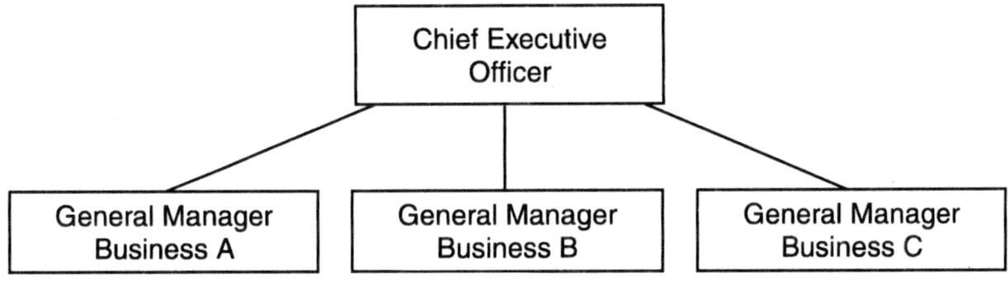

Advantages

- Makes planning and controlling by the corporate staff more manageable
- Decentralizes responsibility, putting it in closer proximity to each business environment
- Enables the CEO to handle other important corporate issues
- Makes for better coordination among divisions with similar products

Disadvantages

- The additional levels of management increase the number of personnel and overhead expenses, and may make communication slower
- Sometimes leads to excessive rivalry for resources and attention
- Creates problems determining which decisions to centralize and which to decentralize

FIGURE 7.4. SBU Structure

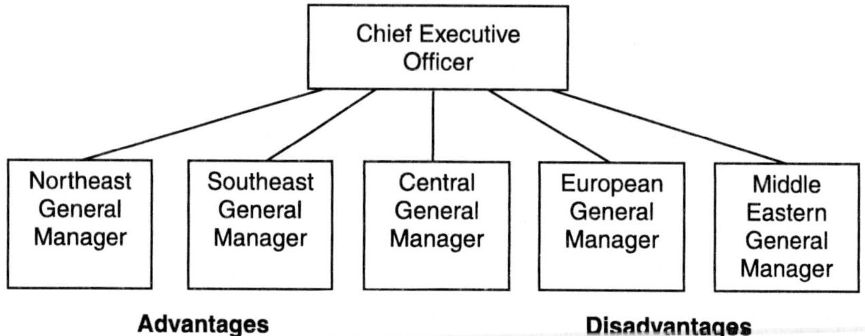

Advantages

- Products and services can be tailored
- More effective responses to technical needs of international areas
- Local customer needs may be better served
- Firm can adapt to the local legal system better

Disadvantages

- May be more expensive because more personnel are required
- Coordination of activities becomes more difficult
- Best interests of company may be overlooked if each geographic manager emphasizes his or her own area
- Adds another layer of management, which can result in duplication of staff services

FIGURE 7.5. Geographical Structure

this difficult situation, efforts must be made to close the gap between the corporate culture and the proposed strategy. Since it is very difficult to change culture, a modification or complete change of strategy may be deemed necessary.

Human Resources and Strategy Implementation

Once the organization has used strategy formulation to decide what it must do, the organization must employ people who have the skills appropriate for those tasks. Since strategies and tasks vary with the situation, specific characteristics of the ideal employee will also vary with situations. There is a need to identify the individual and the group who possess the appropriate skills needed to implement the strategy efficiently and effectively.

Incentives for productive employees should be tied to the objectives and strategies that they are expected to pursue.[4] Since objectives for various SBUs may be vastly different, differing types of behavior will be deemed appropriate and worthy of reward. Essentially, each individual's perfor-

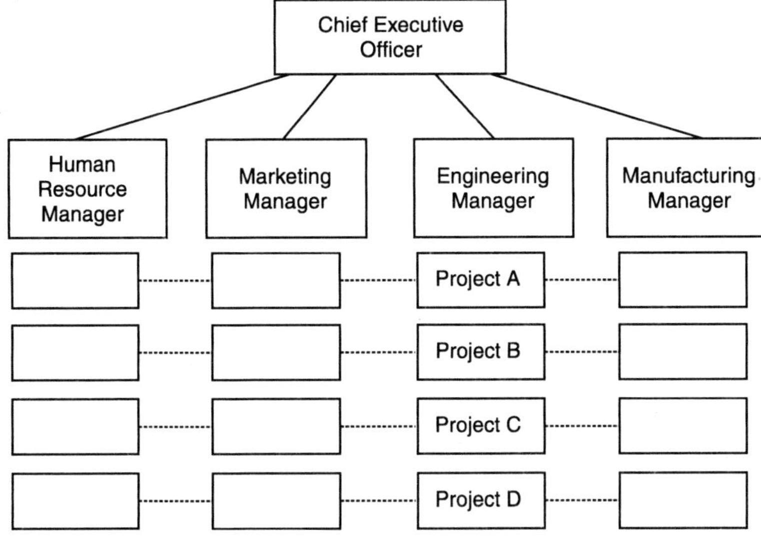

Advantages

- Creates flexibility and speed in dealing with uncertain or rapidly changing products and markets
- Employees are expected to organize their various operations to present a better result
- The employees have the ability to become intimately involved in a project

Disadvantages

- Managing the complex relationships between functions, projects, and products is difficult
- Managers may have different priorities. For example, project managers may attempt to reduce costs while functional managers try to produce quality products
- This structure is very expensive to operate because employees tend to be highly qualified

FIGURE 7.6. Matrix Structure

mance should be measured by criteria that are specific to the situation. Different types of behavior may ultimately receive similar types of rewards.

THE GENERAL MANAGER'S ROLE IN THE IMPLEMENTATION PROCESS

Corporate chief executives are responsible for everything that occurs within their organizations. The CEO must fulfill a variety of roles. In the strategy implementation process, the chief executive officer and the heads of major organizational units are most responsible for strategy implementation even though the implementation process affects the entire organization from top to bottom. Implementation of strategy impacts all of the organization's functional areas and involves the whole management team, not just the senior managers.

Lower-level managers are the most active players in the implementation process. They must determine what is required to achieve successful strategy implementation. These managers not only guide the implementation process in their individual areas of responsibility but also carry out the required day-to-day operations.

If the organization is geographically scattered and/or diversified, it becomes especially important for the lower-level managers to be involved in the process of strategy making and implementation. Therefore, some of the strategy-making responsibility is delegated to lower-level managers who head the organizational subunits where specific strategic results must be achieved. These lower-level managers need to be deeply involved in carrying out the strategy in their areas because they are accountable for strategic success or failure. Therefore, it is hard for them to shift the blame or make excuses for not achieving the target results.

Firms that are diversified into several different businesses usually have four distinct levels of strategy managers:

1. Business-level strategy managers
2. Subsidiary business-level strategy managers
3. Functional area strategy managers
4. Operating-level managers

The business-level strategy managers have primary responsibility and personal authority for strategic decisions affecting the total enterprise. The subsidiary business-level managers exercise a major leadership role in formulating and implementing strategy for the individual businesses they head. The functional area strategy managers have direct authority over a major piece of the business, i.e., manufacturing, marketing, finance, personnel, etc., and therefore must support the business unit's overall strategy with strategic actions in their own areas. The operating-level managers have frontline responsibility for putting together the details of strategic efforts in their areas and for carrying out their part of the overall strategic plan at the grassroots level.

To implement the designed strategy, management will need the cooperation of all members of the organization. How managers proceed with implementation is a function of their experience and accumulated knowledge about the business as well as their ability to lead. Another determinant of the manager's approach to strategy implementation is the context of the organization's situation. The following are examples of factors determining a manager's implementation approach:

Manager's Experience and Knowledge

1. Tenure in the role of manager
2. Network of personal relationships with others in the organization
3. Diagnostic administrative and problem-solving skills
4. Position authority
5. Leadership preferences

The Situation of the Organization

1. Level of seriousness of an organization's strategic difficulties
2. Nature and extent of strategic change involved
3. Type of strategy being implemented
4. Strength of any ingrained behavioral patterns
5. Financial and organizational resources available
6. Configuration of personal and organizational relationships in the history of the firm
7. Pressure for short-term performance
8. The culture of the organization

ISSUES IN STRATEGY FORMULATION AND IMPLEMENTATION

Strategy formulation is primarily a staff activity. It requires competent conceptual, integrative, and analytical skills. Implementation consists mostly of achieving and sustaining commitment to purpose. On the action side of corporate strategy, the skills employed are primarily administrative rather than analytical in nature. But the formulation of strategy is not finished when implementation begins. Feedback from operations signifies changing environmental factors to which the strategy should be adjusted. For example, sales or service people in the field often encounter early clues of the need for change. In a company oriented to innovation, they may report the opportunity through channels deliberately opened to them by people prepared to listen. Without a doubt, effective formulation and implementation are both essential to achieve an organization's objectives. Four possible outcomes of the combination of formulation and implementation exist and are presented in the matrix of Figure 7.7.

	Well-Formulated Strategy	Poorly Formulated Strategy
Well Implemented	SUCCESS	ROULETTE
Poorly Implemented	TROUBLE	FAILURE

FIGURE 7.7. Matrix: Outcomes of Strategy Formulation and Implementation

Success is the most likely outcome when an organization formulates a sound strategy and implements it well. External factors such as risk and opportunities, and internal factors such as strengths and weaknesses will have all been assessed. The strategy has been divided into small workable units, which can be operated effectively. Under these circumstances, the organization has the best chance of achieving its objective.

Roulette refers to situations in which a poorly formulated strategy is implemented well. Two possible outcomes may occur:

1. *Success*—If the management team recognizes the problems early and overcomes the poor strategy by making the proper adjustments, then there is still a chance to succeed. For example, during strategy implementation, the field sales force discovers that the target market has been incorrectly segmented and changes its sales force to the right target to ensure success.
2. *Failure*—Good execution hastens the failure of a poor strategy. For example, rapid production and marketing of a faulty product would cause the strategy to fail sooner. It is difficult to predict whether the organizational objective will be achieved or not.

Trouble occurs when a well-formulated strategy is poorly implemented. Even the most experienced managers fall into this trap. They assume the strategy is incorrectly formulated when things go wrong. Then they most likely go back to reshape the strategy, which makes the real problems more difficult to diagnose. Because of this reshaping, the implementation of the new strategy will fail again.

Failure occurs when a poorly formulated strategy is poorly implemented. In these situations, management has great difficulty getting back on the right track. If the same strategy is retained and implemented in a different way, or even if the strategy is reformulated and implemented the same way, failure will remain the probable result. Strategic problems in this cell of the matrix are very difficult to diagnose and remedy.

This discussion demonstrates that strategy implementation is as important as strategy formulation. To find the cause for a failed strategy, managers should examine both formulation and implementation. Three areas of traps in implementation are summarized here.

Traps in Communicating Strategy

Management may assume that they are the only members of the organization who really have to understand the strategy. When other managers and employees are uninformed about the strategic priorities or long-term direction of the firm, executives often discover that the implementation of their strategy is clumsy and ineffective. Widespread communication of the strategy is the best mechanism for ensuring enthusiastic and creative execution through "buy-in" by others.

Sometimes the strategist may lack the ability to communicate a clear sense of direction. No matter how brilliant the strategy may be, unless the business team understands and accepts it, performance will suffer. Communication of the strategy is incomplete and sloppy when key words, phrases, or strategic concepts are ill defined, thus leaving lower-level managers too much room for misunderstanding. The best way to avoid this strategy trap is to utilize a highly participative approach to strategy formulation and to stress direct, face-to-face communication processes.

A strategy may also suffer from the opposite of the two mentioned communication traps. Executives who fall into this trap are so excited about their business strategy that they fail to involve others in the formulation process. They and their top advisors believe they can sell the rest of the organization on the strategy by using elaborate and eloquent communication mechanisms. However, there is no substitute for participation from all levels in the strategy formulation process. Executives who fall into this communication trap often leave members of the organization unmotivated, uncommitted, and frustrated (lack of buy-in).

Traps in Redefining Standards

Senior managers may fail to upgrade their organization to match the demands of a new strategy. Higher standards must be communicated and enforced with vigor. Meeting financial targets is always important in a high-performance company, but managers should never be forced to act against the best long-term interests of the business to generate short-term profits.

Establishing a cost-leadership position, for example, usually takes time. Market share has to be built, technology has to be upgraded, and so on. In this situation, reducing investment spending is usually the worst thing to do, but it is often the first response to pressure for greater short-term profits.

Traps in Managing the Intangibles

A common assumption holds that professional managers can transfer their skills to any business situation. Many excellent strategies are poorly executed or fail because of the lack of appropriate leadership.

Certain strategies require certain kinds of leadership. Differentiation strategies, for example, usually work best in the hands of a market-sensitive, creative executive. *Differentiation* is the method by which companies allocate people and resources to organizational tasks in order to create value. The greater the number of different functions or divisions in an organization and the more skilled and specialized they are, the higher the level of differentiation. More differentiated companies have more managers in specialized roles and more resources that each manager is required to use in order to perform that role effectively. The more managers in a company, the higher the bureaucratic cost.

Cost-leadership strategies, on the other hand, require more discipline, more structure, and more patience. Paying attention to leadership styles and their impact on the culture and climate of the organization is the only way to avoid this trap. Overall, the most successfully executed strategies match the talents, attitudes, and styles of the managers that exemplify positive leadership traits.

The great volumes of data available in today's business environment can overwhelm even the most action-oriented manager. Such an explosion of information and its accessibility can lead general managers to rely too heavily on data analysis. This often leads managers to hesitate before taking decisive actions. In many organizations, the need to create lengthy and detailed strategic plans further compounds the problem. In the end, senior executives must trust their instincts and sometimes implement strategies without complete knowledge or backup data. This drive to implement sooner leads to increased experimentation and results in increased risk.

Research and experience have also taught that most organizations have distinctive cultures, and that strategies that place new or unusual demands on the values, beliefs, and norms of the organization will not be well executed. Ignoring these intangible factors is a common strategy trap, even though culture management has become a frequently discussed topic. To avoid this kind of strategy trap, the corporate culture must be made more measurable, more understandable, and more tangible. It is important to learn how to avoid these common traps and how to implement the strategy effectively. The actual implementation of strategy can be broken down into six steps. Four of these six steps are discussed in detail in this chapter. The remaining two are discussed in Chapter 8.

ANALYZING STRATEGIC CHANGE

The first step in the implementation process is analysis of strategic change. This step can be broken down into two areas:

I. Analyzing Strategic Change
   A. Determine Necessary Level of Change for Successful Implementation
   B. Classifying Levels of Strategic Change
      1. Continuation Strategy
      2. Routine Strategy Change
      3. Limited Change
      4. Radical Change
      5. Organizational Redirection

Analyzing the degree to which the organization will have to change in order to successfully implement the chosen strategy becomes a very important first step in the implementation process. Some strategies require only minimal changes, such as an organization that selects the market penetration strategy. A *market penetration strategy* entails an increase in marketing efforts (such as increasing advertising or distribution) or a decrease in prices. Such a strategy execution would not change the way the organization operates its day-to-day business; only a few people within the organization would get new assignments. On the other hand, if the organization decides to jump into a variety of new businesses, it would require a new direction for sales growth or stability. However, the implementation of a new strategy may call for the organization to reshape its structure. For strategy implementation purposes, strategic change is divided into the five stages listed in Table 7.1.

A *continuation strategy* is one in which the same strategy that was used in the previous planning period is repeated. This strategy is based on the stability of the existing environmental factors and the fact that no new skills or unfamiliar tasks are involved. In this stage, managers monitor the ongoing activities to ensure that the assigned short-run goals are met on time. Due to

TABLE 7.1. Stages of Strategic Change

Stage	Industry	Organization	Products	Market Appeal
Continuation strategy	Same	Same	Same	Same
Routine strategy change	Same	Same	Same	New
Limited change	Same	Same	New	New
Radical change	Same	New	New	New
Organizational redirection	New	New	New	New

past experience, the learning curve effects will reduce the operating costs and increase productivity.

A *routine strategy* involves normal changes in the appeals used to interest customers. Examples of routine strategy changes include redesigning the product packaging, altering the advertising theme, changing the sales promotion, adopting new pricing tactics, and changing distributors or distribution methods. Implementing such strategies is only part of the managers' routine job. A manager contacts some outside agencies and intermediaries, sets schedules for each activity, and monitors how well each activity proceeds. Coordinating skills are required for managers to ensure that all necessary messages are appropriately handled and all the necessary information is gathered. An important routine strategy change involves positioning or repositioning a product in the minds of consumers. Here, consumer reaction is an indicator to measure the managers' performance in strategy implementation. This approach is powerful, not too difficult to execute, and furthermore does not require a big change in the organization.

A *limited strategy change* offers new products to new markets within the same general product area. Historical data shows that the more successful diversified companies stay with businesses related to their current area of expertise. The rationale is that the experience and competence gained in one part of the portfolio will be valuable to the other business units in the portfolio. Synergy and balance are both involved. How much the organization will have to change to implement this kind of strategy depends upon the degree of difference between new products and existing products.

Radical strategy change involves reorganization, such as mergers or acquisitions between two firms in the same industry. For example, Nestlé acquired Carnation (both were in the food industry) and Procter & Gamble acquired Richardson-Vicks (both in consumer products). Such acquisitions are particularly complex when attempts are made to completely integrate the two firms. The acquiring firm not only obtains new products and markets, but also confronts legal problems, the complexities of developing a new organizational structure, and the need to reconcile conflicting organizational values and beliefs.

Radical strategy changes can also involve numerous changes in the organizational structure, multiple acquisitions, and sales of subsidiaries. For example, when John F. Welch Jr. became chairman of General Electric, GE was regarded as a "GNP company" whose growth and prosperity could never outpace those of the overall economy. Welch set out to create a company that could outperform the economy and prosper even in difficult economic times. He stripped entire management levels from the corporate hierarchy and shifted resources from manufacturing businesses to fast-growing services and high technology. He greatly automated production facilities and eliminated 100,000 employees, more than one-fourth of the workforce. In his first five years as chairman, he sold 190 subsidiaries worth nearly \$6 billion and spent \$10 billion on seventy acquisitions. Clearly, this is a strategy of radical change, which could eventually develop into a total organizational redirection.

In October 2001, software giant Microsoft launched Windows XP, the new operating system that makes it easier to organize music files and gather digital photos, among other improvements. Microsoft hopes to find a niche in the ever-changing video gaming market in offering its recent Xbox game console.

The company was able to earn about \$1.4 billion in the first year of launching these new products. Although this was not as much as Microsoft had estimated it would earn, it was not a disappointment. Microsoft's newest strategy in this market is to produce networking devices, known as routers. These devices will assist in controlling the digitally wired home. Routers will link PCs to game consoles, televisions, and other household devices.

The purpose of the routers is to have all these home devices and appliances connected not only to one another but also to the Internet. Thus, people will be able to download their favorite music and games onto their stereos and computers. Furthermore, families could share a high-speed Internet connection, so teens could swap instant messages while parents are paying bills online. By this means, Microsoft is trying to defend its place as the technology innovator for consumers, against intrusions by other home-networking services. The new strategy is aimed to position the company as the gatekeeper that connects consumers to the multibillion-dollar world of digital entertainment: games, movies, music, and other services.

Microsoft faces intense competition from other companies such as Linksys and Netgear. These two competitors are considered the current leaders in home-networking devices. However, their total sales did not exceed $600 million in 2001. Microsoft allocated about $500 million as a budget for advertising and marketing the new products.

Most of the world's major game publishers, such as Infogames and Sega, are now committed to Xbox. Microsoft is not ready to share the fate of other game console casualties. Previous attempts to take on Japanese game systems have not been successful. 3DO and Philips have both tried and failed. Sega, a major company, was forced out of the console business altogether by the failure of its Dreamcast: it could not get enough third-party game makers to write for its system. Microsoft has also favored larger developers at the expense of smaller operations, as big and small developers pay the same licensing fee.[5]

One form of *organizational redirection* involves mergers and acquisitions of firms in different industries. The degree of strategic change depends on how different the industries are and on how centralized the management of the new firm is to be. For example, when Philip Morris (a manufacturer of cigarettes and beverages) acquired General Foods (a food products manufacturer), the redirection consisted primarily of becoming a more diversified organization operating in two similar industries. When General Motors acquired Electronic Data Systems (EDS), however, considerable differences existed between the industries and between the two companies' views of appropriate business conduct. EDS personnel codes forbade employees to drink alcohol at lunchtime or to wear tasseled shoes. GM employees who transferred to EDS were deeply dissatisfied with such rules, and more than 600 of them resigned. GM Chairman Roger B. Smith had a near revolt on his hands as he attempted to reconcile the two different corporate cultures.

Another form of organizational redirection occurs when a firm leaves one industry and enters a new one. For example, when one small brewery could no longer compete in the beer industry, it redirected its efforts to the trucking and packaging industries. Similarly, American Can Company redirected its business from packaging to financial services and retailing during the mid-1980s. Such organizational redirection involves the most complex strategy implementation. It involves changes in the firm's mission and may require an entirely new set of skills and technologies.

Organizational redirection can also involve multinational acquisitions. Most multinational organizations are highly decentralized in some respects and centralized in others. Activities tied to consumers or operations such as selling, granting credit, pricing, delivery, customer service, bookkeeping, warehousing, and the like, should be adapted to local conditions. Managers of national units should exercise wide discretion to ensure effective implementation of the change.

Blockbuster Inc. currently has 15 percent of the U.S. video rental market with 3,593 video stores throughout the country. In 1996 the video rental market began shrinking at a rate of 10 percent per year due to the rise in pay-per-view movies on cable television and satellite. To combat this loss of the market itself, Blockbuster and Viacom Inc. have agreed to merge in a radical strategy change. Blockbuster's earnings growth posted quarterly increases ranging from 40 percent to 64 percent in 1998 and 1999. This is what made the merger all the more appealing to Viacom. Viacom Inc. presently owns MTV, VH-1, Nickelodeon, and Showtime cable networks. These combined with Blockbuster's video chains, music chains, and two movie studios will bring more revenues to the joint venture. Shareholders will have a stronger investment that has been estimated to rise from $18 to $30 in just one year. The merger between these two corporations integrates their common interests in the entertainment industry, and expands the market by allowing more avenues with advertisement potential.

Blockbuster realized that a change in strategy needed to take place with the depletion of the market itself and performed a radical change to defend its position. Blockbuster is responding to the growth of video games with an ambitious plan to add video console hardware and software sales to its newly expanded DVD retail offering. Blockbuster is also considering the purchase of movie companies and music retailers to broaden its market in the entertainment industry. It was necessary for Blockbuster to merge with a company that already had an established market in these areas and develop new strategies to be competitive in them, despite the fact that it called for radical change.[6]

BUILDING A CAPABLE ORGANIZATION

The second step in the implementation process is building an organization capable of carrying out the strategic plan. This can be broken down into three substeps:

- II. Building a Capable Organization
  - A. Matching Structure to Strategy
  - B. Building Distinctive Competencies
  - C. Assembling a Management Team

Matching Structure to Strategy

The choice of structure must be determined by the firm's strategy. The chosen structure must segment key activities and/or strategic operating units to enhance efficiency through specialization, response to competitive environment, and freedom to act. At the same time, the structure must effectively integrate and coordinate these activities and units to accommodate interdependence between the activities and overall control. The chosen structure should reflect the needs of the strategy in terms of the firm's:

1. Size
2. Product/service diversity
3. Competitive environment and volatility
4. Internal political considerations
5. Information and coordination needs of each component of the firm
6. Growth potential

The philosophy of top management is the primary determinant of strategy as well as the prime source of strategic initiative. Furthermore, without suitable managers, a good match between organizational structure and strategy soon becomes an unrealistic aspiration. With these internal resources, an organization may have a unique ability to overcome one or more special situations.

Building Distinctive Competencies

An organization's distinctive competencies have to be meticulously developed. This development may take years and involves technical skills, habits, attitudes, and managerial capabilities. Superior performance in a few select subunits can significantly contribute to strategic success. "General managers take immediate actions to see that the organization is staffed with enough of the right kinds of people and that these people have the budgetary and administrative support needed to generate a distinctive competence."[7]

Consequently, for a distinctive competency to emerge from organization-building actions, strategy implementers have to push aggressively to establish top-notch technical skills and capabilities for subunits. Superior performance of strategically critical tasks can make a real contribution to strategic success. Once distinctive competencies are developed, the strengths and capabilities that are attached to them become logical cornerstones for successful strategy implementation as well as for the actual strategy itself.

Assembling a Management Team

Assembling a capable management team is an obviously important part of the strategy implementation task. The recurring administrative issues are dependent on the type of core management team that is needed to carry out the strategy in addition to finding the right people to fill each slot. Sometimes the existing management team is suitable. However, sometimes the core executive group needs to be strengthened and/or expanded by promoting qualified people from within or by bringing in skilled managerial talent from the outside.

It is important to assemble a core executive group with the proper balance of backgrounds, experience, knowledge, values, beliefs, styles of managing, and personalities. It is often during the first part of strategy implementation that a company assembles a solid management team. However, until all the key positions are filled with the right people, it is hard for strategy implementation to proceed correctly at full speed.

ALLOCATING RESOURCES TO MATCH STRATEGIC OBJECTIVES

The third phase of the strategy implementation process is the allocation of resources to support the organization's strategic objectives. "Nothing could be more detrimental to the strategic-management process than for management to fail to support approved goals by not allocating resources according to the priorities indicated by these goals."[8] In most cases, changes in strategic objectives will require a change in the allocation of the firm's resources. The general manager must play a central role in determining the distribution and reallocation of resources. The general manager must have knowledge of the types of resources, understand the importance of resource allocation, and effectively distribute these resources:

- III. Allocating Resources to Match Strategic Objectives
  - A. Types of Resources
  - B. Importance of Allocation
  - C. Distribution of Resources
    1. Maintaining Flexible Organization
    2. Overcoming Barriers to Distribution
    3. Utilizing a Combination Approach
    4. Applying the Systematic Allocation Method

An organization's resources can be classified into four groups: financial, physical, human, and technological. *Financial resources* are made up of liquid assets (such as cash, receivables, and marketable securities), liabilities (such as bonds and bank notes), and equity (such as retained earnings and stocks). *Physical resources* include the firm's tangible assets such as plants, equipment, land, and inventory. The organization's employees are its *human resources.* They include managers, engineers, lawyers, and skilled and unskilled hourly workers. *Technical resources* are the knowledge, skills, methods, and tools of the organization used to carry out its business activities. They can include the firm's accounting methods, communication systems, R&D skills, and management information systems.

The organizational subunits must have basic resources to carry out the strategic plans. It is up to the general manager to see that they get these basic resources. For example, if a 10 percent increase in sales for a subunit is part of the strategic objective, the general manager would need to determine advertising and public relations budget changes, manufacturing equipment expansions or improvements, distribution changes, and so forth, to allow the subunit to meet its new goal. If the general manager allocates too little resources to a strategic area, that area may not be able to achieve its strategic objective. If too much is given, waste and inefficiency occurs, and company performance could suffer. The general manager must be willing to redistribute resources to meet goals. If the current strategy is only a fine-tuning of the previous strategy, then less reallocation will be needed. In such cases, incremental changes in budgets, staffing, etc. could be used to reach the desired levels.

A large change in strategy could require big movements of financial and human resources from one area to another. The general manager must be strong enough and determined enough to take risks, as well as to overcome company politics and the overprotection of resources between the units to allow these shifts to take place. The general manager must establish or maintain a flexible atmosphere that, in turn, allows an improved chance for successful strategy implementation. "A fluid, flexible approach to reorganization and reallocation of people and budgets is characteristic of implementing strategic change successfully."[9]

Even if the general manager maintains such a flexible organization, there are two prominent barriers hindering effective resource allocation. The first barrier is the fact that general managers may not possess enough knowledge about the diversified operations to make specific resource allocation decisions. As the organization grows, the general manager's ability to maintain a strong working knowledge of all the organization's operations wanes. This fact forces the general manager to rely on the middle- and lower-level managers to assist in allocation decisions.

This reliance leads to the next barrier hindering effective resource allocation. Lower-level managers are typically more concerned with their particular areas and are even less knowledgeable about the overall strategy. Resource allocation at this level could, therefore, favor the more influential managers, even though their areas may not have the most strategic importance. The result is a resource allocation that does not fit the strategic desires of the organization.

Because of these two barriers, neither a top-down nor a bottom-up resource allocation approach is appropriate. Instead, a combination approach is recommended. Top managers should develop strategic programs, as new strategies are created, which describe what, where, and when resources are needed. The strategic programs are then delivered to the middle- and lower-level managers, who review the programs and use them to prepare formal resource requests. The formal resource requests must be accompanied by statements describing which resources are to be used to fulfill which strategic objectives. Resources are then distributed as deemed necessary, using the judgments of all the managerial levels. This combined approach can be utilized to enhance the resource-allocation phase in the strategy implementation process.

Since the demand for resources exceeds the supply in most organizations, resource allocation should be performed in a systematic manner to achieve optimum results. Resource allocation consists of (1) producing a summary of the available resources, (2) breaking down the summary to show the inventory of resources in each division and department, (3) producing division and departmental resource requests, and (4) determining the allocation of resources to each division and department.

The first step, the summary of available resources, consists of determining what the firm currently has, or what can be made available to it. It includes not only the firm's financial resources, but also its physical, human, and technological resources (see Figure 7.8). The second step indicates the areas in which the resources are currently located. The third step then lists the desired resources of these individual areas. The final step is the actual resource allocation process. It starts by comparing the resource requests with the available resources. Resources can then be distributed in the most efficient manner, with any shortages being felt by those areas that have less strategic significance.

ESTABLISHING ORGANIZATION-WIDE COMMITMENT TO THE STRATEGIC PLAN

The fourth phase in the implementation process is the establishment of an organization-wide commitment to the strategic plan. The corporate culture must support the strategic plan. A mind-set must be developed in which employees energetically and enthusiastically pursue strategic goals. As with all phases of the implementation process, the general manager must play a key role. The general manager must (1) be able to motivate the firm, (2) un-

Financial	
Cash:	$30,000 in the bank
Accounts Receivable:	$15,000 of credit sales
Physical	
Inventory:	$60,000 of merchandise
Buildings:	Two retail stores, one garage
Land:	One cement mill, two three-acre lots
Equipment:	Ten cement mixers, four small trucks
Human Resources	
Employees:	Fifteen truck drivers, five salespeople, five clerical
Managers:	Three managers
Technological	
Computers:	Seven personal computers

FIGURE 7.8. A Total Resource Inventory for Thurston's Cement Company

derstand the corporate culture and develop a strategy-supportive culture, (3) create a results orientation, and (4) link reward to performance.

The first step is to motivate the organization to accomplish its strategy. It is critical that the entire organization, from top management down to the line workers, is committed to successfully implementing the strategic plan. To get this commitment, the general manager may need to use motivational tools such as rewards and incentives. The rewards may be in the form of praise or company recognition, or can come as salary increases and/or bonuses. Other sources of motivation include inspirational meetings and open communication through memos and letters. Examples of other strategy-supportive motivational approaches are:

- At Mars, Inc. (best known for its candy bars), every employee, including the president, gets a weekly 10 percent bonus for coming to work on time every day that week.
- In a number of Japanese companies, employees meet regularly to hear inspirational speeches, sing company songs, and chant the corporate litany. In the United States, Tupperware conducts a weekly Monday night rally to honor, applaud, and fire up its salespeople who conduct

Tupperware parties. Amway and Mary Kay Cosmetics hold similar inspirational get-togethers for their sales force organizations.

- A San Diego area company assembles its 2,000 employees at its six plants first thing every workday to listen to a manager talk about the state of the company. Then they engage in brisk calisthenics. This company's management believes "that by doing one thing together each day [we] will enforce the unity of the company. It's also fun. It gets the blood up." Managers take turns making the presentations. Many of the speeches "are very personal and emotional, not approved beforehand or screened by anybody."[10]

Many companies who applied *management by objectives* (MBO) in their organization have included a reward to motivate employees to accomplish the established objectives. The reward is given when these organizations achieve their goals and objectives efficiently and effectively. This management system involves planning, control, motivation, communication, and the development of employees under a particular system. The system has been frequently discussed and implemented in the past thirty years. It emphasizes the importance of establishing objectives with various managers' and employees' participation, and then continuously evaluating and controlling the various activities. Management certainly must establish a reward system to encourage better results. This system usually improves communication and trust between all levels of the organization, which leads to better job satisfaction among participants. However, such a system might encourage managers to become too critical and/or focus on short-term results and not the long-term objectives of the firm.

CONCLUSION

Structure and strategy are two components that must properly accommodate each other for proper corporate implementation. Corporate culture and human resources are components that aid in achieving the goals of an organization. These are also enhanced by organizational rewards, called incentives, which encourage and reward those working to accomplish the set objectives of the organization. The general manager has one of the most important roles for everything that occurs in the implementation process. Success is most evident when a sound strategy is implemented properly.

Analyzing strategic change is important because it is the basis on which a strategy is formulated. There are five levels of strategic change: continuation, routine change, limited change, radical change, and organizational redirection. Each one is specific to the direction an organization may need to go. After analysis, the next phase in the implementation process is building an organization capable of carrying out the strategic plan. The first step is matching structure to strategy, the second is building distinctive competencies, and the third is assembling a management team. The next phase is allocation of resources to support the organization's strategic objectives. The three components of this phase are types of resources, importance of allocation, and distribution of resources. Commitment to these objectives and motivation are important to get a strategy put into action by employees. The next chapter continues with the corporation's strategy to support organizational goals.

REVIEW QUESTIONS

1. What is meant by organizational structure?
2. Discuss the major types of organizational structure.
3. When does an organization use the product/division structure, and why?
4. When does an organization use the geographical structure, and why?
5. When does an organization use the strategic business unit structure, and why?
6. How is the matrix structure different from other types of structures?
7. Why is an effective implementation of strategy important?
8. Discuss the traps faced during the process of implementing strategy.

NOTES

1. Boseman, G., Phatak, A., and Schellenberger, R. E. (1986). *Strategic Management: Text and Cases*. New York: John Wiley and Sons.

2. Higgins, J. M. and Vincze, J. W. (1993). *Strategic Management: Text and Cases,* Fifth Edition. Orlando, FL: The Dryden Press, pp. 236-237.

3. Chandler, A. (1962). *Strategy and Structure.* Cambridge, MA: MIT Press, p. 24.

4. Coulter, M. K. (1998). *Strategic Management in Action.* Upper Saddle River, NJ: Prentice-Hall, pp. 172-174.

5. Greene, J. (2002). The house that Microsoft is building. *BusinessWeek,* July 22, pp. 40-42.

6. Traiman, S. (2002). Blockbuster rethinks videogame strategies. *Billboard,* 114(27), 57.

7. Thompson, A. A. and Strickland, A. J. III (1996). *Strategic Management: Concepts and Cases,* Ninth Edition. Chicago: Irwin, p. 296.

8. David, F. R. (2001). *Strategic Management,* Eighth Edition. Upper Saddle River, NJ: Prentice-Hall, p. 247.

9. Thompson and Strickland, *Strategic Management: Concepts and Cases,* p. 294.

10. Peters, J. (1993). Business policy in action. *Management Decision,* 31(6), 232.

Chapter 8

Corporate Culture, the General Manager, and Implementation

INTRODUCTION

The building of a strategy-supportive corporate culture is another important task of the general manager. A fit must be developed between the corporate strategy and the corporate culture through the use of rewards, controls, and strategic leadership.

In the first section of this chapter, we look more in detail at the concept of corporate culture. Then we move on to discuss creating a result orientation, linking rewards to strategic performance, installing internal administrative support systems, exerting strategic leadership, and filling the leadership role. This chapter will help the reader understand the importance of the general manager as well as the role he or she plays in building a strategy-supportive corporate culture.

As noted earlier, *corporate* or *organizational culture* can be defined as a set of shared values, beliefs, and methods in an organization. Such elements of a company can be hard to pin down and even harder to characterize accurately because, in a sense, they are intangible and "soft." They manifest in people's attitudes as well as their feelings.[1] Corporate culture is unique to every company—derived from the company's history, the leaders' personalities and styles, and how various tasks are handled.

Motivating the Organization to Accomplish Strategy

Corporate culture can strongly influence the effectiveness of strategy formulation and implementation. When the members of the organization understand the importance of the values and beliefs that are considered to be appropriate behavior, they tend to comply willingly. Organizational culture usually influences the behavior of employees. It motivates people to achieve or surpass organizational objectives. Therefore, for strategic implementation to be successful, corporate culture will have to be considered and perhaps modified or developed to match the strategic plan.

During the strategy development process, it is the general manager's task to ensure that the new strategy fits within the existing constraints imposed by the corporate culture. In the case where a smaller established firm is purchased or acquired, if the smaller firm has a radically different culture, it may be more efficient to keep the different cultures separated to avoid major employee clashes. If a new strategy is to succeed, it must be developed with these constraints in mind.

Building a Strategy-Supportive Corporate Culture

During the implementation phase, the general manager must create and maintain a match between strategy and culture. Corporate cultures can be very inflexible, making the task of change even more difficult.

The general manager has to use a variety of methods to obtain the desired culture. "Techniques used by some companies to develop an effective corporate culture include tolerating mistakes, relocating employees as needed, encouraging informality, acting as community cultural centers, and locating in non-cosmopolitan settings."[2] The appropriate techniques and mechanisms that should be employed by the general manager are a function of the degree of change associated with the new strategic policy.

If the strategic policy is a continuation of the old routine or limited change, it can usually be implemented within the existing corporate culture. For radical strategy changes, major changes in corporate culture may be necessary. These changes could require years to implement.

Creating a Results Orientation

Spelling out objectives leads to the next step in establishing commitment to the strategic plan—creating a results orientation. The results orientation can only be developed if specific targets have been identified and documented, and if all of the individuals involved in the plan have been properly informed. Realistic targets or goals should be provided at all levels, for the entire organization, each organizational subunit, each functional area, each operating line, and ideally each employee. The goals or objectives should be measurable, consistent, clearly communicated, and include time elements. *The targets should be specific, not general.* The annual objectives are more consistent when they state clearly what is to be accomplished, when it will be accomplished, and how its performance will be measured.[3] Goals should be stated in terms of cost, time, quantity, and other measures that are verifiable and clearly stated. This accuracy will increase the likelihood that the organization will achieve its stated objectives.

The goals should be reasonable, but challenging. Organizational resources should be used to their fullest capabilities in reaching the targeted goals. If the goals are unrealistic, morale can suffer and efforts could actually decrease. The number of goals should also be kept reasonable (between two and five is most effective). An excessive number of goals can reduce the focus on those items that are most important for successful strategy implementation.

Although development of a strong results orientation has its benefits, some problems are associated with it. Overemphasis on meeting targets could lead to problems such as deceptive reports, fudging numbers, and letting the goals become ends in themselves. The general manager must be alert to the possibility of these actions and work to prevent them.

Linking Rewards to Strategic Performance

The final step in the establishment of the strategic plan is the linking of reward to strategic performance. "Decisions on salary increases, promotions, and who gets which key assignments are a general manager's foremost attention-getting, commitment-generating devices."[4]

The reward system of any company should align the actions and objectives of individuals and units with the objectives as well as the needs of the company strategy. Reward structures should be clearly directed to the strategy achievers to assist with maintaining the workforce focus on the strategically defined tasks. The success of strategy implementation depends on, among other things, a fair reward system. Since rewards are monitored closely by virtually all members of an organization, they signal the types of behavior and performance the general manager desires. General managers and CEOs can influence employee behavior by aligning the reward system with their performance in implementing corporate strategy.

INSTALLING INTERNAL ADMINISTRATIVE SUPPORT SYSTEMS

The next step in the strategy implementation process is the installation of internal administrative support systems. This process can be broken down into three areas: (1) installation of strategy-related policies and procedures, (2) development of a strategy-related information network, and (3) installation of a formal system of reporting and controls.

Installation of Strategy-Related Policies and Procedures

A change in the firm's strategic direction will most likely create problems at various levels throughout the business. The general manager may respond to these routine problems by installing policies to cope with them.

Policies and procedures specify operating restrictions, state methods, set limits, give guidelines, establish consistency, and document administrative practices that are desired or mandated. Policies clearly communicate to employees what can and cannot be done. Policies can also establish responsibilities and clarify job roles.

Policies can be simple or complex, area specific or applied to the entire organization. Policies exist on three hierarchical levels: corporate, divisional, and departmental. *Corporate policies* are the largest in scope and apply to the entire organization. *Divisional policies* are smaller in scope, but more specific. *Departmental policies* apply only within a given unit, and usually are the most specific in nature. Table 8.1 gives examples of the hierarchy of policies.

When installed correctly, policies and procedures support strategic objectives. Policies work to make the general manager's job easier and enforce strategic implementation in several ways. First, policies act as a tool for establishing practices that support the strategic objectives on an organization-wide basis. They ensure that day-to-day operations work in an efficient manner that matches the desired strategy. Second, policies make the general manager's job easier by limiting the actions employees can take. They set boundaries on subordinates that serve to prevent individuals from deviating from the strategic plan. Third, policies create consistency throughout the organization. They serve to ensure that decisions in one area of the organization match those in another to avoid any conflicting practices and to ensure some degree of regularity and dependability in addressing strategic issues.

Finally, policies help to create the desired work climate. They are a documented form of the corporate philosophy and provide employees with explanations about how things should be done, how people are to be treated, and what the organization believes in. Policies can serve to illuminate the organization's philosophy, and aid in establishing a fit between corporate culture and the strategic objectives (see Table 8.1). "The stronger a company's culture and the more that culture is directed toward customs and markets, the less the company uses policy manuals, organization charts, and detailed rules and procedures to enforce discipline and norms."[5]

A warning is called for when implementing a policy. Too many policies can detract from successful implementation as much as too few policies. Policies can stifle ingenuity and creativity by limiting the actions of the employees.

TABLE 8.1. A Hierarchy of Policies

Stated Strategy and Supporting Policies	Potential Effect of Strategy
Company strategy: Acquire a chain of retail stores to meet our sales growth and profitability objectives.	
1. All stores will be open from 8:00 a.m. until 8:00 p.m. Monday through Saturday.	Could increase retail sales if stores are now open only forty hours a week.
2. All stores must submit a Monthly Control Data Report.	Could reduce expense-to-sales ratios.
3. All stores must support company advertising by contributing 5 percent of their total monthly revenues for this purpose.	Could allow the company to establish a national reputation.
4. All stores must adhere to the uniform pricing guidelines set forth in the Company Handbook.	Could help assure customers that the company offers a consistent product in terms of price and quality in all its stores.
Divisional goal: Increase the division's revenues from $10 million in 2001 to $15 million in 2002.	
1. Beginning January 2002, this division's salespersons must file a weekly activity report that includes the number of calls made, the number of miles traveled, the number of units sold, and the number of new accounts opened.	Could ensure that salespersons do not place too great an emphasis on certain areas.
2. Beginning January 2002, this division will return to its employees 5 percent of its gross revenues in the form of a December bonus.	Could increase employee productivity.
3. Beginning January 2002, inventory levels carried in warehouses will be decreased by 30 percent in accordance with a just-in-time manufacturing approach.	Could reduce production expenses and thus free funds for increased marketing efforts.
Production department goals: Increase production from 20,000 units in 2001 to 30,000 units in 2002.	
1. Beginning January 2002, employees will have the option of working up to twenty hours of overtime per week.	Could minimize the need to hire additional employees.
2. Beginning January 2002, perfect attendance awards in the amount of $100 will be given to all employees who do not miss a workday in a given year.	Could decrease absenteeism and increase productivity.
3. Beginning January 2002, new equipment must be leased rather than purchased.	Could reduce tax liabilities and thus allow more funds to be invested in modernizing production processes.

Development of a Strategy-Related Information Network

When implementing a new strategic plan, the general manager must stay informed about the progress of implementation. The manager must know if schedules are being met, if budgets are being achieved, if customer orders are being satisfactorily delivered, etc. If serious problems are being encountered, the general manager must be informed in time to make the corrections. The manager must have methods of gathering the needed information, which requires the establishment of a strategy-related information network.

There are several sources for this information, including increases or decreases in customer complaints or orders, formal or informal conversations with subordinates, formal reports, special reports, statistical reports, response of the competition, and reaction of investors. Although there are many sources of information, not all have the same degree of integrity. Statistical reports can misrepresent the data. Progress reports may highlight the good news and attempt to cover up the bad news, making things appear better than they are. The more levels an organization has, the greater the tendency for information to get diluted and/or skewed as it travels from the bottom to the top. Accurate and relevant information on the strategic implementation process may be hard for the general manager to uncover. By finding or establishing reliable information channels or networks, this problem can be overcome.

Installation of a Formal System of Reporting and Controls

Strategy implementation must also involve establishing or reviewing the formal system of gathering information. Although an informal information network such as "managing by walking around" has its advantages, it does not and cannot supply all the information needed by the general manager. *Formal information networks* serve to give the general manager concrete figures on the actual performance of each organizational subunit and the overall organization.

Formal information networks include such items as scheduled meetings, letters, memos, and reports. For the formal system of reporting to have value in the implementation process, the information supplied must show several characteristics:

1. The information must be *concise.* The information system must supply only what the manager needs to know. The reports should also flag any negative developments, such as budget overruns or sale losses.

Excess information may overload the general manager and should be avoided.

2. The information must be *timely*. Reports should be generated and distributed in enough time for action to be taken. Timely information can lead to superior decisions by the general manager by giving more time to determine the best response to a given situation.
3. The information must be *accurate*. The information must not be biased by the people generating it or skewed by internal politics. In addition, poor performance in a subunit must not be covered up by inaccurate accounting, false comparisons, or misleading statistics.
4. The information must be *clear*. Reports should be easy for the general manager to understand. Statistics should be used to flag events that are out of the ordinary.
5. The information should be *comprehensive*. Reports and letters should contain all necessary information. If a report shows a large variance in the budget, it should explain the variance. A letter addressing a decrease in sales should give all known reasons for the decrease.
6. The information should be easily *accessible*. The general manager should know where to get the desired information. Computer data banks and programs should be easily obtainable. Files should be kept in order and up to date.
7. The information should generate *early warning signals*. The information system should serve to point out undesirable situations to the manager, who can then take action on them. The information should avoid surprising management by keeping them informed of such events throughout their progress.

EXERTING STRATEGIC LEADERSHIP

The final step in the strategic implementation process is the exertion of strategic leadership by the general manager or the CEO. Implementing the strategic plan is easier said than done. In most instances, the organization must be led through the implementation process. The leader needs to take charge of the task and be the main driving force to ensure that the tasks not only get done, but get done properly. To perform this function, the general manager must understand the issues involved in exerting strategic leadership.

For many companies, the lack of quality in their change caused their downfall. "Forty-seven percent of the companies that appeared on the Fortune 500 a decade ago have disappeared from today's list."[6] If anything, this process is accelerating. CEOs must become the leaders of change. They must leave the traditional organizational system behind and become more progressive and flexible. A leader with a poor outlook and attitude will be reflected in those that work under that manager. For the company to be successful, the top management must believe in and be able to "sell" the vision of the company. This vision is not only for the present, but for the future, too. Starting the change with top management is what companies need to succeed in the future. The old hierarchy and chain of communication must be altered to include the employees of the company.

Robert Eaton of Chrysler Corporation succeeded in taking Chrysler from the brink of death in 1989 to record revenues in 1994-1996. Eaton accomplished this through a number of changes ranging from management to product strategy, but began with a change in the mission statement and corporate culture. "We came up with a statement of purpose, which is to be a car and truck company that designs and builds cars people want to buy, enjoy driving, and drive again."[7] This reflects a leadership with a more simplistic approach to selling cars. Eaton was trying to get away from the distractions that plagued Chrysler in previous years. He overhauled the entire management corporate culture. He gave more autonomy to the workers, emphasized teamwork, and cited the importance of "process thinking." This way of thinking reflected a willingness to take all of the processes of the company apart and restructure them, improving each part as the process continued. Eaton's renovated corporate culture focused on the people in the organization. Of this, Eaton said, "It's how well you train, organize, motivate, and empower those people" that makes the system work.[8]

The general manager has several different methods of implementation approaches to choose from. David Brodwin and L. G. Bourgeois studied several different practices at a number of companies and determined that there are five fundamental approaches that the general manager can use when implementing strategies.[9] These strategies are (1) the commander's approach, (2) the organizational changes approach, (3) the collaborative approach, (4) the cultural approach, and (5) the "crescive" approach. Each of these approaches requires different actions and levels of involvement for the general manager.

When using the *commander approach,* the general manager will apply rigorous logic and analysis to develop the strategic plan. The general manager may do all of the formulation alone, or lead a team of strategic consultants. Once the strategy is formulated, the general manager then "commands" its implementation. The general manager does not play an active role in the implementation phase when using this approach.

The *organizational approach* focuses on how the strategy will be implemented. In this approach, it is assumed that a good strategy is already established and that the manager's present task is to get this strategy implemented. The management team uses behavioral tools such as changing the organizational structure, administrative staffing, organizational priorities, and planning and control systems to facilitate the implementation process.

The *collaborative approach* involves the general manager and the entire management team in the formulation and implementation of the strategy. The general manager's role is to coordinate the team's efforts and to encourage the contribution of a variety of different viewpoints from all those involved.

The *cultural approach* expands upon the collaborative approach by including the lower levels of the organization in the implementation process. In this approach, the general manager establishes a vision of the objectives for the organization and then allows the employees to design their own work and activities in an effort to meet the vision. Once the strategy has been formulated, the general manager serves as a coach, helping and encouraging the different functions and work areas to make decisions in regard to specific operating details that will be used to meet the strategic objectives.

The final approach is called the *crescive approach*. The word "crescive" means growing or increasing, and it describes an approach that, instead of working from the top down, or decreasing, works from the bottom up. This approach works on strategy formulation and implementation at the same time. In this approach, the general manager encourages subordinates to develop and implement their own strategies. The overall strategic plan becomes the summation of all the plans developed at the work level. The general manager serves as a guide, suggesting desirable actions and approving or disapproving action items proposed by the subordinates.

The general manager must analyze the current situation of the firm, compare it with the proposed strategy, and choose which approach and leadership role best fits the situation. The last job for the general manager in the implementation process is to fulfill the leadership role.

FULFILLING THE LEADERSHIP ROLE

The first step in fulfilling the leadership role is the establishment and promotion of enthusiasm in the organizational climate and culture. To establish the desired enthusiasm, the general manager must portray such enthusiasm for others to see. The general manager must display a belief in the strategic plan and work to sell it to subordinates.

The display of support for the strategic plan should take the form of both words and actions. Words are needed to define the cultural norms and to provide documented evidence of the desired climate. This can help when maintaining or changing the existing values. Actions add credibility to words. They set examples and provide a training tool for others in the organization to follow. The greater the changes proposed, the more visible the actions should be. Some examples of culture-establishing actions follow:

- At Delta Airlines, there is a story that a woman inadvertently missed out on a super saver ticket because her family had moved and, owing to a technicality, the ticket price savings were no longer available. She called to complain. Delta's president intervened personally and, being in the same city at the time, met her at the gate to give her a ticket at the super saver rate.
- At IBM, where the goal is "to give the best customer service of any company in the world," corporate officers make sales calls with regularity. A senior financial officer at IBM not only made customer calls, but also insisted that all his people do so as well. His reason: "How's someone going to design a receivables policy if he doesn't know the customer?"
- The past chief executive officer of GE, Jack Welch, transformed the company. He installed a new cultural norm by challenging GE's 250-plus business-level managers to "be better than the best." He translated this theme into a single, overarching performance standard: They must establish their businesses as No. 1 or No. 2 in their industries or else achieve a competitive advantage by virtue of decided technological superiority. All general managers are asked to visit the corporate R&D labs for brainstorming sessions for developing businesses with a clear technological edge. Welch was also able to divest businesses that were unable to meet these standards.

These actions demonstrate that in well-managed corporations the words and actions of the general manager have a significant role in the strategic implementation process, and actions are the more important of the two. The right kinds of actions, displayed on a regular basis, are necessary for establishing the desired corporate culture and climate.

SUMMARY

The six phases of the strategy implementation process involve almost every area and function in the organization. The general manager must give a great deal of time and effort and be extensively involved in every phase. The general manager must use many diverse managerial skills, from budgeting and staffing to coordinating and motivating. With all these requirements, the task of strategy implementation may be considered one of the hardest the general manager has to face. For a strategy to be successful, the general manager must face these challenges head on and lead the implementation process. The implementation process is the action phase of strategic management, and the general manager must ensure that the correct action is taken and maintained.

The implementation process will give the general manager plenty of opportunities to demonstrate creativity and make the job varied and interesting. Organizational success is the reward.

REVIEW QUESTIONS

1. What is corporate culture?
2. How do leaders shape culture?
3. Why must information be timely, accurate, relevant, and reliable?
4. What is the relationship between strategy implementation and the reward system?
5. Provide an example of a company whose culture has helped or hindered its strategy.

NOTES

1. Thompson, A. A. and Strickland, A. J. III (1996). *Strategic Management: Concepts and Cases,* Ninth Edition. Chicago: Irwin, p. 297.
2. David, F. (1997). *Strategic Management,* Sixth Edition. Upper Saddle River, NJ: Prentice-Hall, p. 260.
3. Pearce, J. A. and Robinson, R. B. Jr. (1991). *Strategic Management Formulation, Implementation, and Control,* Fourth Edition. Homewood, IL: Irwin, p. 300.
4. Thompson and Strickland, *Strategic Management: Concepts and Cases,* p. 302.
5. Pearce and Robinson, *Strategic Management Formulation, Implementation, and Control,* p. 346.
6. Moravee, M. (1994). Leaders must love change, not loathe it. *HR Focus,* 71(2), 13-15.
7. Bell, J. (1996). Building the new Chrysler. *Industry Week,* September 16, 10-15.
8. Ibid.
9. Brodwin, D. R. and Bourgeois, L. J. (1984). Five steps to strategic action. In G. Carroll and D. Vogel, *Strategy and Organization: A West Coast Perspective.* Marshfield, MA: Pitman Publishing, p. 174.

Chapter 9

The Control Function

INTRODUCTION

The purpose of *control* is to measure outcomes or outputs to see whether they pass or fail according to the mission, objectives, and strategy. Control is a valuable component of the planning process. It ensures that the organization accomplishes its mission and objectives. Control essentially means making something happen the way it was planned to happen.[1] At the business or corporate level, control is implemented by monitoring the company's progress along a path of change, evaluating the efficiency of that progress, and improving the process of change in order to accomplish the predetermined goals or mission in the most efficient manner possible.

A key component of successful control is the formulation and implementation of a viable business strategy. Business strategies provide direction, goals, and desired results. The plan (the end result of strategy formulation) serves as the tool that management uses to shape the organization's future, as well as a reference to evaluate performance against. Planning can be focused on short-term operational management or long-term strategic management.

To develop an effective control system, it is imperative that measurable objectives are established. This means setting up definitive completion dates prior to determining the system of control. These objectives/goals should be established early in the planning process. The objectives are dynamic and can change as the situation within the business environment changes. Control is in the forefront of any well-managed organization. It will ensure that the ongoing operations meet the goals and standards established by management. Without control, the implementation of a business plan is incomplete. To enhance the chances of success, control must be established to direct the goals of the organization. Success depends upon a control system that is simple and understandable by every member of the organization. The system must be communicated to the personnel responsible for implementation, and those individuals must have confidence in the plan. This means that the individuals/divisions being evaluated must believe in the relevancy of the control system and be given the appropriate opportunity to correct deficiencies before disciplinary action is taken.

The Control Process

Traditional approaches stressed review and feedback of performance to determine degree of achievement. Feedback through inspection is performed by an individual worker or the next person in the process. In some cases, an objective evaluator such as a group leader conducts the inspection. This may be appropriate for operational activities or for companies in stable industries. Feedback requires waiting for the implementation of a strategy before determining how well it is performing. This is not beneficial for long-term strategies. Organizations must instead remain flexible to internal and external environmental changes.

Today, companies have an approach to strategic control that is more future directed. A future-oriented approach that helps anticipate changes is the *feed-forward* approach. This method prevents the worker from making an error that leads to a defect before starting a process, or by providing rapid feedback of abnormalities in the process to the worker in time to correct it. The feed-forward control consists of the development of assumptions that provide a basis for developing strategies. The process also involves constant monitoring of environmental factors to determine validity of previous planning premises. The feed-forward control can also work to recognize past undetected events before they become missed opportunities or serious threats. Therefore, it is created to monitor internal and external events that may threaten a firm's strategy or also may provide opportunities.

The monitoring of external factors can be accomplished through environmental scanning in which the environment is broken down into segments so those trends can more easily be detected. Feed-forward control is a useful technique that works by focusing on inputs to shape outputs. It tries to determine the results prior to implementation. The success of these methods can depend on the company.

To develop an effective control system, management needs to determine which areas need to be monitored. Operations management must identify the part of the implementation processes that need to be monitored and evaluated. The processes must be designed in a way that can be measured periodically and in a consistent manner. The measurements must be applied to all areas of concern in a reasonably objective way. Management usually first ranks these areas based on priority and selects the most critical elements in the ranking. Next management must design acceptable standards of performance (as specific as possible, taking the organizational objectives into consideration). A tolerance range, which represents acceptable deviations from the standards, is specified in the third step. Fourth, management must measure the organizational performance against these standards (reinforce positive performance). Finally, take corrective action when necessary.

If the actual performance is within the standards or the tolerance range, then the measurement process is successfully completed. However, if the results deviate from the expected standards, then corrective action must be taken. The universal control tool is the budget, which is a plan in monetary terms.

The budget is used as a control device by comparing the amount of money that has actually been spent for each item to the amount that is budgeted for it. It is clear that planning and control go hand in hand, with the plan pointing to future achievements and the controls focusing the business's attention on results in terms of the plan. Neither planning nor control can be effective without the other.

LEVELS OF STRATEGY AND CONTROL

Strategy

The three basic levels of organizational strategy are corporate, business, and functional. The corporate level of management is the center for the decision making of the organization. The CEO, the board of directors (BOD), other senior executives, and corporate staff make up the structure of this level.

The business and corporate levels of strategy are the same if the organization is a single business entity. However, in a multibusiness company, the business level is the second tier in the strategic management structure. A business unit is an individually operated entity belonging to the organization, usually containing its own functional departments. On the functional level, the heads of each department are called functional managers, not strategic managers. They are responsible for developing functional strategies and overseeing the specific business functions within the organization. Such functions include personnel, purchasing, production, marketing, customer service, accounting, etc. Functional managers must also implement and execute the decisions made at the corporate and business levels.

Control

Control systems run parallel with strategic levels. There are three basic levels of organizational control. *Strategic control* evaluates the strategies set at the corporate strategy level. *Management control* ensures that the objectives set in the business strategy level are implemented with successful outcomes. *Operational control* measures the performance of individuals or work groups so the outcomes can be ranked with preset standards.

Level Relationship

Interrelationships among the three levels of strategy and control typically found in large businesses are vital for the success of the entire organization. Each level of strategy forms the strategic environment of the next level (e.g., corporate-level objectives, strategies, and policies form a key part of the environment of a division or strategic business unit). The objectives, strategies, and policies of the SBU must therefore be formulated so as to help achieve the plans of the corporate levels. Control systems are then used to determine the effectiveness of this procedure. The same is also true for the functional level.

ORGANIZATIONAL CONTROL

The framework for any successful control system begins with establishing goals and standards of performance for the organization (see Figure 9.1). Determining what must be managed involves identifying the critical factors that make a business successful. Developing or modifying objectives in order to utilize the key success factors in a timely manner is another important issue that can lead to a successful process. Also, it is important to understand what is happening in these important areas by developing communication and tracking systems. This will assist the firm in determining the stage of its critical success factors and how close it is to achieving its established objectives.

The corporate goal must be stated in relevant terms, and every member of management must know *what is to be accomplished*. Standards must reflect the goals that have been established by the organization and will actually indicate the acceptable levels of organizational performance. Once standards of performance are developed, organizational performance can then be measured against these standards. If there is a significant difference between these two, then appropriate measures to improve the process are required. In this case, management investigates various related issues such as the strategy design, the assumptions used, the way the strategy has been implemented, the way it was communicated, and whether resources allocated were sufficient. In some cases, policies, procedures, and rules are modified to ensure effective implementation of the various activities. In other cases,

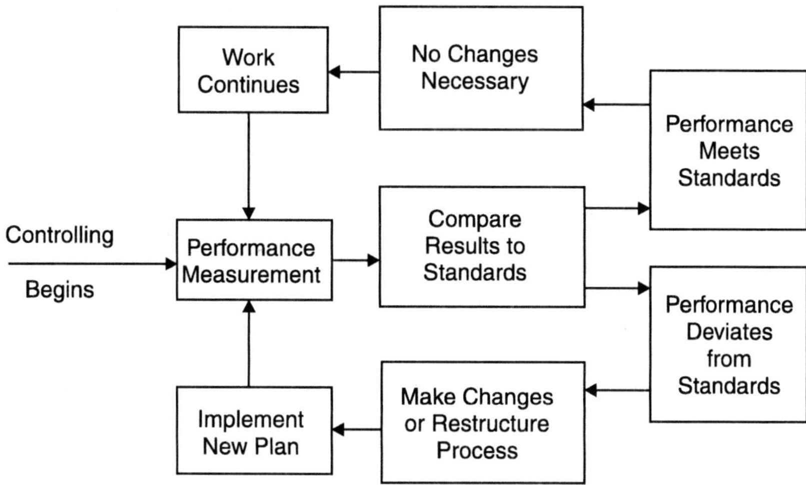

FIGURE 9.1. A General Model of the Control Process

the emphasis is shifted toward performance targets, such as reaching certain quotas in sales or production.

Effective control systems have established standards that must be met to ensure success. Effective control systems and methods must be:[2]

1. *Economical*—Information must be obtained for effective control. However, if too much information is obtained, the control system will become cumbersome and ineffective.
2. *Meaningful*—A control method that does not provide information concerning an objective of the organization is useless. It is not as important to evaluate only what is needed.
3. *Timely*—Information must be provided to management in sufficient time to effectively take any corrective action required. An effort must be made to ensure that any control system obtains the required information without overloading the controllers with superfluous information that bogs down the control process.
4. *Accurate and realistic*—Measure the true character and nature of an activity or function. What is important? What affects the achievement of the goals? Control systems must provide management with a true picture of what is happening.
5. *Informative*—Control systems must provide qualitative information on trends. These qualitative subjects provide management with infor-

mation that can signal problem areas that need further attention, thus facilitating faster resolution of the area of concern.

6. *Facilitate action*—Information provided to individuals lacking the ability or authority to take corrective action is useless and, in fact, detrimental. This detriment results from the manager's perception that the reports are useless. Therefore, the manager tends to ignore a useful report and ultimately wastes resources. The person who receives the report must be able to use it effectively.
7. *Simple*—If the system is so complex that a manager becomes confused and needs to study the mechanics and methodology of the system, then it probably needs to be redesigned. If ideas cannot be expressed in an easily understandable format, they become useless.

Bank of America offers an example of a company that has effectively utilized a control system. In 1987, Bank of America was on the brink of collapse, with $1.8 billion in operating losses since 1985. In late 1986, the board of directors appointed Tom Clausen as the new chairman and CEO. Clausen immediately embarked on a strategy utilizing a stringent control system. Task assignments were confirmed, account abilities were strengthened, and budgetary allocations were tightened. Bank of America maintained strategic control of its objectives by continuous monitoring and surveillance of all feedback mechanisms and by taking timely corrective action ensuring intended outcomes. Overall, Bank of America was transformed from a staggering giant to a well-managed large bank with its feet on the ground and its eye on the future. By 1990, the turnaround was consummated with a net income of $1.05 billion.[3]

FINANCIAL MEASUREMENT METHODS

Three key financial measures are best analyzed through the use of quantitative methods. These three measures are closely related to profit, cash flow, and return on investment. *Profit* is the net of all revenue less all expenses. *Cash flow* is the net of all cash received minus the cash expended. *Return on investment* is a measure of the level of payback on the use of capital.

The importance of profits and cash flow is related to investments and the time value of money. The purchase and depreciation of assets affect these two measures significantly and differently. Return on investment is a measure of the level of payback on the use of capital. It considers the price paid for making the investment. The quantitative measurement brings objectivity to the forefront of the decision-making process. These measurements are commonly used assessments that result in numerical data, which can be organized before a decision is made on the success of current operations. The objective nature of the quantitative data can be lost in the interpretation. The interpretation of the data and a determination of the corrective action required can be difficult to make and are highly subjective.

Return on Investment (ROI)

Return on investment is one of the most commonly used measures of organizational performance. It is usually applied to evaluate the profitability objectives in the organization or in a strategic unit. ROI divides net income by total assets, thus indicating the relationship between the amount of income generated and the amount of assets needed to operate the organization. It has proven to be one of the most important calculations and is defined as follows:

ROI = Average Yearly Profit/Average Fixed Investment
+ Working Capital (During Earning Life)

ROI provides a comparison of the earning power of the business with alternate investments. A single ROI will not provide management with sufficient data to make decisions. Additionally, the successful use of this measurement requires tracking and comparing ROIs for as many consecutive years or quarters as feasible and/or comparing the ROI with those of similar companies. This procedure increases the validity of the conclusions drawn. Comparing ROIs from different industries will lead to incorrect conclusions. The ROI from a pharmaceutical firm will be substantially different from that of a steel-manufacturing firm. The investments required in fixed assets, research and development, advertisements and the cost of sales, etc., impact the return on investment calculation.

To be used effectively, a manager must be familiar with the advantages and limitations of ROI as a measure of organizational performance. The following is a list of advantages and limitations as described by James M. Higgins and Julian Vincze.[4]

Advantages

1. ROI is a single comprehensive figure influenced by everything that happens.
2. ROI measures how well the division manager uses the property of the company to generate profits. ROI is also a good way to check on the accuracy of capital investment proposals.
3. ROI is a common denominator that can be compared with many entities.

4. ROI provides an incentive to use existing assets efficiently.
5. ROI provides an incentive to acquire new assets efficiently.

Limitations

1. ROI is very sensitive to depreciation policy. Depreciation write-off variances between divisions affect ROI performance. Accelerated depreciation techniques reduce ROI, conflicting with capital budgeting discounted cash-flow analysis.
2. ROI is sensitive to book value. Older capital equipment with more depreciated assets has a relatively lower investment base than newer capital equipment, thus increasing their ROI. Inflation can also have an adverse effect on ROI numbers. Further, it is possible for management to manipulate investment rates or dispose of unnecessary assets in order to positively affect ROI performance.
3. In many firms that use ROI, one division sells to others. As a result, transfer pricing must occur. Since, in theory, the transfer price should be based on the total impact on firm profit, some investment center managers are bound to suffer. Equitable transfer prices are difficult to determine.
4. If one division operates in an industry that has favorable conditions and another division operates in an industry that has unfavorable conditions, the former division will automatically look better than the latter.
5. The time span is short. The performance of division managers should be measured over the long run, to match top management's relevant time span.
6. The business cycle strongly affects ROI performance, often despite managerial performance.

The calculation of ROI is very simple and deals with "profits," taking into account all profits forecast during the life of the proposed project. Problems encountered include the fact that there is no universally accepted definition of "capital invested" or "profit," so that different people using the same basic data could report different rates of profitability. This complicates the interpretation of the results.

EPS and ROE

Other popular measures of company performance include *earnings per share* (EPS) and *return on equity* (ROE) and are calculated as follows:

EPS = Net Income / Average Number of Shares Outstanding
ROE = Net Income / Average Stockholders' Equity

Although used by some managers, EPS and ROE by themselves are not adequate measures of corporate performance. For one thing, because alternate accounting principles are available, EPS can have several different but equally acceptable values depending on the computation method. Second, EPS does not consider the time value of money. ROE has basically the same limitations since it is also derived from accounting-based data. There is also some evidence that EPS and ROE are often unrelated to a company's stock price.[5]

Other Control Measures

A popular measure that takes the value created to stockholders through the stock market is called *economic value added* (EVA). EVA *assumes* that the stock market is the ultimate decider of corporate performance. This measure encourages management to especially monitor all forces that can affect stock price and dividend rate. Since the stock market changes throughout the year, stockholder value might not be the accurate measure in the short run. Another limitation of this measure is that it focuses only on the stockholder.

Another measure used is the balanced scorecard, which combines financial and nonfinancial measures. It presents financial data including balance sheet, income statements, and stockholder value. In addition, it shows customer satisfaction with the company's products and services. This measure identifies areas of advantage to the company and shows the capability of improvement in the future. Therefore the scorecard provides much more information than previous traditional measures, such as ROI, ROE, and EPS. However, it is a costly process that leaves management with too many areas to measure and control. The balanced scorecard can be useful if the company can produce a list of priorities that indicates the measures that are most important to the corporation.

Therefore, there is no best measure or group of measures that could be used in isolation. Management needs to first identify the area that needs to be measured, then choose the appropriate tools accordingly.

Stakeholder's Audit

Stakeholders are those people who have a direct interest in the organization. Without their direct interest, the company might not survive. Organizational stakeholders include the following:

1. *Stockholders* interested in the financial position of the company and the value of stocks and dividends
2. *Employees* interested in degree of job security, reasonable wage rates, and other benefit packages
3. *Management* interested in organizational stability and survival as a vital entity
4. *Major creditors* interested in the organization's ability to pay its short- and long-term debts
5. *Major suppliers* interested in retaining the organization as a customer
6. *Government agencies* interested in ensuring that organizations are not violating societal needs and expectations. Also, they consider survival of the organization as important for taxes and other societal benefits.
7. *Social and political interest groups* interested in adopting social norms and expectations, such as activist groups, consumer advocates, and environmentalists.

Management must be concerned about the perceptions of the stakeholders. Stockholders are a specific category who have financial interests in the performance of the organization and must be satisfied before management can consider the organization successful. The goal of management should be to maximize shareholder equity/profits, and the tone and feedback of these shareholders is extremely valuable as a source of information and as an indicator of the organization's progress toward meeting its assigned goals.

REPORTING SYSTEMS

Written reports provide management with the necessary information from every level of management that can be utilized in the control process. These reports can be prepared periodically or regularly as deemed appropriate and/or useful. A brief summary of commonly prepared reports follows.

Daily Management Reports

Timing is essential, but with the exception of certain businesses involved in cash management, there is seldom sufficient justification for a formal daily reporting system. Daily reports and reviews are too frequent and should not be used except in special cases and under special circumstances. Daily reporting relative to a specific situation during a critical period of the operation is acceptable, but it should be discontinued when the critical period has ended. Information needs to be exchanged promptly, but a daily formal reporting system is not normally required.

Weekly Summary Reports

A weekly summary reporting system is a useful communication and control tool in many business situations. A weekly period provides management with meaningful and timely information without overly burdening the administrative workload. These reports can be made even more useful by standardizing the reporting format into a simple summary style. The summary-style report can be easily understood and enhances response time.

Weekly reports from lower-level management seldom exceed one page, and the consolidated organizational report is usually kept to two to three pages. A weekly summary report of each business unit could include items such as sales plan for the month, sales forecast for the coming month, shipments this month, backlog for shipment, and so on. Another report could include the time spent on production, lost time because of accidents, and so on.

Monthly Management Letters

The success of monthly management letters depends on their focus. Such letters must focus on key performance issues and avoid unnecessary detail. These reports are usually limited to two or three pages. However, there is a common format that contains five short sections. These sections contain financial and business highlights, an objectives review, people involved, and a general discussion.

The financial highlights normally provide information pertaining to financial expectations. This section would normally depict the estimate of sales and operating profit for the present month and the upcoming month with a comparison to goals and standards. If appropriate, inventory levels, accounts receivable, and cash flow may be included.

The business highlights review new opportunities, problems, and programs. Very often, a statement on current critical issues is reviewed in this portion of the letter. Each organization can customize the format to best enhance its probability of success.

Monthly Business Reviews

In a business review, responsible individuals gather together to (1) evaluate the business condition, (2) monitor and control key operations compared to the plan, and (3) recognize and appraise major opportunities. The business review team normally consists of managers from the sales, production, technical, marketing, public relations, and finance departments. The addition of at least one junior manager on a rotating basis is beneficial. Exposing junior leadership to the workings of top management decision-making processes provides excellent management training.

Monthly business reviews should address the most important issues and leave lesser issues to subordinates. This process will help management to conduct the review in a timely and efficient manner.

Quarterly Reports and Reviews

Business unit managers or general managers may initiate quarterly reports and reviews, which summarize business unit performance. Like monthly reports, the quarterly report concentrates on critical success factors and is short and concise.

INFORMATION SYSTEMS

An integral part of any successful management operation is the availability of correct and up-to-date information that can be utilized in the various measurements of organizational performance. Every organization develops some method of gathering information. Two methods are discussed in the following sections.

The Management Information System (MIS)

The *management information system* is a formal organization information network that usually utilizes a computer system to generate, qualify, and/or quantify information for management within the organization. MIS can be used by all levels of management to gather information for the various activities within their purview. This information system is designed to provide information that is necessary for performing managerial functions. The MIS collects, records, processes, stores, retrieves, and displays information. For the information to be valuable, it must be relevant, reliable, timely, accurate, and cost effective. The system must also be flexible enough to provide sufficient information for all levels of the organization. In some organizations, the system is called a strategic information system (SIS) or information system (IS).

The Management Decision Support System (MDSS)

Standardization is difficult to achieve in areas where management does not have to make recurring decisions. A management decision support system (MDSS) is an interdependent set of decision aids that assist managers in making unstructured and nonrecurring decisions. An MDSS is an analytical tool incorporating the use of a computer and appropriate software to make subjective decisions. This system provides and organizes information. The manager has the ultimate responsibility to interpret the results and make the final decision.[6] The technological innovation in microcomputers and software has made MDSS available and increasingly popular with the vast majority of managers.

As discussed thus far, there are many ways for management to measure organizational performance. Managers must establish and utilize whatever method best suits their organization. The most important guideline for managers to follow is that organizations monitor and improve performance in the areas affected by their stated goals.

Once top management develops methods to measure organizational performance, they then have a method of comparing the organization's performance against established benchmarks. Organizational goals or standards from which a determination can be made regarding the acceptable level of organizational performance must be established. It is essential that management develop standards in all areas affected by organizational goals.

For example, General Electric has established standards regarding profitability, market position, productivity, product leadership, personnel development, employee attitude, public responsibility, and standards reflecting a balance between short-range and long-range goals. General Electric, like most organizations, feels that both long-range and short-range goals are necessary to maintain a healthy and successful organization. Standards in this area indicate what the acceptable long and short-range goals are, and the relationships among them.

VEHICLES OF CONTROL

Budgets

The administration of the budget is one of the most commonly used methods of control. A *budget* is a plan that assists managers with the coordination of operations and promotes managerial control. Budgeting is the process of identifying, gathering, summarizing, and communicating financial and nonfinancial information about the organization's future activities. The budgeting process provides managers with the opportunity to carefully match the goals of the organization with the resources necessary to accomplish those goals.[7] The budget itself does not control anything. It sets standards by which actions can be measured. The office of the controller in larger corporations usually oversees budget administration. Budgeting helps managers to relate the organization's long-term goals to its short-term activities by allocating resources, tasks, and workloads. It also helps in setting performance measures and communicating responsibilities. It is a plan of action that forecasts future transactions, activities, and events in financial or nonfinancial terms. The owner-manager, office manager, or an independent service organization is usually responsible for the budget in smaller organizations. Management allocates resources to the various activities of the organization through the budgets. At the end of each period, the budget will show how many of these activities were performed and how much they cost. Therefore, the budgets provide continuous feedback, evaluate performance, recognize problems, and coordinate activities.

Budgets, reports, and other programs are used to help the organization apply strategy efficiently and effectively. They also are important means of controlling strategy implementation. The control process starts with identifying the areas that need to be monitored, establishing standards, and continuously monitoring actual performance. Actual performance is compared to the standards, and a correction measure must be taken if there is serious deviation. It is important to find the roots of this deviation before applying any solution. The differences between strategic control and budgetary control are outlined in Table 9.1.

TABLE 9.1. Strategic Control versus Budgetary Control

Strategic Control	Budgetary Control
Time period has long-term range from two to ten or more years.	Time period is usually one year.
Measurements are quantitative and qualitative.	Measurements are quantitative.
Takes both the external and internal environment.	Takes the internal only.
Corrective action is ongoing.	Corrective action may be taken if budget period has elapsed.

Organizational Audits

Audits are also frequently utilized as a control method. Auditing has been defined by the American Accounting Association (AAA) to be "a systematic process of objectively obtaining and evaluating evidence regarding assertions about economic actions and events to ascertain the degree of correspondence between those assertions and established criteria and communicating the results to interested users."[8] These audits generally fall into three basic groups:

1. *Independent audit.* This is usually performed by highly trained accountants who are paid to provide their services. Their primary purpose is to provide an extensive review of the corporation's financial dealings. These individuals can also provide the day-to-day bookkeeping and tax services required to maintain a functioning business corporation. Their audits determine whether the financial statements of the business conform to a predetermined set of rules, called Generally Accepted Accounting Principles (GAAP), and whether the statements fairly represent the activities of the organization.
2. *Government audit.* This is usually performed by one of two government agencies: The General Accounting Office (GAO), which performs audits of government agencies and companies with government contracts, and the Internal Revenue Service (IRS). These auditing agencies make a determination as to the organization's compliance with federal laws, statutes, policies, procedures, and rules. The auditing responsibilities of these two agencies are based upon the function of the organization being audited.
3. *Internal audit.* This is performed by employees within the organization whose task is to assist in determining whether organizational policies and procedures are being followed. These individuals also have the responsibility to safeguard organizational assets. Top-level management of an organization depends upon the expertise of these auditors to assist them in making financial decisions and are the most frequent users of the information they provide.

Another audit commonly utilized is the *management audit.* This procedure can be conducted by outside consultants or through the use of an organization's internal audit staff. The management audit is an attempt to systematically examine, analyze, and evaluate the overall performance of an organization's management team. This type of audit assists top-level management by providing an "outside" view of the management team's procedures and effectiveness.[9]

Chrysler Corporation offers a good example of a company utilizing a strategic control philosophy. After rushing to resolve a series of embarrassing defects on its Neon subcompacts, Chrysler incorporated a new design process. In the old days, individual departments operated in near isolation. The walls between design, engineering, and manufacturing made it easy for problems to slip into a product unnoticed. The emphasis then was to get vehicles out the door. Chrysler switched to a platform design system, where everyone is involved and an engineer is likely to be looking over the shoulder of a designer, ready to point out potential problems while they are still on the computer screen. Chrysler implemented a system to help ensure that its product quality was in line with that of its competitors.[10]

The idea of the *social audit* started in the early 1970s, and it became popular after many companies failed their social responsibility tasks. Traditional financial statements indicate how well the corporation has performed in an economic sense and how shareholder wealth has been improved by its operation. However, these statements do not indicate corporate social performance and its ability to formulate and implement strategy with respect to public policy issues. Social audit refers to the attempt to measure the social performance of the corporation and report this performance in a systematic manner to the stakeholders. Many companies have opened their books to external reviewers who evaluate and report on their social performance just like an independent auditor who evaluates financial records and provides a financial report according to the GAAP. Other companies choose to disclose information about their social programs to their stakeholders. In both cases, companies show that they fulfill their obligation to society that goes beyond financial performance.

Total Quality Management (TQM)

TQM is the integration of organizational functions and processes in order to achieve continuous improvement of the quality of goods and services. TQM means thinking about quality in terms of all functions of the enterprise and is a start-to-finish process that integrates interrelated functions at all levels. TQM strategies and methods are developed as practical, hands-on techniques on how to manage and improve the company's competitive position in an increasingly competitive global environment. There are many variations of TQM. Evidence of the importance of TQM is the enthusiastic response to the Baldrige award, which was initiated in 1988 to recognize high-quality businesses. In a Gallup survey, 73 percent of CEOs believe that

American business is committed to quality and 84 percent of consumers agree with that.[11]

Implementing TQM requires close cooperation among everyone in the organization to ensure the goal of quality. Management is responsible for making the commitment to quality an organization-wide goal. The company needs to identify the customer's needs and expectations and what the company is already providing to the customer. This is followed by an assessment of how close the company is to meeting those needs and expectations. The company must then create a means to measure the quality of its goods and services. A control chart is one of the tools used to ensure the quality of products produced. Other tools used in process control include flowcharts, check sheets, Pareto, and fishbone diagrams. A flowchart is a graphic representation used to trace the flow and sequence of the various steps of a process or part of it; it helps management to detect redundancies in the process. Check sheets are tools used to collect information from various sources and present them in a meaningful format to help management or teams identify problems or inefficiencies in the various activities; they are also used to collect information, not opinion, from internal and external customers about the quality of products and services provided by the organization; data must be cautiously and accurately compiled and presented. Pareto charts are graphic representations that rank problems, deficiencies, and causes from most significant to least significant; the information provided by the check sheets, by the cause and effect diagram, and through brainstorming is ranked by Pareto charts to prioritize the most crucial problems in the organization.

This chart was developed in the nineteenth century by Vilfred Pareto, a socioeconomist who stated that most wealth was concentrated among a few, only 20 percent of citizens, while the great majority, or 80 percent of people, live in poverty. Juran extended this concept to quality-control applications. He indicated that 80 percent of effects come from 20 percent of possible causes. The Fishbone diagram, or the cause and effect diagram, is a tool that helps to identify the relationships between an effect and its possible causes; this diagram is used in brainstorming and other creative thinking activities to assist management and teams in identifying the possible roots of the problems the company faces. After process control, the next step consists of the company setting goals and initiating ways to reach those goals. Creating incentives is one way to assist in reaching goals.

TQM has been accepted in a variety of service industries. However, TQM can be applied to all enterprises, both manufacturing and service. TQM had success in Japan and came with important lessons for American corporations. There are no easy answers to improving U.S. products and services in the domestic and international markets. TQM is a cultural transformation approach; quality and speed are complementary rather than contradictory in nature.

TQM emphasizes the need to recognize defects during the work process, where most defects are likely to occur. Once a defect is identified, the company must locate the source of the error, find the cause, and make corrections to ensure that it does not reoccur. Deming claimed that 96 percent of variations have a common cause, while only 4 percent have a special cause. He contended that as quality improves, costs will decrease and productivity will increase, resulting in more jobs, greater market share, and long-term survival. His main focus was on improving the system, which he believed was the main cause of variations.[12]

Statistical procedures can be utilized to determine variations in the quality of goods and services. An area where poor quality is often found is component parts. To decrease these defects, a company must work with suppliers to improve the quality of the component parts that are being supplied.

The four leading proponents of TQM are Deming, Crosby, Juran, and Feigenbaum. All agree that management must take decisive action to ensure that quality becomes part of the company culture rather than just waiting for it to happen.[13]

If the company commits itself to implementing TQM, the efficiency of its operation will improve tremendously. The quality of the products and services the company provides will improve over the years. Waste and rework, along with the overtime that goes with them, will decrease, and hopefully the employees will be more motivated to work as a team to achieve corporate strategy.

Many quality programs fail to deliver the expected results because top management fails to understand the importance of strategic management in applying TQM concepts. Therefore, most companies will adopt TQM without an in-depth understanding of its underlying strategic foundation, and without the evangelical involvement necessary to sustain the process. The determination of the primary long-term goals and objectives, the coherent vision, the adoption of courses of action, education and training, and a follow-up by managers of all employees is the focus of TQM. A failure rate of 70 percent in the implementation of TQM is an alarming indication of the seriousness of the problem, especially when most managers continue to manage without any fundamental change in their behavior. That is why many companies are reluctant to embrace TQM. Organizations tend to give up when faced with such crises in implementing TQM. This should require companies to examine and analyze the actual causes of failure and deal with them strategically. As the competitive environment is pushing most organizations to their limit, a fundamental rethink and a new approach to the application of TQM is urgently required.

In 1987, the International Standards Association of Geneva, Switzerland, established new quality standards called ISO 9000. Quality is defined as the corporate approach to satisfy, or even exceed, the needs and expectations of customers. ISO 9000 registration is virtually a requirement for doing business in European markets. ISO 9000 deals with the following principles:

1. Customer-focused organization
2. Leadership
3. Process approach
4. Involvement of people
5. System approach to management
6. Factual approach to decision making
7. Mutually beneficial supplier relationships
8. Continuous improvement

ISO 9000 certification may be used as a means to meet requirements for doing business with certain customers in certain markets. However, it can also be a positive intervention for improving organizational effectiveness. Although this approach to quality is usually applied to an entire organization, it can be applied to a particular division or department equally well. TQM is a comprehensive measure of corporate process and quality. ISO first published its quality standards in 1987, revised them in 1994, and then republished an updated version in 2000. These new standards are referred to as the ISO 9000 2000 Standards. Currently, ISO 9000 is supported by national standards bodies from more than 140 countries. This makes it the logical choice for any organization which does business internationally or which serves customers who demand an international standard of quality. ISO 9001 is a quality measure used by companies that design, produce, inspect, test, install, and service items. (For example, a manufacturer that designs and produces furniture.) It is the most comprehensive standard. ISO 9002 is a quality measure used by companies that produce, inspect, test, install, and service items. (For example, a manufacturer that produces but does not design furniture.) ISO 9003 is a quality measure used by companies that must inspect and test items. (For example, an importer or distributor.)

ISO 9004 is a quality measure that is used by all forms of service companies. For example, DaimlerChrysler realized that the key to improving supplier quality was the use of universal quality standards by all automotive suppliers. The U.S. "Big Three" automakers and their suppliers have adopted the QS 9000 standards, which are similar to ISO-9000 standards. The QS 9000 standards include the ISO-9000 requirements along with additional requirements pulled from prior automotive industry quality standards. DaimlerChrysler uses a computerized online system that communicates quality data to suppliers when needed. It will inform suppliers immediately if a shipment is late or if it included defective parts. This is a very effective control measure for both DaimlerChrysler and its suppliers. QS 9000, with its ISO-9000 documentation, is the platform for coordination with suppliers.[14]

Reengineering

Another buzzword in management circles is *reengineering,* which involves the search for and implementation of radical change in the business process. Its chief tool is a clean sheet of paper. Most change efforts, like TQM, start with what exists and fix the existing process. Reengineering starts from the future and works backward, as if unconstrained by existing methods, people, and departments. In effect the question is asked, "If we were a new company, how would we run this place?"[15] Union Carbide used reengineering to eliminate $40 million of fixed costs in just three years. GTE obtained tremendous benefits from applying reengineering techniques. Nonetheless, the process is not for everyone, as many companies are finding out. Complete commitment from top management is necessary for successful implementation.

Two other primary forms of organizational control exist that are necessary for adequate control of a complete corporation. *Management control* assesses whether the major subsystems of the organization are functioning according to the strategic objectives. *Operational control* monitors the behavior of individuals to ensure that it fits their job descriptions. These forms of control are not always clearly separable. Like many other procedures, they frequently overlap.

INTERNATIONAL CONTROL

The international control process presents some unique problems when compared to a typical domestic control process. The first, and probably most difficult, problem is the communication gap. The remote location of a business unit or subsidiary hinders the free flow of information, which is critical to the control process. The communication gap between countries can be narrowed with the plethora of communications technology available today. But the lack of information within the foreign country itself, especially third world countries, concerning marketing data, consumer preference, government data, etc., is different. Usually a company can do little to improve this information gap. Internal monitoring systems designed by the company will either be unable to gather external data or, if they are designed to gather large amounts of external data, will be too costly to operate. Since it is likely that less than ideal amounts of data are available, there are two basic approaches an organization can take to attack international control. One is to be extremely centralized with a global type of operation, and the other is to operate the foreign subsidiary as a separate "domestic" corporation.

Operating with a global centralization strategy is a human resource-intensive operation. To achieve proper control with this approach, an organizational management structure must be present in the foreign country, and a somewhat redundant structure must exist in the domestic headquarters. This allows daily operations to be maintained within the foreign country and provides data sources from which information can flow to the central organization. This also enables central management to incorporate foreign operations into the overall corporate strategic portfolio. Many corporations operate in this manner to ensure that information is properly transmitted between members of management. But great care must be taken to ensure that the decision-making process does not become too cumbersome and slow the reaction time to business challenges of the subsidiary.

Implementation of a multidomestic control structure also has advantages and disadvantages. A multidomestic control structure allows the subsidiary to operate as a self-sufficient corporation. This permits the foreign subsidiary to efficiently structure its goals parallel with the host country's culture and to efficiently react to its environment. The subsidiary was created to benefit the parent company in some way, but if the management structure between the subsidiary and the parent corporation is too loose, the original intention of the expansion may be not served. However, this complicates the aligning of the subsidiary's goals with those of the parent company.

Most multibusiness companies need to develop an explicit, formal process for monitoring strategic performance to ensure that profitability and competitive advantage are maintained over the long term. Multibusiness corporations decentralize to shift responsibility for strategy and results to the specific product market level, but this approach requires some process by which the center can set clear goals and performance standards and determine whether strategies are being successfully implemented. Most companies do not have a formal control process, preferring to set informal performance goals and to use feedback systems. A formal system, however, can engender clearer, more realistic planning, expanded performance standards, better motivated business unit managers, more timely intervention, and better defined responsibilities.

All of the previously discussed control methods will be employed in some acceptable mix within one of these two international frameworks. The only major difference in the control processes of domestic versus international organizations is the difficulty created by the addition of remote operations.

SUMMARY

In conclusion, control is an integral part of the strategic management process. The control process actually begins the moment an idea is conceived for improvement within an organization. It is not formal at this time, but elements that facilitate the control process are already being considered. The ultimate standard of performance is already formulated in the form of the conceived desired result.

As the strategic management process unfolds, certain more manageable facilitators must be incorporated into the process. More definitive standards of performance, time constraints, and resource requirements are just some of the elements of the control process. Then, as the control process is actually designed, further tools are developed. Information gathering systems, management decision support systems, and resource allocation schedules are prepared.

Further, as the strategic management process begins operation, vehicles of control are employed. Management by objectives, time-related control methods, audits, and budget revisions are employed to guide the process to the desired outcome. The desired outcome is also evaluated to ensure that it is really desirable.

If the control process is performed properly, errors in the design of the strategic management process will be corrected, including adjustments for changing external variables. It is imperative that the control process not be omitted from the strategic management process. Controls provide useful, critical links that will ensure that the effort in the strategic management process yields the proper dividends.

REVIEW QUESTIONS

1. In what ways do strategy-related policies help enforce strategy implementation?
2. What is the cultural implementation approach?
3. What are some of the techniques used by companies to develop an effective corporate culture?
4. During strategy implementation, the formal system of reporting must have certain characteristics to have value. What are these characteristics and how are they of value?

5. What are the issues involved in exerting strategic leadership?
6. What are the five fundamental approaches used when implementing strategies?

NOTES

1. Thompson, A. (1976). How to share control. *Management Today,* September, p. 148.

2. Byars, L. (1991). *Strategic Management: Formulation and Implementation,* Third Edition. New York: HarperCollins Publishers, pp. 218-221.

3. Harrison, F. E. (1991). Strategic control at the CEO level. *Long Range Planning,* 24(15), p. 83.

4. Higgins, J. and Vincze, J. (1996). *Strategic Management and Organizational Policy: Text and Cases.* Chicago: Dryden Press, p. 211.

5. Wheelen, T. L. and Hunger, D. (2000). *Strategic Management and Business Policy,* Seventh Edition. Upper Saddle River, NJ: Prentice-Hall, p. 235.

6. Tompkins, B. G. (1985). *Project Cost Control for Managers.* Houston: Gulf Publishing Company, pp. 40-45.

7. Needless, B. Jr., Powers, M., Mills, S., and Anderson, H. (1999). *Financial and Managerial Accounting,* Fifth Edition. Boston: Houghton Mifflin Company, p. 903.

8. Byars, *Strategic Management: Formulation and Implementation,* p. 224.

9. Ibid., p. 225.

10. Eisenstein, P. A. (1995). Chrysler confronts string of embarrassing recalls. *Investor's Business Daily,* February 15, p. 3.

11. Murphy, J. and Taylor, J. A. (1995). Taking quality as seriously as profits. *Industrial Engineering,* 27(1), 28.

12. Anderson, J. C., Rungtusnatham, M., and Schroeder, R. G. (1994). A theory of quality management underlying the Deming management method. *Academy of Management Review,* 19(3), 472-509.

13. Ross, J. E. (1995). *Total Quality Management: Text, Cases and Readings.* Delray Beach, FL: St. Lucie Press, p. 27.

14. Fischer, B. D. and Afifi, R. (2000). Using ISO-9000 certification as a platform for an organizational effectiveness program. *Business Research Yearbook,* Volume VII, p. 451.

15. Hammer, M. (1993). If I had a hammer. *Sales and Marketing Management,* 145(15), 56.

Chapter 10

Strategic Management in Profit and Not-for-Profit Organizations

INTRODUCTION

The key to success for any organization is to have a comprehensive strategic plan. Such a plan should be carefully designed so that all forms of management are directly involved. Systematic strategic planning should develop a proactive culture that increases the probability of developing strategic thinking among the key decision makers. In this chapter, the strategic management process in both profit and not-for-profit organizations is reviewed and compared.

EVOLUTION OF NOT-FOR-PROFIT ORGANIZATIONS

Before 1780, very few corporations existed, and not-for-profit organizations were nonexistent in the British colonies, due to England's control. In the decades following the Revolutionary War, corporations (for-profit) and not-for-profit organizations became more abundant. Until the United States became more unified, however, the status of not-for-profit organizations was ambiguous and varied from state to state. In the early 1900s, not-for-profit organizations existed in a wide variety of areas. Also, at that time, not-for-profit organizations had a more vital role in society and were mostly supported by for-profit organizations. As not-for-profit organizations grew in popularity, the government became more actively involved in their success. Today, not-for-profit organizations are more effective and bigger than ever. The IRS, for charitable deduction purposes, recognizes more than one million. Over three-fourths of all their funding now comes from private individuals, primarily due to the adoption of strategic planning practices.

WHAT IS A NOT-FOR-PROFIT ORGANIZATION?

A not-for-profit (NFP) organization is defined in this chapter as *any institution legally constituted, governmental or nongovernmental, incorporated under state or federal laws as a charitable or not-for-profit enterprise that has been set up to serve some public purpose or cause and is tax exempt according to the United States Internal Revenue Service* (see Box 10.1). Therefore, any organization that is approved by state or federal laws, in order to be considered not-for-profit, must be exempt from paying state or federal tax and have a public purpose. NFP companies usually possess a special legal status that stipulates that all donations made to them are tax deductible.

BOX 10.1. Example of Not-for-Profit Organization: The American Red Cross

In the fall of 1989, the Red Cross mounted one of the largest disaster relief operations in its history to aid the thousands of victims of Hurricane Hugo and the Northern California earthquake. Americans responded with more than $177 million in cash contributions for these and other disasters. The Red Cross faces extraordinary challenges every year. From 1989 through 1992, it dealt with hurricanes, tornadoes, fires, and a major earthquake. The Red Cross also specializes in educating and assisting people infected with the HIV virus, conducting blood drives, and many other projects. As the Red Cross faces new challenges every year, it rises to the occasion with new volunteers, new ideas, new technologies, and new solutions.

Mission of the American Red Cross

As stated in the 1990 annual report, the mission of the American Red Cross is to improve the quality of human life, to enhance self-reliance and concern for others, and to help people avoid, prepare for, and cope with emergencies. It does this through services that are governed and directed by volunteers and are consistent with its congressional charter and the principles of the International Red Cross. The American Red Cross also has established goals in the areas of humanity, impartiality, neutrality, independence, voluntary service, unity, and universality. The Red Cross has been trying to do the following:

1. Improve and innovate new technologies
2. Enhance its volunteer program
3. Increase the amount of funding for disasters and emergencies
4. Establish more natural disaster reduction programs

(continued)

(continued)

5. Distribute public service announcements by celebrities to increase awareness
6. Increase the support of other organizations for the use of their facilities, equipment, personnel, and other resources
7. Reduce expenses to free up more capital for disaster relief projects
8. Do as much as it can for all people in an emergency

Role of the Board of Directors

In 1989, the Red Cross Board of Directors announced three significant actions. The first action was to relocate Red Cross headquarters to Fairfax County, Virginia. This improved communications and efficiency and reduced costs. The second action was that all funding of disaster relief which is designated by a donor for a particular disaster would only be used in that area. The third was the completion of the reversion of the Red Cross pension fund, which had the effect of creating a one-time addition of $152 million to Red Cross net assets. This freed up much-needed capital to be managed by a knowledgeable internal committee for practical new services to those in need.

The board also recognized that they must keep evaluating their performance to maintain excellence. They can no longer rely on their reputation or take their quality service for granted. The Red Cross must constantly examine how they have served the public and determine ways to improve.

Note: Most of this information comes from the 1990 Red Cross Annual Report.

They are also granted a variety of other tax subsidies such as special postal rates, exemptions from property taxation, and other considerations. NFP organizations serve three main purposes:

1. Perform tasks in society that benefit the public interest
2. Fill the void where government and for-profit organizations choose not to participate
3. Influence policy making by governments and other organizations

In many sectors, NFP organizations compete not only with one another, but also with for-profit organizations and government. Today, NFP organizations are almost as competitive as organizations in the for-profit sector. NFP organizations are often protected from their competitors. It is not rare for state and federal government agencies to implement policies to shelter

NFP organizations. If such protection is not provided, it could lead to the extinction of NFP organizations.

To avoid misinterpretation of not-for-profit nomenclature, we must pay specific attention to the NFP organizational structure and its legal status. Organizations that were set up to make profits but have failed to do so are *not* NFPs. Organizations that are government-sponsored and are not-for-profit organizations fall under an umbrella of public not-for-profit organizations.

For-profit organizations produce the major portion of the U.S. gross domestic product. They include public and private corporations. Public corporations issue stock to outsiders, whereas private corporations belong to a single person or partnership (such as lawyers and doctors). Ironically, even though sole proprietorships have the largest market share of the industry, corporations have higher sales volumes. Four major classifications of organizations are listed below.

1. *Private for-profit organizations*. These include corporations, partnerships, and sole proprietorships.
2. *Public not-for-profit organizations* (that trade stocks in a public place). These include state-owned airlines, utilities, and so forth.
3. *Public not-for-profit organizations* (that do not trade stocks in a public place). These include government agencies, public schools, and public hospitals.
4. *Private not-for-profit organizations*. These are organizations that provide services for the good of the society and are supported by private funds. These include private museums, charities, foundations, public interest groups, universities, religious institutions, and hospitals.

Private NFP organizations are referred to as third-sector organizations because they are not-for-profit, nor are they government based. There are eight major categories of private NFP organizations: Religious, social, cultural, knowledge, protective, political, philanthropic, and social cause.[1]

For an NFP corporation to survive as a vital force, it must have the ability to deal with funding crises and, more importantly, to anticipate and plan for the future in this turbulent, complex, and resource-scarce environment. Strategic management is thus equally important to not-for-profit organizations. Without a clear plan, no organization can survive. Strategic planning enables an organization to face unanticipated changes effectively and takes advantage of the existing opportunities. Organizations that competently utilize strategic planning have the greatest chance of survival and endurance. It is important for all organizations to analyze their environment, formulate their mission, goals, and objectives, and streamline resources in the proper manner to meet their goals.

All organizations also must articulate a clear mission. Not-for-profit organizations typically articulate their mission in the public domain. If organizations are to succeed, they must set specific goals and craft a strategy to accomplish their objectives. These attributes may be extremely involved and complex, but they are necessary in both profit and not-for-profit organizations. Organizations require specific skills to meet their objectives and accomplish their mission. In designing strategies, we must consider the following characteristics that differentiate between profit and not-for-profit organizations.

MISSION STATEMENT

A mission statement is a broad assertion of the basic, exclusive purpose and scope of operations that sets the organization apart from others. A mission statement serves many purposes. For managers, it can be a benchmark for success. For employees, it defines a common purpose, nurtures loyalty, and fosters a sense of community. For external stakeholders, such as major investors, government agencies, and the public at large, mission statements help provide unique insight into an organization's culture, values, and future directions. A mission statement helps define the organization and set achievable objectives. Therefore, decision makers should be very careful in designing a clear definition of the mission and purpose of the organization.

Under certain conditions, the mission statement may need revising. General Motors, having faced stiff competition in their main business during the 1970s, moved quickly into other nonautomobile operations. For example, they diversified into space engineering and research, management information services, and computer operations. GM in this case might have decided to broaden its mission from concentrating mainly on automobile productions to include these other operations.

In the short run, any firm with a strategic advantage can survive and prosper. Organizations with a long-term strategic management commitment will continue to succeed. Fortunately, many organizations, both profit and not-for-profit, have begun realizing the importance of strategic management.

NFP organizations focus their mission on service, mutual benefit, and commonwealth rather than profit. Their strategic policy is often vague and qualitative rather than precise and quantitative, as in the for-profit organizations. An example of an NFP mission statement is that of Mercy Medical Center. Its mission is to preserve health care facilities that, in collaboration with the medical staff, are to be devoted to the care of the "total person" and family throughout the life cycle by providing resources for physical, emotional, and spiritual needs, without distinction to religious beliefs, race, natural origin, age, sex, disability, or economic status. In contrast, a for-profit mission statement would encompass product quality, service, and price and profit philosophy. For example, Montana Company's mission is to serve faithfully the needs of the community by providing products and services of superior quality at a fair price to company customers.

Mission statements of NFP organizations appear to have some problems. One problem is the absence of a clearly defined mission and of a clearly stated objective. General goals are more likely to be accepted by the diverse stakeholders. Also, inexplicit goals are less likely to invite close scrutiny and debate than specific goals. This will avoid alienating a potential supporter of the organization. The separation of fund providers from clients and users contributes to the lack of clarity in mission statements. Usually, the contributors often have a great influence on the mission selected. In contrast, the for-profit organization's primary mission is external, focusing on markets and customers, where it typically notes current fields of endeavor. Mission statements simply identify how one business tends to achieve profits and how a similar firm may do in the market. It is easier to measure sales, market share, profits, return on investment, and so on. Usually the mission is a reflection of the CEO's vision.

In an NFP, organization leadership usually changes very frequently, and in most instances will possess different visions. This makes it difficult to formulate and implement a long-term strategy. Employees may not put much effort into a strategy since they know that current strategy may be short-lived. Remember that decisions in NFP organizations are based on providing services to society continuously without any profit or often even an expected outcome. This is not to say NFPs are not concerned with cash flow—they are. But the money raised through donor campaigns and other fund-raising efforts is dedicated to providing services rather than returns to shareholders.

STRATEGIC OBJECTIVES

In a for-profit organization, the broad mission statement is converted into more specific operative guidelines. At the highest level, strategic policies provide general guidance in the formulation of objectives and strategy. Objectives are more specific and measurable than goals and move the organization toward goal achievement. All managers set objectives. Each organizational unit needs concrete, measurable performance targets that specify a course of action in meeting its objectives. By dividing the overall organizational objectives into specific targets for each strategic business unit and holding the operating managers accountable for achieving their part, the organization can efficaciously achieve its overall objectives.

Objective setting is usually driven from the top down rather than from the bottom up. Lower-level managers are given direction so they can formulate objectives and strategy that are in step and support the higher manager's objectives. Using this reasoning, every level of organization and management contribute to the overall objectives of the organization. Both short-range and long-range objectives are necessary. Short-range objectives include objectives that management needs to work toward in the next year or two. Long-range objectives instruct management to consider what they can do now for the long term.

Although NFP organizations are basically the same as for-profit organizations when it comes to objectives, there are some differences. NFP organizations emphasize budgets instead of sales and profit contributions. As stated earlier, the contributors of financial support greatly influence the mission as well as the objectives in NFP organizations. Some services are intangible, hard to quantify, and require good qualitative judgment and therefore are difficult to measure. Many external forces exert pressure for reduced spending while internal forces focus on survival and on achieving the organizational mission within or just above the allotted budget with a hope of acquiring a larger budget in the coming year.

In not-for-profit organizations, the internal components compete among themselves for funding, personnel, clients, audiences, influence, and prestige. Usually, funds allocated to NFP organizations have a political affiliation, as special interest groups, political representatives, or a dominant public figure influences them. Gaining patrons and contributors, clients and customers becomes a high-priority objective for a NFP organization. These objectives, in fact, are its raison d'être. Its other important objectives center on the needs of its employees and satisfaction of customer and client needs at optimal efficiency. Efficiency objectives, which once were not expected of NFP organizations, today are vital for their credibility and growth.

Not-for-profit and for-profit organizations differ in their environments. Sources of revenue for the NFP organization are various, such as contributions, donations, dues, taxes, and the sale of their products and/or services. An NFP center that provides services to the elderly or mentally retarded relies heavily on contributions and donations from the government and from people who may never use the services provided. Because of the limited resources available to various government agencies, financial planning and how to control funds is very important for all NFP organizations.

The business organization's source of revenue is usually the sale of its products and services. When planning, businesses take the various stakeholders (i.e., owners, employees, major customers and major suppliers) into consideration.

NFP organizations deal with a greater number and diversity of stakeholders, including government agencies, legislative bodies, judicial bodies, public interest groups, political pressure groups, volunteers, customers, and the contributors who may never use the organization's outputs. Therefore, management in the NFP has less managerial autonomy than in business organizations.

Management by Objectives (MBO)

Organizations establish many types of specific and general objectives. Typically, top management sets the overall long-range objectives in each performance area in consultation with middle managers. These objectives are communicated by middle managers to the next lower level of appropriate managers, and sometimes even with nonmanagers. Then each participant works out measurable personal achievement targets, which coincide with the organization's overall goals. Middle managers then meet periodically with the participants to discuss their performance in relation to the overall objectives. Finally, all the participants hold periodic meetings to assess the degree of accomplishment so that any corrective measures necessary can be incorporated as a form of feedback and control. This process continues until objectives are realized. George Odiorne popularized this concept of management by objectives. MBO then was updated to include results and rewards (MBORR) in order to facilitate the attainment of objectives. MBORR is similar to the concept of management by results (MBR), which was developed in 1954 by Peter Drucker after he observed the successful functioning of this method at General Motors. This concept can be very effective in both for-profit and not-for-profit organizations.

MBORR has some limitations in the public not-for-profit sector that are not significant in the for-profit sector. First, most of the time the NFP organization's managers can do little to improve rewards. For example, Congress establishes the compensation of federal civil service employees. Therefore, the manager of a civil service organization cannot vary the compensation policy, even though doing so may motivate subordinates to perform better. Another limitation of MBORR in the public NFP sector is that the law preempts many decisions. Therefore, there is less opportunity to participate in setting objectives. For instance, the law sets many forms of reward and recognition. Further, in public NFPs, there is a greater emphasis on seniority than on merit. Finally, limited funds can result in a reduction of staff levels that could hinder MBORR administrative duties and render the organization incapable of offering rewards.

These limitations create a lack of flexibility in making efficient decisions and provide less control in determining one's own accountability and destiny. They often reward the inefficient and punish the efficient. Therefore, managers of most NFP organizations search for better management methods due to increasing pressures from the organization's service users and from its patrons and financial supporters.

CRAFTING A STRATEGY

Every company has some sort of a strategy, although it may not be stated. It may exist only in the mind of the CEO or in some members of top-level management. The methods used to craft a strategy for NFP organizations are considerably different from the methods used by for-profit organizations. When crafting a strategy for an NFP, the concern is not with the money to be made for the shareholders, as in the profit-making organizations, but instead with providing a vital and necessary service to a clientele that may or may not be able to pay for it. The NFP's mission is concerned with mutual benefit and common welfare. Its strategies must therefore reflect its interest and desire in gaining not only needy clients but also concerned contributors and supportive patrons. In the NFP organization, managers have less authority over their subordinates than business managers do. Decisions regarding employee performance evaluation, pay, promotion, termination, and disciplinary action are often subject to rules rather than managerial discretion.

Employees who carry out the strategy of the organization may receive the same rewards as those who ignore the strategy to pursue their own needs. Managers tend to take short-range approaches to strategic management. They may have excellent long-range plans but results do not show up immediately. Immediate results from short-term planning are what get managers reelected.[2]

The strategists in an NFP organization may be any of the following stakeholders: contributors, top managers, board members who are often chosen for their financial contributions, professional staff, clients, politicians, or societal representatives. The strategists may be a mixture between professional managers and volunteer managers, whose objectives as well as management skills usually differ considerably from those of the professional managers. Those responsible for planning must identify, evaluate, forecast, and monitor various events and trends outside the organization, which may impact current or future strategy.

NFPs examine themselves for strengths and weaknesses and assess their environments for threats and opportunities. What they examine, both within the organization and in the external environment, will differ from that of the for-profit organizations. Although most NFPs consider the same internal factors as the for-profits, target groups, techniques, and processes differ somewhat with regard to such economic functions as marketing and such management functions as leadership. The functions may be less sophisticated in the NFPs because the organizations are generally smaller and cannot afford top-level managers or sophisticated management information systems. Additionally, the two groups differ with respect to major power/influence groups. While the for-profit organizations have stockholders, the NFPs answer to contributors, taxpayers, or members whose expectations and influences are appropriately examined when crafting a strategy for the organization.

The major external differences between NFPs and for-profits include the role of government, the definition of competition and the industry, relations with society and reaction to pressure groups, the role of labor, and the influence or absence of influence of the client group. The role of the government significantly increases in NFP organizations since many NFPs are government agencies or receive government funds. Different governmental levels may be competing for the same federal money to fund their projects. The NFPs generally are sensitive to societal demands and to emerging pressure groups. The clients of the NFPs may have tremendous influence on the organization if they are members of a strong pressure group. NFPs are oriented more toward budgets than sales and profits. It is not easy for them to identify units of service, because the units change as the service and client needs change. Historically, NFPs have been less concerned than businesses with efficiency and proper use of resources. Politically motivated people, who feel that the more people under their control (labor) the more important they are, manage most NFPs.

Therefore, crafting a strategy for an NFP organization is considerably different from crafting one for a profit organization. Where a for-profit organization is looking to make money and please its stockholders, the NFPs are looking to provide a service or mutual benefit to clients, contributors, and pressure groups. The word "competition" has a totally different meaning to the two types of organizations, and those formulating and crafting the strategy have different perspectives on it.

Like for-profit businesses, NFP organizations need to assess the internal and external environments before crafting strategies. However, not all not-for-profits look at the same factors to determine strengths, weaknesses, opportunities, and threats because of the wide variety of such organizations. The value of the environmental assessment is largely determined by the value of the information retrieval systems in place, both formal and informal. The budget limits of NFPs often preclude them from having the sophisticated information retrieval systems common in business, such as management information systems and strategic information systems. As a consequence, not-for-profit organizations may have less accurate information and informal sources to help them with determining SWOT.

The internal environmental factors, strengths and weaknesses, have to do with (1) how well the organization has identified its product or service, (2) how well it has marketed it to the target market, and (3) how well stakeholders are satisfied. This evaluation is not always retrospective, but it can predict future expected performance. Stakeholders include any group that has direct interest or investment in the organization. The government itself may be considered a stakeholder. State and federal regulations often play a role in enhancing an NFP's strengths or exacerbating its weaknesses and may even determine its survival.

With for-profit businesses, consumers of the product are also those who support the enterprise. NFPs have the added complication that two different groups perform these functions. That is, the consumers of the products or services often are not those who financially contribute to the support of the organization. This process effectively creates an additional group of stakeholders who can help the organization in assessing its position in the marketplace.

The external environmental factors of the NFPs have to do with competition. Although NFPs do not compete for profits, they do compete (often fiercely) for clients, personnel, funding, prestige, and influence. Government, potential funders (such as the United Way), charitable corporate boards, and foundations receive many more requests for funds from NFPs than they could ever satisfy. The competition for the charitable dollar is intense, with each NFP trying to present the right combination of service or product, efficiency and effectiveness, management expertise, and fiscal accountability.

STRATEGY FOR MULTI-PRIMARY-MISSION ORGANIZATIONS

All organizations, profit and not-for-profit, should have a strategy. The main strategy is the assembly of strategic plans formulated to achieve the organization's strategic objectives. Managers must understand that not-for-profit organizations should be managed as if they were earning profits. Increased earnings increase the amount of service the organization provides.

Missions should be clearly stated and objectives should be defined. Organizational leaders must recognize the need for a strategy and implement it. The main strategy for any organization is broken down into five parts: enterprise strategies, corporate strategies, business strategies, functional strategies, and operating strategies.

The Enterprise Strategy

The enterprise strategy is the overall strategy, a combination of all the other strategies. In formulating the enterprise strategy, the internal and external environmental conditions are assessed and accounted to help the organization achieve its objectives and conform to societal and organizational philosophies.

The Corporate Strategy

The corporate strategy addresses what business or businesses the organization ought to be in and what its conduct should be within that business. An organization that is not driven by its mission will fail. Organizations must focus on what business it is in, which should be ultimately stated in its mission. How the business conducts itself will result in success or failure for the organization. This aspect of the corporate strategy is important. Organizations that are positioned poorly will lead to failure. For example, an instance of risk involves organizations with multiple SBUs, some of which do poorly in highly competitive markets, affecting the performance of the entire organization.

The Business Strategy

The business strategy describes how a business will compete. A firm having a single business will concentrate on the business strategy because competition is its major concern; competition dictates how they will compete. An organization primarily concerned with competition will focus on its distinctive competencies to overcome the competition in the marketplace.

The Functional Strategy

The functional strategy focuses on supporting the organization's business strategies and utilizing its resources efficiently and effectively. There are basically two types of functional strategies. The first type consists of *economic* functional strategies concerned with marketing, operations, finance, human resource management, R&D, etc. The second type is *management* functional strategy, which includes planning, leading, controlling, organizing, problem solving, and communicating.

The Operating Strategy

The operating strategy is more specific and deals with day-to-day requirements of functional area support strategies. For-profit organizations may be involved in one line of business or many, and are usually referred to as single-SBU firms or multiple-SBU firms. Multiple-SBU firms develop the main strategy that covers all areas of the firm. Each SBU will have its own strategy, in terms of product or service and geographical location that cover only the single SBU within the total organization. These strategies usually deal with management techniques and set a limit on policy guidelines.

MANAGEMENT STYLES

Management styles should be pointed out as a clear difference between for-profits and NFPs. Managers in not-for-profit organizations, depending on the size, can be the CEO (or executive director), strategist, and accountant as well as any other title that fits the circumstance. Because NFP organizations depend on charitable donations or contributions, reduced revenue affects the organizational structure. If the NFP had SBUs and funding was reduced, the organization would be more likely to continue operating the SBU because of its public objective, but the additional management responsibility would be transferred to whomever the organization could afford to keep on staff (usually very small and distinct groupings). This is not to say that organizational structures are not affected in private sector for-profit organizations in the same way, but that NFPs are more likely to be affected by reduced revenues. That reduction would affect the management structure more rapidly in NFPs than it would in for-profit organizations.

Leadership roles are often strained in the not-for-profit organization since they are not controlled by the profit motive. NFP organizations have a public purpose and depend on interested individuals to support their effort. Leaders in many NFP organizations are specialists in the service they provide and are less likely to have been educated in business management. This tends to affect the long-term operations of the organization because of the lack of financial or management experience.

STRATEGIC DECISION MAKING IN NFP ORGANIZATIONS

Behavioral factors of the strategic decision process have been determined through the study of not-for-profit organizations. The concept of incrementalism was developed and researched in the government, but carried over into the behavior of for-profit and NFPs. NFPs tend to have multiple major constituents, inaccurate missions and objectives, and inherent bureaucracies.[3] These characteristics sometimes foster the development of incrementalism and decisions based on personality, rather than on information.

Of all decisions required in business operations, strategic decisions involve the greatest uncertainty. Their complexity results from their ability to alter the firm's relationship with its environment. Profit-oriented business firms incorporate issues such as geographical scope, industry position, extent of vertical integration, and orientation toward growth into strategic decisions.[4] Through strategic decision making, top management determines the position of the firm relative to its environment. This orientation to the environment is known as strategic posture.

Management, in addition, employs rational decision making to translate its mission into more specific objectives and to establish major plans of action to reach those objectives. Most discussions of decision making focus on problem solving, but other important issues include recognition, identification, and implementation. Decision making occurs not only as a result of problems but also as the result of opportunities.

EVALUATION AND CONTROL IN NFP ORGANIZATIONS

In general, businesses must be profitable or they are abandoned. Chief executives and their management teams are usually judged by the criterion of performance. What the organization did in comparison with similar firms and how well it performed in its environment are measures of the health and well-being of the enterprise. Harold Geneen, former chairman of ITT, has said:

> Judging the efficacy of management is not a subjective exercise. The Profit and Loss Statement can measure it at the end of the quarter or at the end of the year. You look at the numbers and see what happened. Management achieved either its goal or it didn't. To me everything else is nonsense.[5]

In contrast, it is commonly said that not-for-profit organizations, such as those delivering human service programs, resist effective management because they cannot be held accountable for their results. But most public sector organizations, like private enterprises, have some sort of performance evaluation based on techniques previously discussed in house. Unfortunately they may be poorly designed assessment programs, usually characterized by a lack of objective standards, including wrong or poorly defined performance criteria.[6]

The purpose of evaluation and control is to ensure that organizational performance is in accordance with the prescribed set of plans. Management's job is not complete without evaluation and control. Both are necessary whenever management assigns duties and delegates authority to subordinates. However, management must understand the functions in order to establish an effective evaluation and control system.

There are several requirements of a good evaluation and control system. The first requirement is that the controls must be understandable. Managers throughout the entity must understand the standards to be achieved and how the controls are applied. Another requirement of an effective evaluation and control system is that it must adhere to the organizational pattern. It must be simple enough to identify the responsible manager of the activity under some type of control. The third requirement of this system is that it must be flexible. Regardless of how thoroughly management prepares a plan, it still involves an estimation of the future. This means there is uncertainty.

The system must also be designed to keep pace with the continuously changing environment. The final requirement of the evaluation and control system is that it must give insight into the requisite corrective action. Not only must it expose deviations, it must also show who is responsible for them, and where they have occurred.[7]

An effective evaluation system requires commitment, a great amount of energy, and time to design, implement, and manage. Managers at all levels must embrace positive attitudes toward evaluation efforts and ensure that tailored standards are utilized. Moreover, evaluations should be scheduled, carried out in a timely manner, and be consistent with the priorities placed on the programs being reviewed. Therefore, feedback to upper and lower levels of the organization may provide the most beneficial aspect of the evaluation process, for it affords the opportunity to rethink strategy and develop new strategic objectives.

Essentially, the evaluation and control process involves three basic stages. First, to determine whether performance is in accordance with plans, it is necessary to set standards. *Standards* are criteria for judging results. In planning, management sets the objectives and goals the entity hopes to achieve. These goals and objectives are involved in defining where the business wishes to go and lets the business know when it has arrived. These specific goals become the control standards. Next, there must be a *check on performance.* After standards have been set, actual performance is compared to them. Work is observed, output measured, and figures and reports compiled. This is an ongoing process that, depending on the circumstances, must be performed continuously. The final stage of this process entails taking *corrective action* when deviations from the standards occur. However, if there are no deviations of performance from standards, the system of evaluation and control is fulfilled by the first two steps.[8]

Relevant outcome measurements, therefore, must consist of three specific aspects of program management: the continuous monitoring of program quality; demonstration of program effectiveness; and decisions about program modifications aimed at improving effectiveness. Outcome evaluation involves the capacity to relate program effects to cost, effort and client characteristics, and the application of an active planning process.[9]

A wide variety of evaluation and control measures are available for specific human service programs. The primary consideration is that the dimensions of outcomes are included which are felt to be important by the decision makers that are the intended users of the findings. It is also important that the measurement approach be adequate to detect an effect that has some practical importance. When possible, it is preferable to utilize standard rating scales that have been shown to be sensitive to differentiated service effectiveness.[10]

If evaluations are to effectively influence decisions, it is essential that decision makers participate in the design of studies. The decision makers may be members of the funding agency, heads of particular program components, or a group of line or staff workers. Likewise, program staff participating in the control and evaluation process must be involved in planning the studies. Vigorous interaction is necessary to develop mutual understandings of the outcomes to be measured and the methodologies to be used to report results.

Normally, the evaluation and control techniques used with for-profit organizations are also appropriate for NFP organizations. However, management control measures, such as financial control, are not typically relevant to the NFP organization. The problem of control is increased by the nature of the NFP's planning system, which usually has vague objectives, lacks the ability to quantify and enhance objectives, and employs the budget as the main control device.

Many techniques are involved in the control function of profit-oriented organizations. Some management control measures of profit-oriented organizations, especially profit and ROI, are not relevant to not-for-profit organizations. The control system of NFPs is made more complex by the nature of the planning system. Not-for-profit organizations usually have abstract and vague objectives and sometimes ill-defined plans of action. In contrast, for-profit organizations usually have explicit step-by-step plans that are clear and have a definite purpose of reaching the desired objectives or goals of the organization. Because of the NFP organization's lack of ability to quantify objectives, it often uses the budget as the principal control device. In contrast to the profit-oriented firm, the NFP organization has extremely loose ties between its objectives and its budget. Therefore, the budget approach for NFPs is inappropriate. The primary concern of an organization should be the accomplishment of its objectives, not its expenditures, because when its activities result in achieving objectives and reaching goals, the results could be more funding or recognition for the organization.

IMPLEMENTATION IN THE NFP SECTOR

There are differences in management systems and human resource management at the individual managerial level in for-profit and not-for-profit organizations. Since management systems are usually nonexistent in NFP organizations, the management consists of few people, and the decision-making process is usually complex. Management systems and management development often suffer because of lack of funding in NFP organizations.

Fund-Raising

Money is rarely used in the same way in the not-for-profit sector as it is in for-profit organizations. Funding is the major source of money in NFP organizations. Some types of funding that NFPs use are mail order appeals, life insurance gifts, and special events such as raffles, telethons, banquets, and dances, in addition to charitable tax-exempt donations. In contrast, for-profit organizations obtain much of their funding through the sales of stocks and bonds, and revenues received through sales. Money is rarely used as a motivator in NFP organizations because of the funding process and insufficient funds; in a profit-oriented organization, money motivators such as raises or profit sharing are often used.

Motivation Technique

Motivation techniques are limited in not-for-profit organizations. NFP organizations cannot award bonuses as profit organizations can when they do well. The services that NFP organizations provide are less likely to produce revenues the way a product produces profit in profit-making organizations. If revenues are produced, and they can be in the NFP organization, they are transferred to additional services. Motivation and pay tend to be lower in not-for-profit organizations. NFP organizations should be run like businesses to help combat this stereotype. To have efficient and productive staff, NFPs must realize that skills need to be rewarded. This is not to generalize that all not-for-profit organizations pay little and have low morale, as some are very competitive and maintain a productive workforce.

Therefore, there are evident differences between for-profit and not-for-profit organizations in objectives, leadership, motivation, communication systems, and individual managerial styles.

ROLE OF THE BOARD OF DIRECTORS IN FOR-PROFIT AND NFP ORGANIZATIONS

A key to success in many corporations is a strong board of directors. Failure can often be traced back to a weak board of directors. Stockholder interests are looked after within the company by the board of directors. Stockholders directly elect board members, and under corporate law the board represents the stockholders' interests in the company. Thus, the board can be held legally accountable for the company's actions. Its position at the apex of decision making within the company allows the board to monitor corporate strategy decisions and ensure that they are consistent with stockholder interests.

The roles of the board of directors in profit and not-for-profit organizations are similar. Historically, the roles of the board were to monitor the companies' social and political inputs, elect or remove a chief executive officer, recommend candidates to the board, and approve or disapprove strategic business decisions. However, the board of directors has historically accomplished very little regarding these functions. Even so, the board of directors still executes these functions and now also focuses more on strategic business decisions. They are concerned with overseeing the budget and determining the overall soundness of corporate policies.

The typical board is a mix of insiders and outsiders. *Inside directors* are required because they have valuable information about the company's activities. Without such information, the board cannot adequately perform its monitoring function. However, since insiders are full-time employees of the company, their interests tend to be aligned with those of management. Thus, outside directors are required to bring objectivity to the monitoring and evaluation processes. *Outside directors* are not full-time employees of the company. Many of them are full-time professional directors who hold positions on the boards of several companies. The need to maintain a reputation as competent outside directors gives them an incentive to perform their tasks as objectively and effectively as possible.

In choosing a new board member, management typically picks someone who will be loyal to existing management philosophies. Some critics even contend that the company CEO dominates most boards. In support of this view, they point out that both inside and outside directors are often the personal nominees of the CEO. This can lead to ineffective functioning of the board because the board's primary function is to oversee and evaluate management's performance in running the company. Choosing members based on their loyalty to management may result in biased decision making. The board should be critical of management when necessary and not allow feelings of loyalty to interfere with this function.

Individuals are sometimes invited to serve as directors of a not-for-profit corporation. Some consider this an opportunity to be of service to their community. Others might be reluctant to accept because of the liabilities involved if they fail to exercise due care in carrying out their duties. Careful exercise of the powers vested in a director of an NFP corporation will result in a pleasant experience for the individual and greater benefit to the community and corporation he or she serves.

Guidelines for Future Board Members

1. Before attending their first board meeting, new members should have an opportunity to review corporate documents such as the articles of incorporation or charter, bylaws, auditor reports, financial statements, corporate policies, and management reports. An initial orientation session should be held to train the new board member about corporate policies and expectations.
2. It is the board's responsibility to establish clear job descriptions for the CEOs and other officers along with specifying various committee assignments. It is the board's responsibility to ensure that all critical management areas are detailed and continuous review is taking place. Such areas include planning, organizing, personnel, program operations, tax and legal compliance issues, and financial reporting.
3. If the board wants to stay effective, it should meet regularly and frequently. Board members must be serious about their attendance at board and committee meetings. Before any meeting takes place, board members must do their homework by collecting information about each item on the agenda. It is the board's responsibility to re-

move directors who do not attend meetings or who are not efficient in their job.

4. Board members should be considerate individuals and always seek information from management and others in the community about the operation of the organization. The board is also responsible for judging what information it wants and needs from management. If this is abused and becomes a form of harassment of the staff, it should be brought to the attention of the full board. Corrective action should be taken by the full board.
5. Boards should monitor corporate policies and their enforcement, such as corporate policies to describe and control political campaign and lobbying activities.
6. When conflicts arise, board members need to be objective and responsible. The members should raise issues and concerns, register dissent, and insist that their views be recorded in the minutes.
7. Board members need to be alert and watchful of corporate resources and ensure their utilization in the pursuit of the corporation's best interest.
8. The board should ensure that the corporation has appropriate access to legal counsel and maintains proper accounting practices. The corporation should have an annual audit by an independent auditor (a certified public accountant).
9. When a conflict or reasonable doubts about a course of action occur, the board should seek outside independent advice and counsel from an attorney, certified public accountant, or other expert in the matter.
10. Periodically, boards should verify that all state, federal, and local tax payments, registrations, and reports have been filed in a timely and accurate manner.

Many large organizations, particularly NFPs, often look for big-name businesspeople or stars for their prestige and contacts. Smaller organizations typically look to fill gaps on their boards with community members they know (lawyers, accountants, etc.). Larger corporations have the luxury of being able to get well-recognized business leaders to serve as board members. This not only enhances the image of the company but also brings a wealth of outsider knowledge to the company. This gives it more of a broad view of today's business world, which can give a company a competitive edge in the world or local market. Overall, boards need to go back to their original functions and get involved with organizational strategy formulation and control.

CONCLUSION

In general, profit and not-for-profit organizations have many similarities, but some significant differences as well. One of the main differences is in their strategic management. All organizations must do some type of strategic planning in order to survive. In the NFP organization, service is the major concern, and cost effectiveness is not typically an issue in the mission statement. On the other hand, the for-profit organization believes service and cost effectiveness go hand in hand as the major concern. That is why quality service is often indicated in its mission statement.

One early step in strategic management is developing strategic objectives that indicate the organization's intended results. Not-for-profit organizations place emphasis on budgets instead of sales and profit. Contributions to resource providers take the place of contributions to owners in the for-profit organizations. Usually the people who contribute financial support have great influence on the mission as well as objectives of an NFP organization.

Often, the management of NFP organizations has less freedom in managing due to regulations and laws. Therefore, the formulation of master strategies and objectives must be done within many limitations. Strategic plans must also be made while considering the ever-changing environment in which the organization operates.

A for-profit organization usually expects to make money and please its stockholders. The NFPs are looking to provide a service or mutual benefit to their clients and please their contributors or pressure groups. Competition has a totally different meaning to the two types of organizations, and those formulating and crafting the strategy are coming from different points of view. While profit-making organizations are looking to make money by calculating units of products, the NFPs are looking to stay within a budget and provide units of service.

As far as strategic management and decision making are concerned, there are many similarities between profit and not-for-profit organizations:

1. Both must have strong, successful strategic management to survive.
2. The basic steps of strategic management are the same for both for-profit and not-for-profit organizations.
3. Both have various divisions, each with its own strategy.
4. Both use the power of coalition (the ability of various leaders to exert their strength).
5. Both have varying mission strategies for each profitable division or successful agency.

6. Both use information from the internal and external environment when creating master strategies.
7. Both need cash flow and utilize communication.

For-profit and not-for-profit organizations differ in strategy formulation in the following ways:

1. The major difference lies in the different environments within which the two types of organizations operate. Both are affected by different factors, from competition in the for-profit sector to funding problems in the NFP sector. These and other factors affect their management styles and their formulation of strategic plans, objectives, and goals. Obviously these organizations would have very different master strategies, but the ways in which they develop these plans are quite similar.
2. Profit-oriented firms will get resources for each division from outside the firm, whereas NFP organizations will allocate resources among divisions.

Some similarities in decision making of for-profit and not-for-profit organizations:

1. They both use an incremental, step-by-step approach for decision making.
2. They both contend with the political nature of decision making.

For-profit and not-for-profit organizations differ in their decision-making processes, as well:

1. Behavioral factors of strategic decision making were developed by examining NFP organizations, but the ideas that arose also are applicable to profitable organizations.
2. For-profit firms use more power and strength than NFP firms.
3. For-profit firms' behavioral aspects of strategic decision making are somewhat more complex than those of NFP organizations.
4. For-profit firms use recognition, identification, and implementation, whereas NFP organizations base decisions on personality rather than on information.

Many key factors are necessary for success in not-for-profit organizations:

1. Constituency—the people served or involved
2. Manpower development—recruiting, developing, training, etc.

3. Programs and services—activities to be conducted; improve or expand old, present, or future programs
4. Financial resources—provide necessary current capital funds
5. Physical resources—acquisition and maintenance of land, building, and equipment
6. Community collaboration—join with other agencies to meet local, national, and international needs
7. Governance—provides for the influence of people in organizational decisions

The key factors necessary for success in for-profit organizations:

1. Inventory—where the company is now
2. Planning—what people need to do
3. Available workforce—how to get the right people and how to maximize their performances and potentials
4. Standards of performance—benchmarks to compare actual results to
5. Progress review—how well people perform
6. Development and control—what help is needed
7. Rewards and incentives—how much workers will be compensated

REVIEW QUESTIONS

1. List and describe the four major classifications of organizations. What are third-sector organizations? List the eight major types of private organizations.
2. List four requirements of a good evaluation and control system.
3. List and describe the three stages of the evaluation and control process.
4. Compare and contrast the control function in profit and not-for-profit organizations.

NOTES

1. Higgins, J. M. and Vincze, J. W. (1996). *Strategic Management: Text and Cases*. Chicago: Dryden Press, p. 356.

2. Wright, P., Kroll, M. J., and Parnell, J. (1996). *Strategic Management: Concepts and Cases*. Upper Saddle River, NJ: Prentice-Hall, Inc.

3. Young, D. R. (1983). *If Not for Profit, What For?* Toronto: Lexington Books, pp. 58-59.

4. Higgins and Vincze, *Strategic Management: Text and Cases*, pp. 356-357.

5. Geneen, H. and Moscow, A. (1984). *Managing*. Garden City, NY: Doubleday and Company, Inc.

6. Gordon, R. F. (1985). Does your performance appraisal system really work? *Supervisory Management,* 30(2), 37-41.

7. Scott, W. G. (1983). *Management in the Organization.* Boston: Houghton Mifflin Company, p. 89.

8. Ibid.

9. Franklin, J. L. and Thrasher, J. H. (1976). *An Introduction to Program Evaluation*. New York: John Wiley and Sons, Inc., pp. 123-125.

10. Katz, M. M. and Lyerly, S. B. (1963). Methods for measuring adjustment and social behavior in the community: Rationale, description, discriminative validity, and scale development. *Psychological Reports,* 13 (October), 28.

SECTION II: PREPARING A CASE ANALYSIS

Students should prepare a case study for a company of their choice using the Web site information provided in this section in addition to their own researched sources. There is no preset formula for preparing a case analysis because companies differ in focus, size, and complexity. Students must apply strategic management concepts and techniques to their case analyses. It is important to collect information about the company and its environments from various sources that are relevant and reliable. In writing the report, students are advised to discuss particular issues that will concern the organization, which follow. Students are also advised to avoid vague terminology, redundant words, acronyms, abbreviations, and biased language in writing and presenting their reports. Tables, figures, and charts may be used to help communicate important issues.

The case study may be prepared individually or may be undertaken as a group project. Each member of the group might research two or more of the steps and compile the information to formulate a strategic management plan for the company's future. Students must remember that their research should be done with the idea that they are acting as consultants to the organization or as top-level management. The following issues are relevant to each case listed in this section. Students must identify current sources for each of these companies and use them to write and analyze their cases.

IMPORTANT STEPS IN PREPARING A COMPREHENSIVE CASE ANALYSIS

1. Explore the history of this company from its origins to the present.
2. Identify the company's existing missions, visions, goals, objectives, and strategies.
3. Develop a mission statement for the organization.
4. Identify the company's strengths, weaknesses, opportunities, and threats.
5. Define and discuss this company's major competitors.
6. Discuss the current problems facing this company.

7. Determine what steps this company should take to improve its competitive position in today's marketplace.
8. Discuss how this company serves its community and its employees.
9. Determine the strategy you would use if you were CEO of this company. Recommend specific strategies and long-term objectives.
10. Specify how your recommendations can be implemented.
11. Justify your recommendation and why you think it will work.

Case 1

Ben & Jerry's

Founded by childhood friends Ben Cohen and Jerry Greenfield, Ben & Jerry's Homemade Ice Cream Shop opened on May 5, 1978, in downtown Burlington, Vermont. Ben & Jerry's is now an international company that strives to produce high-quality all-natural ice cream made from Vermont dairy products, to operate on a sound financial basis of growth, and to improve the quality of life of its local, national, and international communities. Ben & Jerry's treats its employees well and is concerned about social responsibility to society.

SUGGESTED SOURCES

Bayles, Fred (2000). "Reviews in on Ben & Jerry's Sweet Deal." *USA Today;* Arlington. April 20.

"Ben & Jerry's Homemade, Inc. Announces 1999 Fourth Quarter and Year-End Results." Press Release, January 26, 2000. Available online: <http://lib.benjerry.com/fin/qtr/1999/Q4-99.html>.

Haukebo, Kirsten (2000). "Sweet Suitor Buys Slim-Fast, Ben & Jerry's Unilever Wins Favor by Donating to Foundation." *USA Today;* Arlington. April 13.

"Ice Cream Makers Are 'Responsible' Capitalists." *USA Today;* Arlington. December 21, 1999.

"Report: Ben & Jerry's Is Takeover Target." *USA Today;* Arlington. April 10, 2000.

"Unilever Completes Ben & Jerry's Homemade Tender Offer." Press Release, May 16, 2000. Available online: <http://www.unilever.com/news/pressreleases/englishnews_1083.asp>.

U.S. Securities and Exchange Commission Web site: <www.sec.gov>.

Case 2

Blockbuster

The very first Blockbuster store opened in Dallas, Texas, in 1985. After acquiring Errol's Video, Inc., in 1990, Blockbuster started the following year with over 1,500 operating stores. By the end of 1992, Blockbuster had grown to include more than 3,300 stores.

The success of the company continued through 1995 by introducing the Blockbuster Entertainment Network, the Blockbuster Visa (the world's first electronic entertainment card), and the first electronic Blockbuster gift card.

In 1996, Blockbuster opened the first Blockbuster store within major retail locations at Wal-Mart Super Centers in Texas. They also joined with *The New York Times* to launch the monthly magazine for Blockbuster members, titled *Blockbuster Entertainment Feature Magazine.* By the end of the year, Blockbuster was operating more than 5,300 stores.

As of April 2001, Blockbuster has employed approximately 95,800 individuals to work in 7,200 stores worldwide. Blockbuster is a company that promotes franchising opportunities with their large number of stores and franchises in twenty-six countries.

SUGGESTED SOURCES

"Blockbuster Inc. Announces Agreement with Universal Pictures to Distribute Movies over the Blockbuster Entertainment on-Demand Service." *PR Newswire,* February 27, 2001.

"Blockbuster for Real." (2000). *Hudson Valley Business Journal,* 11(3), p. 23.

Blockbuster Web site: <http://www.blockbuster.com>.

Fitzpatrick, Eileen (2000). "Blockbuster Suits up for 'Phantom' Kickoff." *Billboard,* 112(16), p. 89.

Griffeth, Bill (2001). "Blockbuster and Radio Shack Chairmen & CEOs—Interview." *Power Lunch* (CNBC), February 28.

Jackson, Bechetta (2000). "NAACP, Blockbuster Video Plan to Team up for Voter Registration Effort." *Knight-Ridder/Tribune Business News,* September 1.

Sweeting, Paul (2000). "Blockbuster Eyes Blanket in Chill of VOD Battle." *Variety*, 381(5), p. 70.

Yahoo Finance: Blockbuster Profile. Available online at <http://biz.yahoo.com/p/b/bbi.html>.

Case 3

Tootsie Roll Industries, Inc.

Tootsie Roll Industries, Inc., has an extensive history that spans over 106 years. The company is the producer and distributor of a line of top-quality candy products known as Tootsie Rolls, along with many other items associated with the Tootsie Roll brand name. Tootsie Roll Industries, Inc., is still a fairly small business that has a niche market in the candy industry. Clara "Tootsie" Hirschfield, Leo's five-year-old daughter, inspired the candy's name. Children are the focus of Tootsie Roll's marketing because as consumers they create the greatest demand for confectionery products. The company still produces the same candy as it did back in 1896.

Successful sales have been attributed to Tootsie Roll's recently acquired brands, successful marketing promotions, and pre-Halloween sales programs. The company's internal cost-control programs also contribute to its impressive sales record. Tootsie Roll has been able to stay competitive in such a large and vast industry as the candy industry by producing a top-quality product.

SUGGESTED SOURCES

Marker, Mike (2000). "Tootsie Roll Industries, Inc., Purchases Assets of Andes Candies, Inc." May 15. Accessed online February 15, 2001: <http://www.tootsie-roll.com/newsPR20000418.html>.

Tootsie Roll Industries, Inc. (2001). *Financial Earnings Report.* February 12. Accessed online February 23, 2001: <http://www.tootsie-roll.com/financialER01022.html>.

Tootsie Roll Industries, Inc. (2001). "New Products—Charms Way 2 Sour Blow Pops." Accessed online February 25, 2001: <http://www.tootsie-roll.com/newsPR19990920.html>.

Tootsie Roll Industries, Inc. (2001). "New Products—S'Moresels." Accessed online February 25, 2001: <http://www.tootsie-roll.com/newsPR19990528.html>.

Case 4

Southwest Airlines

Southwest Airlines was founded in 1971 by Rollin King and Herb Kelleher. Their idea was to establish an airline company that flew between major Texas cities with low fares and no frills. The company started with only three Boeing 737 aircraft in 1971 and went public in 1975. The Airline Deregulation Act of 1978 allowed Southwest Airlines to enter markets outside the state of Texas. In the 1980s, Southwest's annual passenger count tripled. At year-end 2001, Southwest was operating 355 Boeing 737 aircraft and providing services to fifty-nine airports in fifty-eight cities in thirty states throughout the United States.

Air Transport World magazine named Southwest Airlines the Airline of the Year in 1992, stating, "Southwest has demonstrated excellence over the years in disciplines required for safe, reliable, and fairly priced air transportation." Prestigious *Fortune* magazine also devoted its cover and feature article to Herb Kelleher and Southwest Airlines. Between 1989 and 1993, the airline industry lost $12 billion. Southwest alone showed a profit. At Southwest, Fridays are not the only day casual attire is allowed—casual attire is an everyday policy. Southwest Airlines' employees are often compared to the cast of *Saturday Night Live.* Line-level training exists at Southwest: flight attendants train other flight attendants; secretaries train secretaries, etc. Other airlines have tried to imitate Southwest's success, but they are facsimiles of the real thing. Southwest is *the* low-fare airline. Southwest Airlines continues to grow and to dominate the airline industry and has shown a profit for twenty-six consecutive years.

SUGGESTED SOURCES

Applegate, Jane (1996). "Quirky CEO: Think Like an Entrepreneur." *Triangle Business Journal,* 12(11), p. 13.

Burns, Matthew (1999). "Southwest Boom Spurs RDU Parking Plans." *Triangle Business Journal,* 14(41), p. 7.

Cariaga, Vance (1999). "Southwest's Move into the Triangle." *Business Journal Serving Charlotte,* 13(49), p. 78.

Corry, Carl (1999). "Southwest Leads Way in 2nd Record." *Long Island Business News,* 46(39), p. 1A.

Rose, Sarah (1999). "How Herb Keeps Southwest Hopping." *Money,* 28(6), p. 61.

"The Top 25 Managers of the Year" (2001). *BusinessWeek,* January 8.

U.S. Securities and Exchange Commission Web site: <http://www.sec.gov/Archives/edgar/data/92380/000095013402000776/d93658e10-k.txt>.

Weil, Dan and Pounds, Stephen (2001). "The Airline Everyone Seems to Like." *Palm Beach Post,* January 20.

Yung, Katherine (2001). "Southwest Exec Flies Under the Radar in Checking Out New Cities to Serve." *The Dallas Morning News,* May 4.

Zellner, Wendy (2001). "After Kelleher, More Blue Skies." *BusinessWeek,* April 2.

Case 5

Airborne Express

Airborne Express was founded in 1946 as Airborne Flower Traffic Association of California. Its original purpose was to transport fresh flowers from Hawaii to the United States mainland. The company has been publicly traded on the New York Stock Exchange since 1975. For more than fifty years Airborne Express has served the shipping needs of business customers around the world. It is the third largest and fastest-growing air express delivery carrier in the United States. Airborne also serves as a freight forwarder in international markets.

Airborne's management believes that customer service and close contact with clients is the way to ensure that customer needs are met. Part of Airborne's sales strategy includes telephone representatives who call customers to solicit business. This technique has worked extremely well for them in doing business with smaller, low-volume shippers. Competition in the air express industry includes internationally strong companies such as Federal Express, United Parcel Service, DHL, and the United States Postal Service. In 1999, Airborne formed an alliance with the United States Postal Service, thus allowing shipping competitors to share the costs of logistics services. Airborne employed over 24,149 people worldwide in 2001.

SUGGESTED SOURCES

"Airborne Warns of Larger Loss" (2001). Accessed online, April 16: <http://news.lycos.com/headlines/business/article>.

"Consulting Firm Forecasts Air Cargo Revolution" (1999). *Journal of Commerce,* July 27.

"DHL Forecasts Strong Asia-Pacific Air Express Growth" (1999). *Air Transport Intelligence,* August.

Linn, Allison (2001). "Airborne to Begin Ground Services." Accessed online, April 19: <http://news.lycos.com/headlines/business/article>.

U.S. Securities and Exchange Commission Web site: <http://www.sec.gov/Archives/edgar/data/1172672/000089843002003186/d424b1.htm#toc>.

Case 6

Snapple

Snapple began selling all-natural juices in 1972 in New York City. Snapple is named after a carbonated apple soda that was part of the original beverage line. Revenues for Snapple grew dramatically during the early 1990s. Quaker Oat acquired Snapple in 1994 to help Quaker round out its beverage offerings, which include Gatorade. Quaker ultimately was not happy with Snapple's sales performance. They sold Snapple to Triarc Companies in 1997 for $300 million. From 1997 to 2000, Triarc worked on producing new products for Snapple. They have developed new Snapple candy—Snapple Beans, Whirls, Fruits, and Snapplets. Snapple beverages are distributed by more than 300 distributors across the United States. As of 1999-2000, Snapple products were also available in Asia and the Pacific, Europe, Latin America, and the Caribbean. The end of 2000 concluded Snapple's prior expansion objectives: Japan, Ireland, and Australia now have Snapple products.

SUGGESTED SOURCES

"Ameet Sachdev, British Candymaker, Buys Snapple, Others" (2000). *The Dominion Post Newspaper,* September 19.

Snapple Web site: <http://www.snapple.com>.

U.S. Securities and Exchange Commission Web site: <http://www.sec.gov/Archives/edgar/data/892563/0000950117-99-002621-index.html>.

Case 7

PepsiCo, Inc.

In the late 1890s, Pepsi-Cola was founded by Caleb Bradham. In 1965, PepsiCo, Inc., was created through the merger of Pepsi-Cola and Frito-Lay. PepsiCo is among the most successful consumer products companies in the world, with revenues of over $20 billion and 125,000 employees in the year of 2000. PepsiCo serves consumers in several major businesses, including beverages, snack foods, and juices. The company consists of Pepsi-Cola Company, the world's second largest soft drink business; Frito-Lay Company, the largest manufacturer and distributor of snack chips; and Tropicana Products, the largest marketer and producer of branded juice. PepsiCo brands are among the best known and most respected in the world and are available in about 190 countries and territories.

In 1996, PepsiCo faced many crises. Pepsi's biggest soft drink rival, Coca-Cola, took over two key markets in Russia and Venezuela. Almost overnight, Pepsi's largest foreign bottler, Baesa, was essentially bankrupt. The restaurant division at the time accounted for over 30 percent of the company's expenditures, yet returned only 18 percent of profits. Market share in relation to Coca-Cola was at its lowest point in twenty years, and net income was down 15 percent for the year. However, since then Pepsi has been making strides to gain a larger share of the soft drink market, including its January 2001 acquisition of 91 percent interest in South Beach Beverage Company (SoBe).

SUGGESTED SOURCES

McKay, Betsy (2001). "Sports Drinks Refresh Rivalry For Coke, Pepsi." *Wall Street Journal,* Eastern Edition, May 8, p. B1.

Noonan, David (2001). "Red Bull's Good Buzz." *Newsweek,* 137(May 14), p. 39.

"Pepsi and Tricon U.S. Restaurant System Renew Long-Term Alliance" (2001). Company Press Release, May 3. Accessed online: <www.pepsico.com>.

"Pepsi Bottling to Expand Plant" (2001). *The Wall Street Journal,* Eastern Edition, May 14, p. 1.

"Pepsi Takes New Twist on Cola" (2001). Company Press Release, June 7. Accessed online: <www.pepsico.com>.

"PepsiCo" (2001). *Standard and Poor's,* June 9.

"PepsiCo Buyout of Quaker Oats Could Be Delayed by FTC" (2001). *The Wall Street Journal,* Eastern Edition, May 9, p. A8.

Case 8

Pillsbury

In 1869, Charles Pillsbury dealt with farms personally from a wooden shack. The Pillsbury Mill showed a profit the first year. At the time, millers marked the finest grades of flour with three Xs. Charles Pillsbury and workers felt that their flour was the best, so they used four Xs. This commitment to quality has symbolized the famous trademark, "Pillsbury's BEST." By the end of the 1870s, millers were exporting as much as 35 percent of their production in Minneapolis. Pillsbury's giant "A" mill, the world's largest, set a one-day production record of 5,107 barrels on October 12, 1882. Five years later, Pillsbury was the largest flour miller in the world.

In 1967, Pillsbury became the first major U.S. food company to enter into the restaurant business, when it acquired Burger King. By 1979, Pillsbury acquired Green Giant and became one of the largest processors of branded vegetables in the world. The company makes grocery items, including frozen foods and refrigerated dough products. On October 31, 2001, General Mills completed the acquisition of the worldwide businesses of Pillsbury. On November 13, 2001, International Multifoods Corporation (IMC) purchased the Pillsbury dessert and specialty products businesses as well as certain General Mills brands and the General Mills Toledo production facilities for $316 million. Today, Pillsbury products can be found in more than seventy countries worldwide. Pillsbury has sales of $6 billion and employs more than 17,000 people worldwide.

SUGGESTED SOURCES

"New Cereal Bars, Fruit Snacks Doing Well for General Mills" (2001). *Candy Industry,* 166(3), p. 10.

Niedens, Lyle (2001). "U.S. Business Brief: Multifoods to Buy Several Pillsbury Brands." *Futures World News,* May 21.

Egerstrom, Lee (2001). "Pillsbury to Close Atlanta Plant, Lay Off 146 Employees." *Saint Paul Pioneer Press,* June 1.

"Pillsbury Plans $12.6 Million Expansion for Joplin, Mo., Plant" (2001). *The Kansas City Star,* May 9.
Pillsbury Web site: <http://www.pillsbury.com>.
U.S. Securities and Exchange Commission Web site: <http://www.sec.gov/Archives/edgar/data/40704/000089710102000567/genmills023880_10k.txt>.

Case 9

Hershey Foods Corporation

Hershey Chocolate Company was established in 1894 by Milton S. Hershey. By 1901, the chocolate industry was growing rapidly. Hershey sales reached $662,000 that year. The company expanded by adding new factories and acquiring others. By 1960, Hershey had become a household word. Net sales have increased from $4,220,976 in the year 2000 to $4,557,241 in 2001.

Today, Hershey Foods Corporation is engaged in the manufacture, distribution, and sale of consumer food products. The corporation's operations are concentrated in two divisions: Hershey Chocolate North America and Hershey International. Hershey Chocolate North America is the nation's leading domestic producer of chocolate and nonchocolate confectionery products as well as chocolate-related grocery products. Hershey International oversees all of the corporation's international interests. Hershey Foods Corporation exports products to over ninety countries worldwide, including Japan, the Philippines, Korea, and China. As of December 31, 2001, the corporation had approximately 14,400 full-time and 1,600 part-time employees, approximately 6,000 of whom were covered by collective bargaining agreements.

SUGGESTED SOURCES

Ball, Deborah, Frank, Robert, and Ellison, Sara (2002). "Nestle CEO Cool to Hershey Deal." *The Wall Street Journal,* August 30.

"Hershey Foods Corporation Does Not Endorse Mini-Tender Offer" (2002). *PR Newswire,* August 8.

"Hershey to Acquire Nabisco's Intense and Breath Freshener Mints and Gum Businesses" (2000). Accessed online August 14: <www.CBS.MarketWatch.com.>.

Hersheys Investor Relations on Hershey Web site: <www.hersheys.com>.

Johnson, Tom (2002). "RPT-Hershey Auction Turns Bitter; Actual Sale in Doubt." *Forbes,* September 1, p. 15.

"Tough to Swallow WSJ: Nestle CEO Says Hershey Merger Is Unlikely" (2002). *MSNBC:Business,* August 30.

U.S. Securities and Exchange Commission Web site: <http://www.sec.gov/Archives/edgar/data/47111/000004711102000069/form10k_2001.htm>.

Case 10

H. J. Heinz

In 1869, Henry John Heinz and his friend Clarence Noble launched Heinz & Noble. Its first product was Henry's mother's grated horseradish, bottled in clear glass to reveal its purity. By 1876, ketchup had been added to the company's condiment line. In 1946, Jack Heinz, grandson of the founder, made the company public. Heinz's leading power brands (sales exceeding $100 million) command number-one or number-two market shares in more than fifty countries. Heinz varieties are marketed in more than 200 countries and territories. The Heinz label is one of the most powerful global brands in the food industry. Heinz's most recent international ketchup expansion was the acquisition of two leading privately held food companies, based in San Jose, Costa Rica—Productos Columbia, S.A. and Distribuidos Banquete. This acquisition will allow Heinz to expand ketchup sales, as well as other popular Heinz brands and products throughout Central America. On January 29, 2001, Heinz acquired Vlasic Foods International. On March 1, 2001, Heinz acquired Cornucopia and Central Commisionary Inc., who produce and market refrigerated and frozen food products. Heinz manufacturing plants are found all over the world. Today Heinz markets more than 5,700 varieties in over 200 countries and territories and employs on a full-time basis, as of May 1, 2002, approximately 46,500 persons around the world.

SUGGESTED SOURCES

"Fresh Catch As John West Tuna Pouches Are the First to Hit UK Stores" (2001). *Business Wire* News Release found online at <www.heinz.com>, March 26.

"Heinz French Unit Recalls 2.3 Mln Tins of Mackerel" (1999). LEXIS-NEXIS. October 6.

"Heinz Further Builds Its European Tuna Business with Acquisition of Italian Brand" (1996). *Business Wire* News Release found online at <www.heinz.com>, May 21.

"StarKist Debuts Advertising for New Tuna in a Pouch; Spokesfish 'Charlie the Tuna' Promotes Convenience and Fresher Taste" (2001). *Business Wire* News Release found online at <www.heinz.com>, January 16.

"StarKist Rides Innovation Wave" (2001). Accessed online April 20: <www.heinz.com>.

U.S. Securities and Exchange Commission Web site: <http://www.sec.gov/Archives/edgar/data/46640/000095015202005732/j9491701e10vk.txt>.

Case 11

Gap Inc.

Gap Incorporated was founded in 1969 in San Francisco, California, with a single store and a handful of employees. Today, Gap Inc. is a global company with three distinct brands, including Gap Inc., Banana Republic, and Old Navy, and revenue topping $13.6 billion. Gap Inc. is a leading international specialty retailer offering clothing, accessories, and personal care products for men, women, children, and babies. As of February 2, 2002, Gap Inc. operated 2,932 Gap brand store concepts at 1,858 locations in the United States, Canada, the United Kingdom, France, Germany, and Japan. Banana Republic operates more than 300 stores in the United States and Canada including factory stores. Gap Inc. started Old Navy to create a whole new shopping experience. Old Navy addresses the family-oriented market that seeks value-priced clothing.

SUGGESTED SOURCES

Coleman, Calmetta (2001). "Gap Posts 34% Drop in Profit, Issues Warning," *The Wall Street Journal,* Eastern Edition, March 21, p. B5.

"Gap Inc." (2001). *The Wall Street Journal,* Eastern Edition, March 13, p. B14.

"Gap Inc. Selects Hempel As the Marketing Chief for Its Flagship Brand" (2001). *The Wall Street Journal,* Eastern Edition, March 28, p. B8.

Gap Inc. Web site: <www.gap.com>.

"Gap's Old Navy Sets Sail With Items for Dogs" (2001). *The Wall Street Journal,* Eastern Edition, March 2, p. B5.

U.S. Securities and Exchange Commission Web site: <http://www.sec.gov/Archives/edgar/data/39911/000102140802004717/d10k.txt>.

Case 12

Intimate Brands, Inc.

Intimate Brands, Inc. is the leading specialty retailer of intimate apparel, beauty products, and personal care products through the Victoria's Secret and Bath & Body Works brands. The company was established by Roy Raymond and his wife in 1977. Victoria's Secret was based in San Francisco, California, at the time of inception. The business was aimed at making men feel comfortable buying lingerie for their significant others and providing women with an appealing environment in which to purchase intimate apparel. Currently Victoria's Secret consists of Victoria's Secret shops, catalogs, and beauty company. Leslie Wexner, of the Limited, Inc., bought Victoria's Secret in 1982. Victoria's Secret products are available in stores, through its catalog, and online. As a result, the Victoria's Secret brand reaches millions of customers every day. Intimate Brands has been traded publicly on the New York Stock Exchange since October 1995.

SUGGESTED SOURCES

DeMarco, Donna (2000). "Victoria's Attraction No Secret to Millions of Internet Viewers." *The Washington Times,* May 19, p. B9.

Intimate Brands, Inc. Web site: <www.intimatebrands.com>.

U.S. Securities and Exchange Commission Web site: <http://www.sec.gov/Archives/edgar/data/945676/000091205701510239/a2044947z10-k405.htm>.

Case 13

Nike

Nike is one of the most successful sports apparel manufacturers in the world. The company has proven to produce quality sports shoes, clothing, and equipment that meet the demands of both professional athletes and increasingly health-conscious consumers. Nike markets its merchandise in a nontraditional manner. Rather than promoting individual product lines, Nike focuses on enhancing its image as the number-one sport and fitness company. The company has been successful in marketing with respect to brand recognition. Most manufacturing of Nike products is done outside the United States to reduce production costs. To improve profit margins, the company may eliminate jobs companywide and seek a more efficient corporate structure through which to operate.

Nike has experienced some problems such as complications arising from the implementation of its demand and supply system and processes, which resulted in product excesses and shortages, and shipment delays.

Nike was the first company to join former President Clinton's Coalition on Fair Labor Practices. Nike pledged to abide by the Apparel Industry Partnership's Workplace Code of Conduct and vowed to help the industry eradicate sweatshops in the United States and abroad.

SUGGESTED SOURCES

"Earnings at Nike Plummet 33% in the Latest Quarter" (2001). *The New York Times,* Late Edition (East Coast), March 21, p. C4.

Furchgott, Roy (2001). "Logos Worth a Thousand Words." *BusinessWeek,* April 30 (Industrial/Technology Edition), p. 10.

"Nike Inc." (2001). *Standard & Poor's Stock Report,* June 9.

"Nike Inc." (2001). *The Wall Street Journal,* Eastern Edition, March 13, p. B14.

"Nike Names New Leader for United States Operations" (2001). *The New York Times,* Late Edition, March 16, p. C4.

Nike Web site: <www.nike.com>.

Case 14

Rite Aid

Wholesale grocer Alex Grass founded Rack Rite Distributors in Harrisburg, Pennsylvania, in 1958 to provide health and beauty aids. In 1968, Rite Aid went public and adopted its current name. The store's rapid growth is attributed to acquisitions and new stores. Rite Aid continued to increase its store count as well as the number of neighborhoods and customers it serves. The company has over 80,000 employees from thousands of local communities that staff Rite Aid's stores and eight distribution centers. Rite Aid realizes that when customers shop, they are looking for convenience, quality, and value. The company has trained about 10,000 pharmacists to counsel customers on natural remedies and is opening small General Nutrition Company (GNC) stores within 1,500 Rite Aid drugstores. The company has over 1,000 drive-thru pharmacies.

In 1996, Rite Aid closed several markets in Massachusetts and Rhode Island; in 1998, it closed several smaller stores. In late 1998, Rite Aid bought competitor PCS Health Systems from drug maker Eli Lilly for $1.5 billion. Rite Aid partnered with GNC in 1999. In January of 2000, Rite Aid appointed Christopher Hall senior vice president and chief accounting officer.

SUGGESTED SOURCES

"California; Rite Aid Settles Lawsuit Over Practices" (2000). *Los Angeles Times,* April 14.

Excite Money & Investing by Quicken (n.d.). Accessed online at <http://www.quicken.excite.com/investments/comparisons>.

Glasner, Joanna (2000). "Drugstore.com Sells Big Stake." Online at <http://www.wired.com/news/story>.

Rite Aid. 2000. http://www.riteaid.com/company_info.

"Rite Aid Addresses Associate 'Quality of Life Issues' " (2001). *Lebhar-Friedman, Inc. Drug Store News.* LEXIS-NEXIS. January 15.

"Rite Aid Corporation" (2000). *Hoover's Company Profile Database—American Public Companies.* Hoover's Inc.

"Rite Aid Shares Rise After Rebuilding Plan Announced" (2000). *Anchorage Daily News,* accessed online at <http://www.nando.net/24hour/and/busin>.

Case 15

Circuit City Stores, Inc.

Since 1949, Circuit City has been serving the home and mobile electronics needs of consumers across the country. Today, Circuit City operates over 630 stores spanning forty-six states. Circuit City became one of the first customer service stores in its time. Circuit City Stores, Inc. is a large retailer of brand-name consumer electronics, major appliances, personal computers, music, video, and software. The company also owns 77.5 percent of the CarMax group; a large retailer of used cars and light trucks, and has been investing in a new home medium known as Divx. On February 22, 2002, the CarMax auto business was separated from the Circuit City consumer electronics business. Circuit City hopes to maintain its low-price image, excellent product selection, and commitment to customer service. In addition, the company has a customer service information system that keeps a historical record of individual customer transactions. Circuit City is considered one of the market leaders in the industry. This is important because many consumers are already familiar with the Circuit City name and know about its reputation for quality products and service.

SUGGESTED SOURCES

"Charter Communications & Circuit City Sign 63-Store Broadband Retail Agreement; Displays to Give Consumers Chance to Test Drive High-Tech Services" (2001). *Business Wire,* June 6.

"Circuit City Cited for Rain Checks" (2001). *Associated Press Online,* June 6.

"Circuit City Stores, Inc. Releases Earnings Expectation For the Circuit City Business" (2001). *PR Newswire,* February 28.

"Circuit City Stores, Inc. Reports First Quarter Sales and Earnings Expectations for the Company, the Circuit City Group and the CarMax Group" (2001). *PR Newswire,* June 6.

"Circuit City Stores, Inc. Reports Fourth Quarter and Fiscal Year 2001 Sales for the Company, the Circuit City Group and the CarMax Group" (2001). *PR Newswire,* March 6.

Circuit City Stores, Inc. Web site: <www.circuitcity.com>.

U.S. Securities and Exchange Commission Web site: <http://www.sec.gov/Archives/edgar/data/104599/000104324602000011/ccfy02_10k.txt>.

Case 16

Gillette

Known as the world leader in male and female grooming products, the Gillette Company was founded in 1901 by King Gillette. Gillette celebrated its 100th anniversary in 2001, marking the end of its first century of preeminence in the global marketplace and the start of its second. Gillette is famous for the manufacturing and marketing of a large variety of consumer products. These products include razors and blades, toiletries, Duracell batteries, Braun appliances, and Oral-B products. Today, Gillette is a globally diverse consumer products company. It has thirty-four manufacturing facilities in fifteen countries, and its products are distributed in more than 200 countries and territories around the world. The Company employs more than 39,000 people, nearly three-quarters of them outside the United States. Gillette posted steady and healthy growth during the 1990s. It is estimated that Gillette's global market share in the shaving market stands at an impressive 65 percent. Gillette's major competitor worldwide in blades and razors is Pfizer's brand line known as Schick.

SUGGESTED SOURCES

"Company, Investors, Community, Press Room, Products" (2001). Gillette Company Web site: <http://www.gillette.com/annual_report 2001.asp>.

"Duracell Relaunches Duracell CopperTop Batteries with $100 million Strategic Initiative" (2001). Accessed July 4: <www.duracell.com>.

"Financial Summary: Gillette" (n.d.). Accessed online: <www.yahoofinance.com>.

The Gillette Company Web site: <www.gillette.com>. See "Mission and Values."

Rayovac Corporation Web site: <http://www.rayovac.com>.

U.S. Securities and Exchange Commission Web site: <http://www.sec.gov/Archives/edgar/data/41499/000095013502001673/b41814gce10-k.txt>.

Case 17

Harley-Davidson

In the early 1900s, William Harley, age twenty, and Arthur Davidson, age twenty-one, began experimenting with taking the work out of bicycling. Arthur's brothers Walter and William soon joined them, and Harley-Davidson was formed. Harley-Davidson became the largest motorcycle manufacturer in the world by 1920. They had dealers in sixty-seven countries and had produced 28,819 motorcycles. In 1965, Harley-Davidson ended family ownership and went public. By 1989, Harley-Davidson had 60 percent of the super heavyweight motorcycle market. Harley-Davidson's branded line of merchandise is available only at Harley dealerships and through their catalogs. It seemed that customers would pay almost anything to get the Harley-Davidson logo. In October 2000, Harley-Davidson launched its new Web site, including a Harley-Davidson store. At this site, Harley-Davidson has earned additional profits from the sale of motorcycle accessories and merchandise. Harley enthusiasts can also learn about new products offered by the company, view pictures of motorcycles and other products, and apply for the Harley-Davidson credit card. A unique feature of the site is its link to local dealers to connect prospective motorcycle customers to dealer outlets. All Harley-Davidson employees take part in a gain-sharing program, earning cash incentives for attaining quality, profitability, and product delivery goals.

SUGGESTED SOURCES

"Fans Pressure EU to Call Off Tariffs on U.S. Bike" (2002). *The Wall Street Journal,* April 25.

Harley-Davidson Web site: <www.harley-davidson.com>.

Helyar, John (2002). "Will Harley-Davidson Hit the Wall?" *Fortune,* August 12.

U.S. Securities and Exchange Commission Web site: <http://www.sec.gov/Archives/edgar/data/793952/0000912057-00-014049-index.html>.

Case 18

Home Depot

Founded in 1978 in Atlanta, Georgia, by Arthur Blank and Bernard Marcus, the first Home Depot Store opened on June 1979. Home Depot, known for its orange color scheme, is credited as the world's largest home improvement retailer and the third largest retailer in the United States. Home Depot grew to encompass stores in Georgia, Florida, Louisiana, Texas, and Alabama within its first five years. Growth continues to this day, with more than 1,400 stores open throughout the United States, Canada, and Mexico. By the end of 2003 Home Depot expects to operate over 1,900 stores in the United States alone. Home Depot services three primary customer groups: do-it-yourself customers, buy-it-yourself customers, and professional customers. Home Depot empowers employees, creates superior customer service, and expands business growth through its leadership training and community programs.

SUGGESTED SOURCES

Bergen, Kathleen (2001). "FAA Proposes $60,000 Penalty Against Home Depot for Hazmat Violations." Federal Aviation Administration Web site accessed April 11: <http://www.faa.gov/apa/ASO/2001/homedepot.htm>.

Home Depot Web site: <http://www.homedepot.com>.

"Home Depot's and Lowe's Battle over Which Offers Lowest Prices" (2001). *The Atlanta Journal and Constitution,* March 31.

"Market Guide: Home Depot" (n.d.). Accesses online: <http://biz.yahoo.com/p/h/hd.html>.

Oguntoyinbo, Lekan (2002). "Understanding Reached with The Home Depot." Accessed online September: <http://www.michigan.gov/mdcr/0,1607,7-138-4952-16150—,00.html>.

"Social Responsibility Report" (1999). Accessed online: <http://www.homedepot.com>.

Case 19

Lincoln Electric

The Lincoln Electric Company is the world's largest manufacturer of arc-welding products and a leading producer of industrial electric motors. The company was created in 1895 by John Cromwell Lincoln to manufacture electric alternating current (AC) motors, and then shifted its resources during World War II to manufacture arc-welding products. The culture of the organization is characterized as one of high wages, high productivity, and high levels of trust between management and employees. Headquartered in Cleveland, Ohio, the company employs about 6,300 workers worldwide in seventeen countries.

There is a sense of ownership of the company for all employees. There are four major parts to Lincoln Electric's incentive system. They are piecework, annual bonuses, guaranteed employment, and limited benefits. Lincoln and its employees have watched millions of people lose their jobs in other companies that once seemed secure. Guaranteed employment does not mean rewarding the lazy or the incompetent; it means providing security to the people who give all for the job and the company, who work well, who continually improve their skills and knowledge, and who come up with new and fruitful ideas.

The company expanded its customer base and introduced new-tech products in the past decade. Lincoln's shareholders saw the company's value almost double from 1995 to 1998.

SUGGESTED SOURCES

Elliot, Jay (1995). "A Whole New World." *CFO,* May.

Hach, John J. (1995). "Less Warehousing, Better Distribution." *Transportation and Distribution,* March.

Hasting, Donald F. (1999). "Lincoln Electric's Harsh Lessons from International Expansion." *Harvard Business Review,* May/June.

Hodgetts, Richard M. (1997). Discussing Incentive Compensation with Donald Hasting of Lincoln." *Compensation and Benefits Review*, September/October.

Lienert, Anita (1995). "A Dinosaur of a Different Color." *Management Review*, February.

Lincoln Electric Web site: <www.lincolnelectric.com>.

Case 20

Motorola, Inc.

Motorola is one of the largest providers of electronic equipment in the world, including cellular telephones, pagers, and two-way radios. The original company was established by Paul V. Galvin in 1928 and was known as Galvin Manufacturing Corporation. The name of the company was officially changed to Motorola in 1947. The company has branched off into the computer chip, microprocessor, and integrated circuits market. Motorola continues its success despite having many competitors. Globally, Motorola's toughest competitor is the Japanese market. The Japanese government has pledged a lot of help to this sector of the industry. In wireless communication, it interchanges the top spot with AT&T and Ericsson. Motorola is always on the cutting edge of technology. Some of the mainstream companies that use Motorola semiconductor products include Apple, Sega, and many of the new cars heading out of Detroit. On January 5, 2000, Motorola and General Instrument Corporation completed their previously announced merger. This merger places Motorola as a leader in the convergence of voice, video, and data technologies. On February 21, 2001, Motorola announced that the Motorola Computer Group will acquire Blue Wave Systems, Inc.

SUGGESTED SOURCES

Business Wire (2001). February 21, p. 1.
"D&B Business/Credit Reports: Motorola, Inc." (2002). *D&B,* September 1.
Electronic Business News (2001). February 12, p. 8.
Motorola, Inc. Web site: <www.motorola.com>.
"Technical Analysis for MOT " (2002). *OptionSmart,* September 1.

Case 21

Microsoft

Founded in 1975, Microsoft is the worldwide leader in software, services, and Internet technologies for personal and business computing. The company offers a wide range of products and services designed to empower people through great software—any time, any place, and on any device.

Microsoft's first major breakthrough as computer software manufacturer came with the brilliant licensing deal and strategic alliance that its co-founder Bill Gates struck with IBM concerning Microsoft's MS-DOS operating system. On May 22, 1990, Microsoft, after a decade of improving upon its MS-DOS platform, finally introduced a new window-based product that made computers friendlier to the general user. Windows would later prove to be one of Microsoft's most valuable assets.

Building on the popularity of its operating system, Microsoft started to market improved versions of Windows in 1995, 1998, and 2000, further improving the system's ability to support Web and network communication. The company also introduced Windows XP as a part of series of its newest Microsoft launches. Other products will soon hit the market, including Visual Studio and NET; and Xbox, its much-hyped video-game console, has been moderately successful already. To ensure its long-term growth, the company is moving into new markets, such as digital entertainment, enterprise software, and Web services.

SUGGESTED SOURCES

"Microsoft Annual Report" (2001). Microsoft Corporation. Available online: <http://www.microsoft.com/msft/ar.htm>.

"Microsoft Corporate Profile and Organizational Structure Overview" (n.d.). Microsoft Corporation. Available online: <http://www.microsoft.com/presspass/corpprofile.asp>.

"Microsoft Extending Its Tentacles" (2001). *The Economist,* October 20, pp.70-71.

Index

Page numbers followed by the letter "b" indicate boxed text; those followed by the letter "f" indicate a figure; and those followed by the letter "t" indicate a table.

SPECIAL 25%-OFF DISCOUNT!

Order a copy of this book with this form or online at:

http://www.haworthpressinc.com/store/product.asp?sku=4759

STRATEGIC MANAGEMENT

Formulation, Implementation, and Control in a Dynamic Environment

_______in hardbound at $52.46 (regularly $69.95) (ISBN: 0-7890-1809-8)

_______in softbound at $29.96 (regularly $39.95) (ISBN: 0-7890-1810-1)

Or order online and use Code HEC25 in the shopping cart.

COST OF BOOKS________

OUTSIDE US/CANADA/ MEXICO: ADD 20%________

POSTAGE & HANDLING________
(US: $5.00 for first book & $2.00 for each additional book) Outside US: $6.00 for first book & $2.00 for each additional book)

SUBTOTAL________

IN CANADA: ADD 7% GST________

STATE TAX________
(NY, OH & MN residents, please add appropriate local sales tax)

FINAL TOTAL________
(If paying in Canadian funds, convert using the current exchange rate, UNESCO coupons welcome)

☐ **BILL ME LATER:** ($5 service charge will be added)
(Bill-me option is good on US/Canada/Mexico orders only; not good to jobbers, wholesalers, or subscription agencies.)

☐ Check here if billing address is different from shipping address and attach purchase order and billing address information.

Signature________________________

☐ **PAYMENT ENCLOSED:** $________________

☐ **PLEASE CHARGE TO MY CREDIT CARD.**

☐ Visa ☐ MasterCard ☐ AmEx ☐ Discover ☐ Diner's Club ☐ Eurocard ☐ JCB

Account # ________________________

Exp. Date________________________

Signature________________________

Prices in US dollars and subject to change without notice.

NAME________________________

INSTITUTION________________________

ADDRESS________________________

CITY________________________

STATE/ZIP________________________

COUNTRY________________ COUNTY (NY residents only)________________

TEL________________ FAX________________

E-MAIL________________________

May we use your e-mail address for confirmations and other types of information? ☐ Yes ☐ No We appreciate receiving your e-mail address and fax number. Haworth would like to e-mail or fax special discount offers to you, as a preferred customer. **We will never share, rent, or exchange your e-mail address or fax number.** We regard such actions as an invasion of your privacy.

Order From Your Local Bookstore or Directly From

The Haworth Press, Inc.

10 Alice Street, Binghamton, New York 13904-1580 • USA
TELEPHONE: 1-800-HAWORTH (1-800-429-6784) / Outside US/Canada: (607) 722-5857
FAX: 1-800-895-0582 / Outside US/Canada: (607) 722-6362
E-mailto: getinfo@haworthpressinc.com

PLEASE PHOTOCOPY THIS FORM FOR YOUR PERSONAL USE.

http://www.HaworthPress.com BOF02